# WILLIAM JAMES
## ON
## HABIT, WILL, TRUTH,
### AND
## THE MEANING OF LIFE

# WILLIAM JAMES
## ON
# HABIT, WILL, TRUTH,
## AND
# THE MEANING OF LIFE

Edited and with an Introduction by

James Sloan Allen

FREDERIC C. BEIL

SAVANNAH

2014

Printed in the United States of America

LIBRARY OF CONGRESS CATALOGING-IN-PUBLICATION DATA
James, William, 1842–1910
[Works. Selections]
William James on habit, will, truth, and the meaning of life /
edited and with an introduction by James Sloan Allen.
pages cm
Includes bibliographical references and index.
ISBN 978-1-929490-28-8 (cloth : alk. paper)
ISBN 978-1-929490-45-5 (ppk. : alk paper)   .
ISBN 978-1-929490-46-2 (ebook)
1. James, William, 1842–1910
2. Pragmatism. 3. Psychology—Philosophy.
4. Life. 5. Habit. 6. Will.
I. Allen, James Sloan. II. Title.
B945.J21A543   2014
191—dc23

2014014914

To the memory of my father, Mark Knight Allen,

who first taught me to read William James

# Contents

# ACKNOWLEDGMENTS

I am grateful to two people for awakening me to William James. First, my father, to whom this book is dedicated, took James as a mentor in psychology and encouraged me to appreciate James's wisdom and wit in many subjects. Second, the late historian and cultural critic Jacques Barzun, who taught me much and bestowed on me many favors, prompted me to see James as a thinker of penetrating insight into the particularities of life and the intellectual courage to fight the wayward attraction of pretentious academic jargon and mind-clouding abstractions.

I wish to thank my publisher, Frederic C. Beil, for carrying his own interest in William James into the idea for a book of James's writings on habit, and for his indulgence in my expanding on that theme, as well as for his patient and exemplary editing.

I also again thank my wife, Elizabeth, for supporting me in this task and in all things.

# INTRODUCTION

## WILLIAM JAMES: A PHILOSOPHER FOR OUR TIMES

"Every moment of immediate experience is somewhat absolutely
original and novel."

"The highest ethical life consists at all times in the breaking of rules
which have grown too narrow."

"Be not afraid of life."

When William James died in the late summer of 1910 at the age of
sixty-eight, the brightest light in American intellectual life went out.
But its energy radiated on. Preeminent psychologist, revolutionary
philosopher, intrepid modernist, spiritual exponent, self-help guide,
inspiring teacher, popular speaker, James touched the lives and minds
of countless people inside academia and out, at home and abroad, while
he lived and afterwards—among them grateful students like Gertrude
Stein, W. E. B. Du Bois, and Walter Lippmann, as well as a cofounder
of Alcoholics Anonymous, a host of European intellectuals, and, to
dubious effect, Benito Mussolini. Fifteen years after James's death,
his former student the philosopher Horace M. Kallen announced in
an early anthology of James's writings that "the world" viewed James
"not merely as the greatest American philosopher, but as the greatest
philosopher of America." A half-century later, finding James's shadow
lying across the epochal "reconstruction of European social thought"
in the early twentieth century, the distinguished intellectual historian
H. Stuart Hughes concluded, "I doubt whether ever before or since an
American thinker has enjoyed such prestige on the European continent."
But William James was more than the most celebrated and influential
American thinker of his times. He was a thinker for everyone in our
times—and beyond.

That is because James teaches us much about how to navigate the
surrounding and often treacherous sea where we live our lives: the sea

1

of experience. James dove into that sea to explore it with ecumenical curiosity, intellectual audacity, and generous humanity. For he was convinced that experience not only measures reality, it *is* reality, in all of its dimensions. That conviction led him to some radical conclusions— he would name his philosophy "radical empiricism"—about how to understand experience and make the most of it. This also inspired him to insist that we should not shrink from experience, however it might unsettle our expectations, but meet it with inquisitiveness and courage, will and action. "Be not afraid of life," he declared in one of his popular essays (emblematically entitled "Is Life Worth Living?"†*). That might have been his credo.

Life, James wrote in a notebook when he was sixty-one, is "a muddle and a struggle, with an 'ever not quite' to all formulas, and novelty and possibility forever leaking in." He thought this all to the good. For "if this life be not a real fight in which something is gained for the universe by success," he asserted in the essay above, "it is no better than a game of private theatricals from which one may withdraw at will." And in this fight, nothing arms us better than believing we can prevail. "Believe that life is worth living," James promises, "and your belief will help create the fact."

The lines I have quoted nearly state the gist of William James's vision of life. For they disclose, or imply, how eagerly James embraced the variousness of experience, the unpredictability of existence, the rewards of effort and action, the efficacy of belief, the pragmatic test of truth, and, I might add, the potency of free will and good habits of mind that serve everything else. Some of this vision allied James with fellow pragmatic philosophers like Charles Sanders Peirce and John Dewey—and made him a forerunner of phenomenology and even of postmodernism. But it also put him in the company of less academic modern philosophical and literary figures for whom life was a perilous adventure demanding keen exertions of imagination and will. The tormented, probing, spiritually yearning Fyodor Dostoevsky was one of these—who brought his dark masterpiece of psychological and moral fiction, *The Brothers Karamazov* (1880), to a climax with the same affirmation that James would use: "Do not be afraid of life." Friedrich Nietzsche was another. Two years younger than James, Nietzsche wrote flashy philosophical aphorisms on the rewards of suffering, strength, and will as he assailed all conventional moral assumptions and comforting intellectual pieties. In many ways, James was the American Nietzsche (Nietzsche's atheism aside), and Nietzsche was the German James—Oscar Wilde was their British counterpart. Mark Twain, eight years older than James and dead four months earlier, could fit here too. Both endowed with a gift for muscularly vivacious prose, a keen eye for the ways of the real world, a provocative sense of humor, and a taste for irreverence, James and Twain were the most radical, prominent American authors of their generation (albeit Twain leaned to a cynicism over human nature and society that the charitable James did not).* Jean-Paul Sartre is yet another intellectual confrère. James shared with Sartre an existential (if not entirely existentialist) belief in human freedom and a commitment to responsibility for creating our lives and our morality in an uncertain universe.**

These few names signal some of the more daring modern intellectual company that James's vision of life keeps. And yet, while James saw life as an existential struggle, and he attacked philosophical conventions blind to the varieties of experience, he wielded in battle a dauntless good nature and a winningly genial rhetorical style. It was a very personal style that mirrored his character and philosophy. Conversational, often colloquial, in tone and sparkling with lively anecdotes and arresting metaphors, it engagingly captured the concrete particulars of human experience that James believed engulf our lives—unlike the philosophical abstractions that, he said, betray "the gaping contrast between the richness of life and the poverty of all possible formulas." James also frequently addressed his words to common readers and listeners because he found in almost every psychological fact and philosophical truth grounds for what he sometimes dubbed "hortatory ethics" ("little sermons," his former student and colleague George Santayana wryly labeled them) on how to understand human life and how to live it in the great "muddle and struggle" that is our existence. All of this makes William James among the most delightful, enlightening, and life-giving thinkers we can read.

But James paid a hefty price for his worldly wisdom. He was roiled by troubles, physical and *nervous*—as *depression* was known in those days, long before modern pharmaceuticals could assuage it—almost all his life. And in his young adulthood he suffered compounding philosophical agonies as well, tempting him to suicide. How he became the thinker from whom we can learn so much today is a story of how, as James said again and again, ideas grow from temperaments schooled by experience, and from how we engage in the fight for our lives.

## THE PHILOSOPHER IN THE MAKING

Outwardly, William James had a privileged youth only dreamt of by many a young man. His father, Henry James, Sr., had inherited wealth from his own enterprising father, who had become one of the wealthiest men in New York State. Freed from labor, inclined to intellectual pursuits and spiritual yearnings, and remarkably open-minded, Henry Sr. desired to give his own children an expansive cosmopolitan education. That desire begot a stimulating, if rather peripatetic, existence for his family.

William, born in New York City in 1842, first sailed to Europe at the age of twenty months with his father, mother, and six-month-old brother, Henry. They stayed for almost a year and a half then returned to New York City, where William's childhood unfolded amidst that burgeoning metropolis and its flowering cultural life, which Henry, Sr., expected his children to share with him. In 1855 the family, now counting five offspring, headed back to Europe, remaining there for three years while the older children learned French and German and imbibed European culture in a variety of settings and schools. A subsequent year in America at a new home in Newport, Rhode Island, closed with yet another sojourn in Europe, this time cut short after a year by William's wish to resume the art studies he had begun in Newport with the painter William Morris Hunt, a plan not to his father's liking but to his grudging consent.

These foreign travels gave William James the education his father had intended for him, as well as an attachment to Europe that William would renew with repeated, often lengthy visits for the rest of his life.* But he would on occasion actually rue his itinerant education for allowing him to skate on the surface of learning and not compelling him to master any subject. "I feel as if the greater part of the last ten years had been worse than wasted," he complained in a letter of 1867, "my habits of mind have been so bad." James was, in fact, very much a self-educated man. And his biographers understandably agree that this contributed to the kind of thinker he became—for the better, not the worse. By temperament, James was, among other things, an inquisitive, restless, energetic character eager for experience, and his education let his mind range freely across many subjects at his own rapid pace and to perceive them from his own point of view. It also gave him a certain distrust of institutions and authority. He came to cast a wary eye on the budding professionalization of education in his day, modeled on the German research university, which he derided in his essay "The Ph.D. Octopus." And he later promoted pragmatism in this same spirit, touting it as a blazing intellectual revolution setting a torch to desiccated philosophical conventions.

But James's unconventional education also left him for a long time at loose ends in the search for a career. He had made a tentative move toward one at the age of eighteen when he returned from Europe to study painting in Newport. Planning to give himself a year or two to learn if he had the talent to succeed as a painter, he soon proved to possess only an amateur's aptitude, and gave it up. Unintentionally, he became an artist of another kind.

From art, James turned to science, then to medical studies at Harvard. Yet he did this with no clear ambition, avidly reading literature, history, science, and philosophy. When the opportunity arose in 1865 to spend nine months in Brazil with the famed naturalist Louis Agassiz, he jumped at it. Agassiz was a skilled observer of nature and a resolute anti-Darwinian, unpersuaded that organisms evolve through godless natural selection. James admired Agassiz's close scrutiny of nature but became himself an ardent, albeit not godless, evolutionist. After returning from Brazil (where, as so often, he got seriously ill), James resumed his medical studies for a year, then lived another eighteen months in Europe to study and improve his health, and he finally obtained his medical degree (such as it was in those days of book-learned medical education) in 1869. But he didn't enter the medical profession. He still could not decide what he wanted to do with his life. Depression set in. Then a series of emotional and intellectual disturbances brought a turning point that set him on the professional course he would follow, in his own meandering manner, thereafter. But that crossroads lay far ahead when James was growing up under the ruling influence of his father—more than of his mother, who favored young Henry. Henry James, Sr., not only dedicated himself to his children's cosmopolitan education. After a spiritual crisis during that first European trip with his two young boys had delivered him to the mystical religiosity of Emmanuel Swedenborg, he set himself to teach humankind the truth about good and evil, God and the universe, and how to gain redemption through Swedenborgian spirituality. In time he would write and publish at his own expense nine books propounding his convictions. William didn't cotton to his father's philosophy, but he wrote a long, respectful introduction to an unfinished tenth volume of Henry Sr.'s writings. And, as his father lay dying in 1882, William wrote him a letter professing, "All my intellectual life I owe to you."

That was a bit of filial piety. But William's expansive and eccentric education had come at his father's hands, not the least of it at home. And spirituality only punctuated it. Henry, Sr., was also a man of the world who cultivated friendships with many of the leading thinkers and social reformers of his day. Ralph Waldo Emerson became a close friend—and William's god-father. Henry David Thoreau and Bronson Alcott visited the James homes in New York and later in Cambridge, Massachusetts, where the family finally settled in 1866 to be with William at Harvard. The newspaper publisher Horace Greeley and the editor-poet William Cullen Bryant came to share thoughts with Henry, Sr., on social reform and the abolition of slavery. Henry, Sr., converted to Fourier's utopian socialism through some of these impassioned companions. In London he made a point of getting to know Thomas Carlyle, Lord Tennyson, and John Stuart Mill. These and other associations gave the James home, wherever it was, an atmosphere of intellectual ferment that William breathed throughout his youth and early adulthood.

William even got from his father some of the very agility of his mind and sparkle of his verbal style. Henry, Sr., was an engaging conversationalist with a sharp wit and a facile way with words, along with a penchant for tongue-in-cheek exaggeration that all of his children, most conspicuously William and Henry, Jr., inherited. The correspondence of these two famed brothers abundantly displays this practice—which has misled some critics into taking their words too literally.*

William inherited a portion of his father's spiritual nature, as well. This surfaced most dramatically in one of the emotional disturbances I mentioned above, closely resembling his father's spiritual crisis. Just as Henry, Sr.'s crisis had brought an idiosyncratic conversion to Swedenborg, William's discord opened new perceptions of life that would shape his future. Religion would play a lasting role in these perceptions. But William did not suffer only a spiritual crisis. He experienced a philosophical conversion, and it gave him a new intellectual and moral life. That was the crossroads.

This dramatic passage in James's life took place over a period of months probably from late 1869 to April 1870. James turned twenty-eight years old that January. By this time the Civil War had come and gone— James's two youngest brothers had fought in it, but he and Henry had not—and James had received his medical degree the previous May. Now he was in a discomfiting limbo, reading widely while suffering from a chronic back ailment, insomnia, eye trouble, and a general feeling of inertia over what his next move should be. Then the ground fell away under his feet.

In *The Varieties of Religious Experience*† James describes an episode of existential despair that he attributes to an unnamed Frenchman. He later confessed that this experience had been his own,* and his son Henry, who incorporated it in his collection of James's letters, calculated that the episode had occurred around this time. James has the Frenchman say that in a "state of philosophical pessimism and general depression of spirits about my prospects," he was seized suddenly one evening by "a horrible fear of my own existence." He saw a desolate image of himself that struck him with "horror" and reduced him to "a mass of quivering fear." For days afterwards he awoke "with a horrible dread at the pit of my stomach" from a sense of "the insecurity beneath the surface of life." The fictional Frenchman turns to religious belief as a way out. James did, too. But more than that, the experience gave James an appreciation for the psychology and religion of what he would name the "sick soul" afflicted by existential dread. Although James's own feelings of dread faded, that appreciation never disappeared. For he had ineffaceably experienced the dark side of life, the reality of evil, and the redemptive power of religious belief—about which he would write at length in *Varieties*.

But equally, perhaps more, important in changing the course of James's life was what happened in the spring of 1870. James was then going through a spate of troubles, both intellectual and emotional. The intellectual troubles grew from the materialist doctrine of the day that James had absorbed from his scientific and medical studies. This doctrine defined reality as merely matter governed by deterministic laws, reducing human beings to mechanistic automatons and dismissing free will, human motivations, and moral responsibility. "I feel that we are Nature through and through," James had lamented to a friend in 1869, "that we are wholly conditioned, that not a wiggle of our will happens save as the result of physical laws." And he didn't like it. For that doctrine clashed with James's own nature. With all his physical sufferings, emotional distress, and philosophical anguish, James persistently relished intellectual adventure, welcomed variety and change, and brimmed with a good-natured vivacity endearing to everyone who knew him—his sister said he could "lend life and charm to a treadmill."* A conflict in him between determinism and free will was bound to erupt.

Describing his intellectual turmoil, he wrote in his diary on February 1: "Today I about touched bottom, and perceive plainly that I must face the choice with open eyes: Shall I *frankly* throw the moral business [free will] overboard . . . or shall I follow it, and it alone?" To pick himself up, he opted for freedom and responsibility and thinking of "useful ends," like "salutary habits," as "occasions for my moral life to become active." But he didn't yet know how to use ideas as "occasions" to spur free moral action.

While laboring over these philosophical predicaments, William suffered another blow. This was emotional. A young cousin, Minny Temple, whom both he and Henry adored for her spiritedness and intelligence, died. Henry admitted that he used her as the model for two of his finest female characters, the idealistic Isabel Archer in *The Portrait of a Lady* and the ill-fated Milly Theale in *The Sign of the Dove*. William was likely in love with her, and her death devastated him anew. But it also helped push him forward. Minny had been ill for some time and had gone through her own moral and religious angst, which she exposed in heartfelt letters to William. Her last missive to him concluded: "The question will always remain, what is one's true life—and we must each try and solve it for ourselves." That question—What is one's true life?—was to be her legacy to William James.

Two weeks after Minnie died, James wrote an elegiac message to himself about what she now meant to him. "Minnie, your death makes me feel the nothingness of all our egotistical fury," he railed, but he vowed to "use your death (or your life, it's all one meaning)" to find his own true life. "Since tragedy is at the heart of us," he went on, we should "go to meet it, work it to our ends, instead of dodging it all our days. . . . May I feel that every torment suffered here passes and is as the breath of the wind—every pleasure too. Acts and examples stay." Accept suffering and tragedy as conditions of life, but do not succumb to them. They pass. Acts and examples stay. Here is James's moral imagination in embryo.

An experience a few weeks later took James further along that path. For it led him beyond the materialistic determinism that had oppressed and thwarted him. He recorded this experience in a striking diary entry of April 30.

"I think yesterday was a crisis in my life," he again wrote ominously. But the crisis turned out to be an epiphany. For he discovered the secret of free will and how it could give him the confidence to live an active moral life. "I finished the first part of [Charles] Renouvier's second 'Essais'," he explained, "and see no reason why his definition of Free Will—'the sustaining of a thought *because I choose to* when I might have other thoughts'—need be the definition of an illusion. At any rate, I will assume for the present—until next year—that it is no illusion. My first act of free will shall be to believe in free will" (which he had already done without recognizing it). And for the rest of the year he would "abstain" from gloomy speculations and "voluntarily cultivate the feeling of moral freedom, by reading books favorable to it, as well as by acting." James was now a pragmatist before the name: if the idea of free will worked in experience, it must be true.

James then coupled this commitment to free will with a particular principle of action. This was the principle of habit. For now he saw that will and habit go together in creating an active and good life. He would never forget that. "Recollect," he advised himself in the same diary entry, "that only when habits of order are formed can we advance to really interesting fields of action—and consequently accumulate grain on grain of willful choice." Happily, he continued, "today has furnished the exceptionally passionate initiative which [Alexander] Bain posits as needful for the acquisition of habits," since habits arise through "accumulated *acts* of thought." Equipped with that "passionate initiative" from Renouvier's idea of will, James would thereafter make a habit of free will in accumulated mental acts of choosing some ideas and resisting others. And "I will go a step further with my will," he effused, "not only act with it, but believe as well; believe in my individual reality and creative power" and spurn the former bad habits of mind that had set him adrift and made "suicide [seem] the most manly form to put my daring into." Now, he pledged, "I will posit life (the real, the good) in the self-governing resistance of the ego to the world. Life shall [be built on] doing and suffering and creating." William James had found the way to his own true life.*

As he acknowledged in this momentous diary entry, James owed much inspiration for this new perception of life to the two authors Charles Renouvier and Alexander Bain. Renouvier was a French Neo-Kantian philosopher whose works James had first encountered while in Europe in 1868. But it was reading later Renouvier's discussion of free will in the second volume of his *Essais de critique generale* (1854–64) that awakened James to free will as Renouvier defined it. James wrote to thank Renouvier for his "reasonable and intelligible conception of liberty," and before long the two began corresponding. They became quite close during the next few years, exchanging ideas and promoting each other's works, and James taught courses on Renouvier's theories. They eventually drifted apart over what James called Renouvier's "philosophical manner and apparatus," but James dedicated his final book, *Some Problems in Philosophy*, published posthumously, to this mentor. "Feeling endlessly thankful as I do for the decisive impression made on me in the seventies by his masterly advocacy of pluralism [i.e., free will]," James proclaimed that without Renouvier "I might never have got free from the monistic superstition [determinism] under which I had grown up."

James did not warm so much to Bain, a severe and prolific Scottish philosopher and psychologist whom he met only once. But James respected Bain's fervent empiricism, and Bain's chapter on "The Moral Habits" in *Emotions and the Will* (1859) had seeded the ethical thoughts on habit that sprouted in James's epiphany. James also taught courses on Bain's works and quoted his words whenever he wrote about habit. James never stinted in paying homage to his intellectual benefactors.

When James married the ideas of Renouvier and Bain (and he published an appreciative article on them both in the *Nation* in 1876), he found that by believing in free will, and by repeatedly exercising it with "accumulated acts of thought" that hold to some ideas and reject others, he could develop "salutary habits" of mind and enter "really interesting fields of action." This revelation freed James to build his own true life on habits of will and doing and suffering and creating. In one way or another, this family of ideas would influence James's life and thought from then onwards.

James's epiphany of April 1870 brought a related insight that also brightened his future. He did not explicitly describe this in writing. But he later mentioned it to his father, who reported it in a letter of 1873 to Henry, Jr. One day, William had come to his father in exceptionally high spirits. Asked why, he had explained that reading Renouvier was the first reason. Reading Wordsworth was another. "But especially," Henry, Sr., wrote, "his having given up the notion that all mental disorder required to have a physical basis," for he now "saw that mind did act irrespectively of material coercion, and could be dealt with therefore at first hand." Affirming free will had taught William that mind itself has an autonomy independent of matter, enabling it to cause "mental disorder" and to cure it. Although he never wholly resolved the puzzling connection between mind and body, or brain (he would conclude his chapter "The Mind-Stuff Theory" in *The Principles of Psychology* with the words, "nature in her unfathomable designs has mixed us of clay and flame, of brain and mind," and "the two things hang indubitably together and determine each other's beings, but how or why, no mortal may ever know"), his decision that the mind possesses a degree of autonomy enhanced the mental and moral life for him. It also paralleled the discovery of Sigmund Freud in 1897 that neuroses do not necessarily grow from physical experiences but often from imagined events and repressed desires. Freud would expand this discovery into his theory of psychoanalysis.

But between the time of his epiphany about free will and his father's positive letter about him three years later, James continued to suffer bouts of "philosophical hypochondria," as he put it to Henry, and depression, mainly over the direction of his life. It was not enough for him simply to affirm his free will to live an active life. He had to find an active life to live. In short, he needed a vocation, a way to "make my *nick*," he had told a friend, "and so assert my reality." At close to thirty years of age, and despite holding a medical degree, he still had no career—while the younger Henry was acquiring a promising reputation as the author of nearly two dozen excellent short stories. That started changing for William when he taught his first class at Harvard in January 1873.

Harvard was just then embarking on its transformation from a provincial college to a sprawling research university under the direction of its new president, Charles W. Eliot—eight years James's senior and creator of the graduate Ph.D. program that James would revile. James hesitated to accept Eliot's invitation to teach a class in Natural History, but once he consented, his life began to acquire the beneficial "habits of order" that he had hoped would lend structure and purpose to his life. "It is a noble thing for one's spirits," he granted to Henry while preparing for the class, "to have some responsible work to do." Three months after James walked into the classroom, his father wrote the letter about his improved morale, noting "Willy goes on greatly with his teaching"—a class of fifty-seven students. Teaching this class, an astute recent biographer observes, was "the first regular work James had done in his life."

The emotional effect that this dawning career had on him suggests that whatever else James had suffered in his late twenties, one of his maladies was what the pioneering sociologist Emile Durkheim would name *anomie*. In his famous book *Suicide* (1897) Durkheim described anomie as a condition of aimlessness aroused by the absence of purpose or goals and the constraints these impose on the mind. It feels like the depression of amorphous emptiness. And it is typical of many suicides. Its cure is to set specific, immediate, attainable goals for the mind to grasp and for actions to pursue. James suffered anomie and got the cure. Had he read Durkheim, which he seems never to have done, he would have recognized anomie as at least an ingredient in his previously suicidal moods. A few generations later the psychologist Erik Erikson would give the term "identity crisis" to part of the same disoriented state of mind. And he would repeatedly point to James as an example because "James's life history" shows "a protracted identity crisis as well as the emergence of a 'self-made' identity."

As James's teaching responsibilities grew—he ascended to assistant professor of physiology in 1876 and then of philosophy in 1880—James's life gained order from other sources, as well. The year 1878 marked a watershed. That year James married Alice Howe Gibbens, with whom he was to share a mostly contented life and father five children. And he signed a contract with the publisher Henry Holt to write a textbook on psychology for Holt's new series of such books on the sciences. James reckoned he could complete the book in two years. It took twelve.

That same year, James published the first of the articles that would later become part of this textbook. And he started making serious ventures into philosophy, which was not far to go when psychology remained a branch of philosophy. These philosophical ventures plumbed ideas that had been with James since his intellectual crisis. In thinking them through and starting to write about them, he was staking out terrain that he would continue to explore ever more widely for the next thirty years. He was at last settling into the intellectual life that would bring him an "identity" and fame.

It is to that life of ideas and works that we now turn. I broadly map out James's course but dwell on some salient ideas that deeply mattered to James and that make him most generally worth reading today—and that give form to this anthology.

## WORKS AND IDEAS

One of James's philosophical essays of 1878 threw down the gauntlet of free will and the power of mind at the feet of the philosopher Herbert Spencer, an evolutionary materialist who treated mind as merely a passive organ that reacts to sensations. That is nonsense, James scoffed. "There belongs to mind, from its birth upward, a spontaneity, a vote. It is in the game, and not a mere looker-on." What is more, "mental interests, hypotheses, postulates, so far as they are bases for human action—action which to a great extent transforms the world—help to *make* the truth which they declare." Here already speaks the lively, combative James we know in style and argument. The next year, James went after the avid Darwinist T. H. Huxley for his similar contention that because human beings, like the lower animals, are material creatures, they are "automata" who have consciousness but act without genuine will and autonomy. James, of course, would have none of this. Drawing on Renouvier's notion of the will—and foreshadowing his own theory of consciousness—he asserted in "Are We Automata?" that "whoever studies consciousness, from any point of view whatever, is ultimately brought up against the mystery of interest and selective attention" that causes us to give some experiences "peculiar accentuation, and to ignore the rest." No automaton could do that. We are no "impotently paralytic spectators of the game," he swore in what was becoming one of his favorite metaphors.

James expanded these pugnacious, anti-deterministic ideas in a more sustained essay called "The Dilemma of Determinism" (1884). There he argued that if you believe in a deterministic universe where everything fits together and necessity reigns, you must either sink into pessimism over the existence of evil and unhappiness, and banish hopes for human motivation and morality, or you must pretend that determinism somehow serves a higher good, which you can only imagine but never experience (Marxist materialism was zealously taking that imaginary flight in those very years). As an alternative, James proposed believing in an undetermined "pluralistic, restless universe" where "chance" exists, events can unfurl in various ways, free choices can happen, and humans can live moral lives of action and responsibility. James did not presume to prove the reality of his undetermined, pluralistic universe because neither determinism nor indeterminism can be clinchingly demonstrated in this world. We pick one or the other, he said, as a matter of belief. The point is, he explained with his fledgling pragmatism, "the *difference*" between believing in "a world with chances in it" and believing in "a deterministic world" where there are none. He exhorted readers to "follow my own example in assuming [the pluralistic universe of chance] true, and acting as if it were true. . . . In other words, our first act of freedom, if we are free, ought . . . to be to affirm that we are free."

James would make the same case many times—not just the case for freedom and chance, but for acting on our beliefs to make them true. His first collection of philosophical writings years later, *The Will to Believe* (1897), which included this essay on determinism, would be a monument to that argument. That book would also contain a farther-reaching seminal essay on these and related themes from his philosophical beginnings, "The Sentiment of Rationality."†* There James rebuked rationalist biases, probed human nature, slammed abstract thinking, and upheld faith as a road to truth. It is full of good, and very Jamesian, ideas, on how to think—and write—and merits a longer look.

Rationalists, James said there, have always convinced themselves that their lofty mode of thought rises above the lower, emotional parts of human nature to attain immaculate truth. But that is no more than a self-serving, self-deceptive bias. All thought, philosophical and otherwise, James contended, is entangled in feelings, temperaments, and self-interest—like the rationalist bias itself. This was hardly a new idea, as James well knew. Francis Bacon and the French moralists of the seventeenth century had given it modern currency. But the dominant philosophers and scientists of James's day, both idealists and materialists, didn't buy it. Nowadays it is a commonplace of the social sciences, thanks to James and other revolutionary social theorists of the late nineteenth and early twentieth centuries.** And what sensible person can deny its truth? But James had his own philosophical purposes for staking this claim—as did Nietzsche, who took on some of the same intellectual enemies at the same time.

Rationality itself, James elaborated, is a kind of *feeling* born of a "passion for simplification" in truth and for comforting unity in existence. To satisfy this passion, rationalists try "to comprehend the whole" through an "abstract way of conceiving things" that contents them with "blurred outlines." This "feeling of rationality" gives its exponents a sense of certainty and makes them "feel at home" in the universe—which holds for religious believers no less than for philosophers because "the peace of rationality" can be found in "ecstasy when logic fails."

James contrasts those who have this "sentiment of rationality" to those who have a "passion for distinguishing." Eschewing the abstractions and "blurred outlines" of rationalism, the distinguishers strive "to be *acquainted* with the parts" of existence and to see the "clearness" of "particulars" in the "teeming and dramatic richness of the concrete world." They cannot feel as serenely at home in the universe as the self-satisfied rationalists, but they feel closer to reality.

James recommended a certain balance of the two ways of thinking, but his own temperament plainly favored the "passion for distinguishing." He recoiled from both the metaphysical idealism that enfolds all particulars in a cloudy cosmic absolute (or monism), and the scientific materialism that subordinates all particulars to deterministic physical laws. James could live only amid that *teeming and dramatic richness of the concrete world* where, as he said, "no abstract concept can be a valid substitute for a concrete reality," and where "the entire man . . . will take nothing as an equivalent for life but the fullness of living itself."

Playing out his own "passion for distinguishing," James always tried to grasp the particulars of experience, whatever their messiness, and describe them with plain, concrete language—although his rationalist rivals professed not to understand what he was saying. And he would never cease flailing the taste for abstraction as a bad habit of mind that inflates thought into murky hot air, contrives a language of pretentious gibberish, and blinds people to the actualities of existence. James inveighed against this habit in a choice letter of 1905. "The awful abstract rigamarole in which our American philosophers obscure the truth," he wrote, "will be fatal. . . . It means utter relaxation of intellectual duty, and God will smite it. If there's anything he hates, it is that kind of oozy writing." Imagine what James would say of the language that too often passes for respectable thought and writing in academia today. His warning should steel every student and aspiring thinker against it.*

Leaving the philosophical biases and abuses of rationalism, James moved on to the efficacy of faith for living in this teeming and dramatic concrete world where no absolute truth can be found, but where people nonetheless need to feel a certain sense of at-homeness. James did not restrict this efficacy to religious faith. He had in mind faith as a belief—standing between absolute truth and terminal skepticism or paralyzing doubt—that gives us confidence to act. "We cannot live or think at all without some degree of faith," James assures us, because "faith is synonymous with working hypothesis." We use such hypotheses all the time to make sense of life and to live it. Maybe this or that is true of life, we say. Let's find out. That entails a measure of uncertainty and risk. After all, James says, "a certain amount of uncertainty" is not a bad thing, for "risk lends a zest to worldly activity." Besides, "in the total game of life, we stake our persons all the while." That makes faith "the same moral quality which we call courage in practical affairs."

In a burst of existentialist imagery, James further punches why we need the courage of faith. "Naked, [man] is flung into the world," he declares, "and between man and nature there are no rules of civilized warfare." In this unpredictable universe, faith gives us moral hypotheses to live by and the courage to act on them, and that action validates their truth. "Again and again," James writes, "success depends on energy of act; energy of act again depends on faith," and that is how "faith thus verifies itself"—"The truths cannot become true till our faith has made them so." Above all, we create the moral truth of the world by acting to create it. "This world is good, we must say, since it is what we make it—and we shall make it good."

James was not serving up a bromide of positive thinking here, as critics have sometimes accused him. He just wanted people to see the inextricable bond of will, belief, courage, action, and moral truth in living our lives. "All that the human heart wants is its chance," James concludes, repeating another of his gaming metaphors—a chance to succeed in a universe of moral uncertainty, where "all the evidence will not be 'in'" until "the last man has had his say and contributed his share to the still unfinished x," and where human beings have an "inalienable right to run risks."

The principal ideas in "The Sentiment of Rationality" would flower in most of James's future writings. But that would become conspicuous only in the 1890s when, after publication of *The Principles of Psychology*, James became renowned as a philosopher and popular author and speaker. Meanwhile, the decade of the 1880s would be increasingly consumed by the writing of that masterpiece, along with early publication of several chapters of it that James figured would find an audience.

The two bulky volumes of *The Principles of Psychology* rolled off the presses at last in September of 1890—a slight four months after James had submitted the mammoth manuscript. James joked to his publisher that it was "a loathsome, distended, tumefied, bloated, dropsical mass," for "*no* subject is worth . . . 1000 pages." It contained twenty-eight chapters, from "The Scope of Psychology"—opening with the line, "Psychology is the Science of Mental Life, both of its phenomena and their conditions"—to a chapter on theories of how "we may have come by the peculiar mental attributes which we possess," concluding that no one knows. "It was a tolerant, curious book," said James's colleague and magisterial biographer Ralph Barton Perry, because James was "so promiscuously hospitable" to experience and so inclined to ruminate on its varieties and its philosophical implications. James did not claim scientific originality for the book—and he had no patience for laboratory experiment. It was a synthesis of wide reading, close observations, and forceful ideas. But what a synthesis. No one could have written it but William James. Glittering with his radiant rhetoric and intellectual ingenuity, it far surpassed its sources as a book of knowledge and insight, wisdom and delight. I will outline some of its contours, accentuating a few ideas, chiefly those pertaining to habit and will so essential to James and useful to anyone.

First, readers should know that in writing the book James aspired to make psychology a science rather than leaving it a branch of philosophy. To do this he had to apply the deterministic laws of the natural sciences. "Let psychology frankly admit," he explained in his Epilogue to the abridged edition (popularly known as the *Briefer Course*) "that *for her scientific purposes* determinism must be claimed." But his heart was not in this. And he quickly equivocated: "ethics makes a counter-claim; and the present writer, for one, has no hesitation in regarding her claim as the stronger and in assuming that our wills are 'free.' For him, then, the deterministic assumption of psychology is merely provisional and methodological." Empiricist and nascent pragmatist that he was, James could proceed in no other way. He then makes a startling confession. When "we talk of 'psychology as a natural science' we must not assume" that it truly is one. For it has "not a single law in the sense in which physics shows us laws. . . . This is no science, it is only the hope of a science."

That scientific defect of psychology actually proved a boon to James. For it permitted him to explore "the mental life" without the strict restrictions that a true science imposes. That latitude freed James to rely "first and foremost and always" on "Introspective Observation"—that is, scrutinizing his own experience and consciousness for clues to mental life in general, while skirting "the Psychologist's Fallacy" of confusing himself as observer with the thing observed. It also allowed him to extrapolate repeatedly, in his words, "ethical implications" from his findings and to philosophize on his favorite topics, taking swipes at his philosophical adversaries. And it gave him license to draw on anecdotes and incidents from other people, even from literature, and to give his earthy rhetorical style free rein. In all, James proceeded as a philosophically minded observer and interpreter of human psychological experience—not unlike Freud would do—or a novelist, giving rise to the quip that he wrote psychology like fiction and that his brother Henry wrote fiction like psychology. George Santayana said flatly: "This is a work of imagination . . . evoking vividly the very life of the mind." All of these things made *Principles* the rich and unique study of human nature that it is.

After defining his subject in chapter one, James went on to five chapters he labeled "physiological preliminaries": a pair on errant theories of the mind and brain and three on how the brain receives stimuli and prompts behavior. In these latter three he describes the reflex arcs that convey stimuli and responses along nerve channels devoid of deliberate thought. This thoughtless physiology accounts for the most common and elemental types of human behavior: instinct and habit.

James considered these to be two forms of the same thing. And the chapter he devoted to habit here (number four) became the most widely read and reprinted part of the book. But that popularity had nothing much to do with the physiology. It had to do with James's memorable account of the role of habit in the conduct of life—or James's "hortatory ethics." For James found the ethics of habit, no less than the physiology, to be the matrix of the lives we live.

James first published the chapter on "Habit" as an article in *Popular Science Monthly* in 1887. He cracked to a friend at the time that it was "a mere pot boiler, which I had long had, written, in my drawer. No new thing in it." That arch, self-deprecating tone typified many of James's letters. Perhaps the piece had nothing technically new in it. But it was fresh as air, especially when James turned from the physiology of habit to the "practical remarks at the end," as he told another friend, for "something pithy and real . . . composed with the view of benefiting the *young*." Those "practical remarks" were his "hortatory ethics," or, more formally, "the *ethical implications of the law of habit*." But first a few more words on the physiology.

James begins with a catchy assertion. "The laws of Nature," he says, "are nothing but the immutable habits" of "matter" in its mindless "actions and reactions." However, he continues, within nature, organic things have a "*Plasticity*" that gives their reactions a flexibility foreign to inorganic matter. This plasticity allows organic things to change, and it makes organic evolution possible. Human beings have the most plasticity of anything. Our plasticity resides in the human nervous system and its responses to stimuli. Those responses, or our behavior, actually alter our nervous system over time through deliberate or inadvertent repetition. This is our blessing and our curse.

Our primary reactions to stimuli come from instinctual physical reflexes, like sneezing or pulling your hand from a flame. James equates those instincts with habits: instincts are innate habits of behavior. Other reactions are learned by choice or accident. But all truly habitual behavior occurs without thought. This happens through "systems of reflex paths" between stimuli and reactions. The more often we react in the same way, the deeper the path (plasticity at work), the more automatic the behavior, and the harder it is to change that behavior if we want to. Consider a deliberately *learned* habit. The first language we speak, for instance, seems almost natural as words and grammar take root in the previously untouched plasticity of our nervous system. But learning a new language taxes us because the habits of that first language stand in the way. And yet, through practice the new language can become habitual, too, automatically springing to mind. But we should be aware that if practice makes perfect, as the cliché goes, the practice has to be perfect, or every imperfection of the practice becomes a bad habit.

"In habitual action," James explains, "the only impulse which the intellectual centres need send down is that which carries the command to start." The action then proceeds pretty much as a reflex. Most of our daily routine works like this. Only if something goes amiss in that routine does our attention become aroused. Words we do not know, a wrong note on the keyboard, a misstep on the sidewalk, and the like, will shake us from our habitual performances. But make no mistake, James says, whether deliberately chosen or not, habits add up to more than repetitious actions; they give us patterns of behavior inscribed deep in the physiology of the nervous system. So, habit is not just "second nature," he quotes Lord Wellington saying, "Habit is ten times nature."

This brings James to the "hortatory ethics" that invariably appeal to readers. Given the physiology of habit, he says, we should "*make our nervous system our ally instead of our enemy.*" In the first place, we should take advantage of what habits can do for us. They ease our lives by sparing us the mental labor of pondering our every move, and this helps us feel at home in a confusing world. They also free "our higher powers of mind . . . for their own proper work," and they train us to do the right thing. But, by the same token, we should see how they can undo us. Because we are, in a manner of speaking, "walking bundles of habits" where every "stroke of virtue or vice leaves its never so little scar," there is danger in bad habits. "The hell to be endured hereafter," James warns gravely, "of which theology tells, is no worse than the hell we make for ourselves in this world by habitually fashioning our characters in the wrong way." A person might say when doing something derelict, "I won't count this time," and "a kind heaven may not count it," James adds, "but it is being counted all the same" down in the "nerve-cells and fibres . . . storing it up to be used against him." This is why our habits largely make us who we are and can be as hard as rock to break.

To nurture good habits and guard against bad ones, James offers several maxims on the fruits of repetition and the imperatives of self-control. The last of these maxims counts most. It concerns effort. The idea of effort holds a prominent place in James's psychology and ethics, going back to his own efforts to control his wayward mind and to his early article, "The Feeling of Effort" (1880). For James viewed effort as the engine of the most important things we do—none more important than nurturing good habits and thwarting or breaking bad ones. We should, therefore, he said, acquire the habit of effort itself. This prepares us to exert ourselves whenever circumstances demand. How do we acquire this habit? It is simple, if not easy: "*Keep the faculty of effort alive in you by a little gratuitous exercise every day.*" That is, do "something for no other reason than that you would rather not do it." Imposing this everyday rule of "asceticism" requires more an act of conscious effort and will than of automatic habit, but it fosters the habit of exerting effort, which underlies all mental discipline. Those who have this underlying habit can summon it automatically to "stand like a tower when everything rocks around" them; and the youth who nurtures it by keeping "faithfully busy each hour of the working day" can be sure of "waking up some fine morning, to find himself one of the competent ones of his generation."

James's hortatory ethics of habit were, as he knew, hardly novel, however novel his rendering of them. Not only had James's contemporaries Alexander Bain and the self-help guru Samuel Smiles written prominently about this—as had the French thinkers Felix Ravaisson and Maine de Biran earlier in the century—and empiricist philosophers led by John Locke had long held that habit "associates" ideas in the mind, but at the origins of Western philosophy, Aristotle had placed habit at the very heart of ethics. Pointing out that the Greek words for *ethics*, *character*, and *habit* are variations of the same word, *ethos*, Aristotle explained that we form ethical character through habitually good actions. Consequently, he said, "it is a matter of no small importance what sort of habits we form from the earliest ages, it makes a vast difference, or rather it makes all the difference in the world." It is peculiar that James never mentions Aristotle's *Ethics*, with whose "practical aims" (*pragmatia*) and anti-idealist slant he had so much in common (notwithstanding James's disapproval of Aristotle's metaphysics). Aristotle would surely have agreed that, in the words of the proverb James scrawled in his own copy of the *Briefer Course*: "Sow an action and you reap a habit; sow a habit and you reap a character; sow a character and you reap a destiny."

I should mention that James was pretty hard on people who develop virtuous habits of *mind* and *feeling* without correspondingly virtuous habits of *effort* and *action*. He faulted Rousseau, for instance, for prescribing techniques of child rearing while hustling his own children off to a foundling home. And he condemned the habits of "excessive novel-reading and theater-going" and "excessive indulgence in music" for their "relaxing effect upon the character"—like the Russian lady who weeps "over the fictitious personages in the play, while her coachman is freezing to death on his seat outside." The antidote to this sentimental aestheticism, James said, is never to have a feeling aroused by art that you do not act upon with at least a gesture of kindness, "if nothing more heroic offers." Artist though he was, James spurned sentimentality and aestheticism as passive experiences that breed bad habits of self-indulgence.

A final point about James's idea of habit. This might seem contradictory. It concerns the virtue of breaking habits. In an oft-cited passage, James says that habit is "the enormous flywheel of society, its most precious conservative agent," anchoring traditions in place and resigning people to sometimes sorry lives. He even warns that habit "dooms us all to fight out the battle of life" in our settled ways because "it is too late to begin again." In the chapter on instinct he reiterates the warning. "Outside of their own business," he says, "the ideas gained by men before they are twenty-five are practically the only ideas they shall have in their lives. They *cannot* get anything new" because "the mental grooves are set" and novelty arouses "a sense of insecurity." These statements imply that we are nothing more than a "bundle of habits" that cannot be undone. But James did not believe that. How could he have believed it in a pluralistic universe of chance? He just wanted us to see how firmly habits can grip us and why we should foster good habits early. In fact, he saw not only a potential for changing habits but a human need to do it.

The chapter on conversion in *The Varieties of Religious Experience* testifies to this. James explains there that although the "ideas and habits" in "the habitual centre" of an individual's "personal energy" resist change, they can be broken and replaced by new ones. This can occur when "dead ideas" and "dead habits" yield to a "new set of moral and spiritual habits," usually through some kind of stimulus, "especially violent . . . emotional occasions." When true conversion happens, it leaves old habits in the dust. James even said in a popular essay that the "solid meaning of life" depends in part on our imagining and rising to an "unhabitual ideal."

James acknowledges other exceptions to the hold of habit as well. One is genius. In the chapter on Attention, he says that genius does not rely on normal "habits of voluntary attention" because genius uses its own intense powers of concentration. "Genius, in truth," he remarks elsewhere, "means little more than the faculty of perceiving in an unhabitual way," unlike the "old fogeyism" blinkered to everything but the habitually conventional. It is no surprise that James championed the iconoclastic ideas of pragmatism as the rejection of "a lot of inveterate habits dear to professional philosophers."

James saw another exception to habit in human nature itself. "Man lives *by* habits, indeed," he said in a speech in 1904, "but what he lives for is thrills and excitements" because "the only relief from Habit's tediousness is periodical excitement." For this reason, he went on, people have welcomed war. And he suggested that society provide peaceful excitements to avoid war, a thought he would spell out in "The Moral Equivalent of War."†

James had embraced the idea of habit when his epiphany about free will converted him from negative habits of mind to more positive ones. This incident had opened his eyes to how bad habits, like addictions, can destroy us, but how good habits give us control of our lives. The most important of these are the habits of *effort*, *attention*, and *will*, which are the making of all good habits—including the deliberate practice, perhaps even the habit, of breaking bad habits. We shall look further at these good habits of mind when we reach the Will after first visiting James's conception of consciousness.

Following the "physiological preliminaries" in *Principles* that went far beyond physiology, James proceeded to a couple of methodological chapters then to pivotal chapters headed "The Stream of Thought,"† "The Consciousness of Self," and "Attention,"† followed by chapters on several types of cognitive activity, among them conception, discrimination, association, perception of time and space and reality, memory, sensation, imagination, reasoning, and finally to chapters on movement, instinct, emotions, will,† and hypnotism. This arrangement was not, James conceded, strictly logical, but it charted his quite intuitive journey through the mental life. Or his own "stream of consciousness," an idea central to the book and to James.

Every educated person has heard of "the stream of consciousness." This was James's inventive term (replacing "Stream of Thought" as the title of the chapter on consciousness in *Briefer Course*) for how consciousness works. And it encompasses everything in the mental life. Consciousness, James said, does not merely house ideas that come from sensations and get "associated" there, as traditional empiricism had it. Consciousness consists of all human experiences, along with relations among them (the unconscious lies in the shadows on its fringe). Within consciousness these experiences flow together as in "a 'river' or a 'stream'." "Let us call it the stream of thought, or consciousness," James said, which is in "constant change." Because these experiences flow together in this stream, they cannot wholly diverge—thoughts from feelings, sensations from memories, fantasies from facts, and so on. "Every definite image in the mind is steeped and dyed in the free water that flows around it." This account of consciousness jibed with James's long-standing contention that rationality and all claims to truth float on undercurrents of feelings. It also deprives consciousness of a fixed structure, rendering it impossible to get firm hold of. Years later, James would go so far as to ask, "Does consciousness exist?" And he would answer: No, it does not. Consciousness does not exist as a thing or entity. It is a function or a process. Something that happens. Lest we miss the radical intellectual implications of this idea, James said in *Principles* that his very purpose was "the reinstatement of the vague to its proper place in our mental life," remedying the errors of "traditional psychology" that had equated mind with an inert mechanism. Understandably, some readers have judged James an "impressionist" (an epithet, by the way, that Henry James accepted for his own writings), and James came to be identified with modernist authors who wrote fiction in the "stream of consciousness" style—early among them, we might say, his admiring student Gertrude Stein.

Within the "stream of consciousness," we form "the consciousness of self" and organize the lives we live. We do this through the "reinforcing and inhibiting agency of attention" that selects from the stream what we will use and what we will reject or neglect. Hence the next crucial quality of mind is *attention*. And it leads to the *will*.

"*My experience is what I agree to attend to*," James writes. For attention "is the taking possession by the mind . . . of one out of what seem several simultaneously possible objects or trains of thought" that flow in consciousness. Some of these grab our attention involuntarily. Others attract us more voluntarily with what, years earlier, he had called "the mystery of interest and selective attention" that arouse our notice. And "only those items which I *notice* shape my mind—without selective interest, experience is an utter chaos" of unfocused attention. That is to say, our attention must be trained. For our attention shapes our lives. "What is called our 'experience'," James says, "is almost entirely determined by our habits of attention." So, "each of us literally *chooses* by his way of attending to things, what sort of universe he shall appear to himself to inhabit." These decisive "habits of attention" show us where the will comes in. Although James leaves his discussion of will to near the end—and makes it the climax of the *Briefer Course* and his *Talks to Teachers*—we can best take it up here.

Echoing Renouvier, James says that we exercise our will when our mind, or consciousness, chooses to adopt some ideas and reject others. Sometimes an act of will leads to the "*direct* outward effects" of physical movement through what James and others called "ideo-motor action." That is, a physical action issues directly from the will seizing an idea, almost like a reflex. But whether the act of will triggers immediate

movement or not, that act "is a psychic or moral fact pure and simple.
. . . The whole drama is a mental drama." That makes every act of will
a drama of thinking. "*To think*, in short," James says in the chapter on
will in *Talks to Teachers*, "is the secret of will." But not just any kind of
thinking. Identifying which kind calls for more of James's hortatory
ethics.

The true test of thought and will, James explains, comes in the
mental drama of choosing which ideas to hold onto and which to resist.
The outcome now depends on both attention and that power of mind
James had made a key to good habits: effort. In order to hold to an idea
that has rivals in our minds, we must fasten attention on it. Doing this
calls for mental effort. At bottom, "attention and effort," James remarks,
"are but two names for the same psychic fact." Accordingly, "*effort of
attention is thus the essential phenomenon of will.*"

James was surely right that the effort of attention is something to
make a habit of. It enhances all of our powers and intensifies life. And
it is not far from the Hindu and Buddhist idea of mastering the mind
with powers of concentration, which James commended in several
places. It also gives us a psychological clue to morality: morality consists
in resisting ideas that stir immoral actions and in clutching ideas that
inspire moral actions. As James writes in the chapter on the stream of
consciousness, "The ethical energy *par excellence*" is choosing "which
*interest* [or idea] out of several, equally coercive, shall become supreme."
Therefore, he says, "*Will you or won't you have it so?* is the most probing
question we are ever asked." The "strong-willed man" has trained
himself to answer it with an habitual "effort of attention" that molds a
"heroic mind" and is "the measure of our worth as men." Such a person
plays "the game of human life" with the fervent affirmation: "*Yes, I will
even have it so!*" And with the "effort demanded" to do this, he "makes
himself one of the masters and the lords of life."

These exuberant words, urging the mental effort of attention and
will, recall again the epiphany that had set James on his philosophical
journey twenty years earlier, and they anticipate his future advocacy of
"the strenuous life." *Attention, effort, will,* and disciplined *habits* make
up a quartet of mental attributes that we need in order to keep our
minds alert (*awake!* in Buddhist parlance) and to govern our lives well.

Unfortunately this quartet performs with diminishing resonance in the young nowadays amidst the habitual mental scatterings and distractions of omnipresent electronic technology and entertainment. James's writings on the quartet should be required reading for the young today more than ever (and they are featured in this anthology).*

Even the selective and impressionistic outline of the *Principles of Psychology* that I have given demonstrates that it is more than a textbook. It is a philosophical adventurer's explorations of the mental life (marking another kinship with Freud, who once referred to himself as a "conquistador") as human beings make their way through experience. It is also a kind of philosophical self-help book on how to do this. Several psychologists and philosophers at the time, objecting to its frequently informal tone, failed to appreciate its intellectual substance and durable wisdom. But history has sided with James. *Principles* remains the seminal classic in psychology, and it feeds new minds in every generation.** The renowned historian and critic Jacques Barzun spoke for generations of admirers when he said it is "a masterpiece in the classic and total sense" of needing no qualifying adjectives to place it in a category because it stands on its own.

James was justly proud of it—"especially from the literary point of view," he remarked to Henry Holt, jesting, "I begin to look down on Mark Twain." But he and Holt knew that at well over 1,000 pages it ran longer than most students would tolerate—even in that pre-electronic-media age. They had, in fact, been considering an abridged edition for some time, and the next summer James whittled the *Principles* down to what became known as the *Briefer Course* (officially: *Psychology*. American Science Series—Briefer Course). This omitted long quotations and elaborate footnotes, combined some chapters, added boldface headings, revised some phrasing, accentuated certain ideas, replaced the last chapter with an Epilogue on "Psychology and Philosophy," and attached, as James told Holt, some "wretched twaddle about the senses" at the beginning "to satisfy the market." The new edition ran to about a third of the original. It became the leading psychology textbook in America for decades. It also raised the curtain on James's career as a public speaker presenting his versions of psychology and philosophy to teachers, students, and Everyman.

During the 1890s James gave abundant lectures of this popular type. In 1897 he published a volume containing several of these, along with some of his previous papers, under the title *The Will to Believe and Other Essays in Popular Philosophy*. This book expanded James's reputation and remains a classic of its own. In the Preface, James said its contents exemplified what he now called "radical empiricism." This term bespoke his conviction that all human experience, inside and outside, is in the game, as he liked to say, and is open-ended, for no truth is absolute. In all, the book thumped James's arguments on such topics as how determinism amounts to abstract folly, pluralism reflects concrete experience, belief has efficacy in the quest for truth, religion can give meaning to life, morality arises from the lives we live, and individuals play an indispensable role in the historical evolution of human kind. Having already commented on "The Dilemma of Determinism" and "The Sentiment of Rationality" in this collection, I will say a little about three other pertinent and closely related essays in it: "The Will to Believe,"† "Is Life Worth Living?"† and "The Moral Philosopher and the Moral Life."†

"The Will to Believe," based on a lecture of 1896, reads like a sequel to "The Sentiment of Rationality." James later remarked that perhaps he should have named the essay "The *Right* to Believe" since it defends the intellectual right to affirm beliefs shy of scientific evidence. But *will* was the term he originally used, and it betokened his long occupation with that idea. The question he focused on now was: "Can our will either help or hinder our intellect in its perceptions of truth?"

He opens with the assertion that anything we might believe is a "*hypothesis*" giving us "*options*" between it and other hypotheses. If these options do not greatly affect our lives, we can ignore them and the related hypotheses. But if they do affect us enough that our lives hang in the balance, we have to act. "*Moral questions*," James explains, pose hypotheses and options of this compulsive kind. For they concern what we should do with our lives. Faced with such questions, we "cannot wait for sensible proof" before choosing which hypothesis to act on. And not to choose is to choose. Either way, we are choosing a moral hypothesis in the absence of knowledge. That makes the choice an act of will, not a judgment of reason or intellect. "The question of having moral beliefs at all or not having them," James asserts, "is decided by our will."

For that matter, James reminds us, consciousness being the stream it is, the search for truth of any kind relies on "our non-intellectual nature," including the will. And he chides rationalists again for overstating the cognitive purity and intellectual certainty of their purported truths. Then he clinches his case. Finding truth in moral life—if not science— depends, he says, above all, on our will to believe in that truth in the first place. For in moral life "*faith in a fact can help create the fact.*" James had already made this point in "The Sentiment of Rationality." And he had elaborated on it in an article entitled "The Psychology of Belief" (1889). Wielding his fertile conceptions of will and attention, he said there that because "the will can change the relative power which objects have of compelling our attention," it "can end up by making us . . . *act* as if they were real." That action then verifies the belief with rewards in experience. "Belief and will," James sums up, "are thus inseparable functions."

This is how *the will to believe* delivers the empirical truth of beliefs. Applied to religion, the method works like this. "The religious hypothesis" proposes, first, that "eternal things" matter most in the universe, and, second, that "we are better off even now if we believe" the first proposition. Whether we accept or reject this hypothesis, or stay neutral, "we *act*, taking our life in our hands" by deciding how to live. For his part, James had no doubt what to do. "I do not wish," he said, "to forfeit my sole chance in life of getting upon the winning side" by dismissing a belief in religion that can bring rewards now and that "might be prophetic and right." The "risk" of error, he said, is worth it in the game of life, where winning is everything.

"The Will to Believe" did not persuade the rationalists, who denounced it as rank irrationalism.* But it heightened James's reputation as both a radical and a religious thinker—and took him further on the road to pragmatism. In the related essay, "Is Life Worth Living?" from a lecture given near the same time as "The Will to Believe," James recast the same themes for people who doubt that life is worth living—as he had done years before. We "have a right to believe," he said, in "an unseen spiritual order" that accounts for the "physical order," if for no other reason than that "thereby life may seem to us better worth living."* For "not a victory is gained except upon a maybe," and often "our faith beforehand . . . [ed.] *is the only thing that makes the result come true."* After all, he says, "it is only by risking our persons from one hour to another that we live at all." And he concludes with an upbeat existentialist pronouncement, part of which I quoted at the beginning. Life, he says, "*feels* like a real fight" in "a half-wild half-saved universe . . . in which we dwell alone with our willingness and unwillingness, our faiths and fears." But we should "be not afraid of life" because to "believe that life is worth living . . . will help create the fact," just as confidence that we can succeed at anything takes us a long way toward success.

This essay makes an apt companion to "The Will to Believe." But James's assurance that we can verify the truth of a moral belief by acting on it left open a stubborn question. In science, material evidence settles questions of truth, at least provisionally, until proven wrong. Lacking that evidence in the moral life, how do we choose between competing beliefs when they prove equally true in experience to their adherents? Do tyrants and suicide bombers validate their beliefs with the purposeful lives they feel that they live and the deaths and mayhem that they deliberately cause?

James knew the problem. But in writing about religion, he aimed only to justify religious belief in general as a way of giving purpose to life. He never picked theological sides. As a believer himself, he was decidedly nonsectarian and heterodox. At the same time, he repeatedly denounced fanaticism. In "The Psychology of Belief" and later in *Principles*, he emphatically declared, "The greatest proof that a man is *sui compos* [self-controlled] is his ability to suspend belief in the presence of an emotionally exciting idea"—one that induces a person to believe: "Nothing which I can feel like *that* can be false." That suspension of belief is an act of will: resisting seductively self-satisfying ideas. "To give this power" of mental resistance, James says, "is the highest result of education." For it insulates us against mind-twisting fanaticism, imperious ideologies, and corrosive self-deception. James even concluded "The Will to Believe" with an appeal to pluralism and tolerance. Given the absence of absolute moral truth, he said, we should "respect one another's mental freedom" in the "spirit of inner tolerance" that is "empiricism's glory." This principle of tolerance would become a prominent theme in his writings. And the troubled world we live in today could gain much from what James had to say about it.

Still, we might reasonably ask: Besides advising restraint when confronted with emotionally exciting ideas, and urging respect for "one another's mental freedom," did James have no other standard of good among competing moral ideas? If not, then anything goes, except intolerance. But James did have other moral standards. His many excursions into the hortatory ethics of habit and will alone demonstrate that. And he took a shot at more formal ethical philosophy in "The Moral Philosopher and the Moral Life," a talk he gave in 1891. It is a tantalizing and provocative piece showing James's empiricist mind at work on that historically rocky ground.

James alerts readers right off that there can be no "ethical philosophy dogmatically made up in advance," since, like all truth, moral truth depends on experience. Not only that, "there can be no final truth in ethics . . . until the last man has had his experience" because people create ethics as they live, opening the door to new moral truths every day. This is a strikingly existentialist notion of ethics, again bringing James close to Jean-Paul Sartre, who declared in *Existentialism Is a Humanism* that human beings invent ethics with every choice they make, like artists creating works of art.

But James goes on to say that philosophers must do more than allow this moral inventiveness. They must search for a more general "*system of truth*" to aid people in their ethical lives. Naturally, James looked for clues to such a system in ordinary experience. This showed him that the moral life arises from people's everyday "judgments of good and ill and [their] demands upon one another." Whenever two people get together, ethics crop up. God has nothing to do with it. "Whether a God exist, or whether no God exist, in yon blue heaven above us," James hymns, "we form at any rate an ethical republic here below." For "ethics have as genuine and real a foothold in a universe where the highest consciousness is human, as in a universe where there is a God as well." Theist though he was, in morals James was also something of an existentialist and ethical humanist.

Still, the question remained: How do we decide which of these human judgments and demands is the most ethically good? To answer it, true to his empiricist principles, James cuts through the history of philosophical ethics with an observation of prosaic fact: everybody agrees that "*The essence of good is simply to satisfy demand.*" And "the demand may be for anything under the sun." In other words, people have desires, and they judge satisfying them to be good. This commonsense idea pulled the rug from under conventional ethics. James goes on to conclude that the only general ethics possible is to "satisfy at all times *as many demands as we can*" and to produce the "*best whole . . . at the least cost.*"

This might sound like moral anarchy tempered by the Utilitarian idea of the *greatest good for the greatest number.* James had a certain anarchist streak in him, but he was no Utilitarian social engineer tooling to maximize quantities of pleasures and minimize quantities of pain. As he wrote in a short essay called "The Importance of Individuals" (in *The Will to Believe*), "I for my part cannot but consider the talk of the contemporary sociological school about averages and general laws and predetermined tendencies, with its obligatory undervaluing of the importance of individual differences, as the most pernicious and immoral of fatalisms." This charge targeted the same kind of deterministic assumptions that today reduce human behavior to social or psychological influences. James spurned anything smacking of determinism. In the morality essay he invited social and ethical experiments to show "by what sort of conduct the maximum amount of good can be gained and kept in this world," while heeding the benefits of custom, but he stated unequivocally: "The *highest* ethical life—however few may be called to bear its burdens—consists at all times in the breaking of rules which have grown too narrow." This was James the revolutionary—and breaker of habits. And yet, as always, he would let experience tell us whether or not any experiment or action—customary or revolutionary—worked in the world. Like science, ethics must "be ready to revise its conclusions from day to day." Unsettling as this open-endedness may be, the ethics of radical empiricism requires it.

James's ethical philosophy in "The Moral Philosopher and the Moral Life" will not satisfy those who want definite truth and trusted authority to guide their moral lives. James is here admittedly imprecise, adamantly antiauthoritarian, capaciously pluralistic, profoundly tolerant, predominantly pragmatic (without the term), and fundamentally humanistic—although, in a parting gesture praising "the strenuous mood" over the "easy-going" for helping us get "out of the game of existence its keenest possibilities of zest," he said that nothing can "let loose in us the strenuous mood" better than religious faith. James acted on his own ethical principles with virtually everything he wrote, and by opposing any system of authority—intellectual or political—that would limit learning from experience and deprive people of living their own lives to the full. In portions of his next book, James applied these principles to a few common experiences with exceptionally evocative imagery and detail.

This book comprised a series of lectures James had been giving to teachers since 1892 based on the *Principles of Psychology*, plus three talks to students on the moral life. He published the collection two years after *The Will to Believe* under the unassuming title *Talks to Teachers on Psychology: And to Students on Some of Life's Ideals* (the lectures there on "The Laws of Habit" and "The Will" and two of the talks to students appear below).*

The first of those talks to students, "The Gospel of Relaxation," is a slight piece (with a title taken from James's frequent adversary Herbert Spencer) on a topic popular in late nineteenth-century America: the "over-tension and jerkiness and breathlessness and intensity" and "absence of repose," as James put it, ailing many Americans. Dismissing the usual attribution of this condition to the climate or the hurried pace of modern American life, James blamed it on—what else?—"*bad habits,* nothing more or less." He prescribed good habits of "harmony, dignity, and ease" as the cure. This prescription might seem to contradict James's demands for effort and the strenuous mood—he even cautioned his listeners against trying "to become strenuously relaxed." But, appreciating human nature as he did, James could encourage strenuousness and still recommend relaxation to restore energy.

The second talk, "On a Certain Blindness in Human Beings,"† has more weight. And James counted it among his most important moral statements, providing "a definite view of the world and of our moral relations to the same." It examines an ordinary but consequential human experience. That is "the blindness with which we all are afflicted in regard to the feelings of creatures and people different from ourselves." Through a skein of examples from life and literature, James illustrates this blindness and the common "stupidity and injustice of our opinions, so far as they deal with the significance of alien lives." This blindness (he says at the beginning of the next talk) "is the root of most human injustices and cruelties, and the trait in human character most likely to make the angels weep," just as recognizing it "is the basis of all our tolerance, social, religious, and political." Aware of this blindness, he wound up the talk on it, we can "tolerate, respect, and indulge those whom we see harmlessly interested and happy in their own ways, however unintelligible these may be to us." Like his metaphysics, James's ethics were always pluralistic.

In its modest way, this essay on our blindness to others made another case for James's conviction that "the truth is too great for any one actual mind . . . to know the whole of it." By the time the essay appeared in 1899, it also had direct political relevance. In the previous year the Spanish-American War had broken out, fueling a frenzy of jingoistic imperialism that James condemned as a blatant political eruption of the blindness leading "our nation to inflict its own inner ideals and institutions" on others around the globe. This imperialism violated precepts his philosophy shared with democracy itself: "respect for the sacredness of individuality" and "tolerance of whatever is not itself intolerance." James's ethical philosophy of empiricism and pluralism had become a political philosophy as well.

The third of those talks to students captured the spirit of James's philosophy of life more concisely than any other single work. It takes on no less a topic than "What Makes a Life Significant?"†* James had been asking himself this question since a visit to the ideal community of Chautauqua in New York State where he had given a lecture in the summer of 1896. There he had found all at peace and everyone smiling, free from crime, disorder, and discontent, "without a blot, without a tear." Here thrived, he says, the utopia mankind has always wished for. But upon leaving, James felt relief swell in his breast at escaping "this atrocious harmlessness of all things." Chautauqua lacked, he mused, the "heights and depths," the "intensity and danger" of "the wicked outer world" where "strength and strenuousness" and "heroism" flourish, making life more significant—give him, he wrote to his wife, "the flash of a pistol, a dagger, or a devilish eye, anything to break the unlovely level of 10,000 good people." And he regretted that modern society seemed to be drifting toward that same benumbed condition.

Then a group of hard-working laborers caught his eye, and it dawned on him that these rustic fellows did live strenuous lives of challenging, dangerous work. He began to idealize them, he says, rather like Tolstoy—whom he esteemed for literary and philosophical reasons—idealized the Russian peasantry. But he later wondered if their lives felt any more significant to those laborers than the lives of Chautauqua's blissful inhabitants felt to them. Admitting his own blindness to everyone else's internal self, he decided that the feeling of significance in life must be an "inner meaning which passeth show." And he wondered what gives rise to this inner meaning that can burn in such disparate lives.

It then dawned on him that whatever else kindles this inner meaning, it would have to include some kind of ideal—an aspiration, a principle, a belief, a desire. But not an ideal alone. Ideals in themselves supply us little more than a morally pleasing pat on the back. To work for us, ideals have to engage reality. As James wrote in a letter a few years later, "Ideals ought to aim at the *transformation of reality*—no less!" To do that, he said in the essay, we must summon none other than "the active will" and a little "pluck." This involves effort and attention, of course, even strenuous energy, and it might cause some pain. In words James had written long ago and reprinted more than once, we need "the particular mood called seriousness, which means the willingness to live with energy, though energy bring pain." At the same time, James suggests, we should search for "new ideals" to energize us when we need them and to shake us out of dead habits. Only then can we fully grasp the truth that "the solid meaning of life is always the same eternal thing—the marriage, namely, of some unhabitual ideal, however special, with some fidelity, courage, and endurance; with some man's or woman's pains." As he had said earlier, "the *highest* ethical life consists" in breaking rules that have grown too narrow.

"What Makes a Life Significant?" at once cautioned against mis-judging other people's lives and urged the creation and re-creation of meaning in our own lives through the *active will* to find *unhabitual ideals* and through the *effort* to courageously put them into practice. Here again the habit of effort would have to break dead habits and form new live ones. This talk to students was James at his most hortatory—and wise.

In the years surrounding these wholesome talks to the young on life's ideals, James had also become engrossed in a very different kind of subject: abnormal psychology. In writing *Principles*, he later explained, he had chosen not to address the "harmful . . . mental activity" of psychologically "ill 'adapted'" human beings because that was the province of "'Psychiatry.'" His primary interest at that time lay in the "preservative" functions of more normal, conscious "mental life"—his short chapter on hypnotism merely described the phenomenon, and James deleted it from the *Briefer Course*. This inclination put James roughly in the tradition of future ego psychologists like Anna Freud and Erik Erikson and personality theorists like Gordon Allport and Carl Rogers occupied with conscious adaptations of the ego to the world rather than, like Freud, with pathological intrusions of the unconscious. But, beginning with his own time of crisis, James always had a lively curiosity about the dark, mysterious, wild side of the psyche as well—or, as he described it in a letter near the end of his life, the "twilight region that surrounds the clearly lighted center of experience." As a psychologist in the late nineteenth century, he could hardly have lacked that curiosity. This was a time of ascending occupation with mental pathology and the "buried life" (a term James identified in "The Gospel of Relaxation" with an anonymous "Viennese neurologist of considerable reputation," namely, Sigmund Freud). James exhibited his own curiosity by studying a wide variety of abnormal psychology, and he gave a series of lectures on them in 1896, ranging from dreams and hysteria to witchcraft, demoniacal possession, and multiple personality. He also wrote appreciative reviews of works on hysteria by both Freud and Pierre Janet (who coined the term subconscious and with whom James corresponded). And he was a leading member of The Society for Psychic Research, whose studies of the occult he reported in *The Will to Believe*, evincing the existence of "a 'subliminal' self" that "may make at any time irruption into our ordinary lives." In another essay, entitled "The Confidences of a 'Psychical Researcher'," published ten months before his death, James went farther. "I am persuaded," he wrote, "that the greatest scientific conquests of the coming generation will be achieved" through study of "the facts called 'psychic'." But James's interest in the "subliminal self" and the "twilight region" of mental life did not lead him to a comprehensive theory of the unconscious and psychopathology, as it did Freud (fourteen years younger than James)— first published in Freud's *The Interpretation of Dreams* (1900). Instead, it conducted James down another trail where he brought forth a second psychological classic characteristic of him. This was *The Varieties of Religious Experience*,† presented as the Gifford Lectures in Edinburgh, Scotland, 1901–02. It made James an internationally celebrated figure.

Like "The Will to Believe," *Varieties* defended religious belief. But this was almost the least of it. Subtitled "A Study of Human Nature," it cast the light of James's distinctive scrutiny into some penumbral quarters of human life, disclosing unseen realities and delivering useful truths. This time James got into the trenches, as he told a friend, to "defend . . . 'experience' against 'philosophy' as being the real backbone of the world's religious life." He jocularly told his colleague, friend, and amiable idealist adversary Josiah Royce, "When I compose my Gifford lectures mentally, 'tis with the design exclusively of overthrowing your system, and ruining your peace."

The experiences James located as the "backbone" of religious life were not those of "your ordinary religious believer," whose "religion has been made for him by others" and is "retained by habit." They were instead "the original experiences" of "individuals for whom religion exists not as a dull habit, but as an acute fever." These individuals are "'geniuses' in the religious line," often of "neurotic temperament" and "subject to abnormal psychic visitations." For these very reasons they worship at the fount of religious life, which James broadly defined here as "the belief that there is an unseen order, and that our supreme good lies in harmoniously adjusting ourselves thereto."

James suspected that this most authentic religious experience arises from the "subconscious and non-rational" regions of human nature (or, as he put it in a letter, from "an extended subliminal self, with a thin partition through which messages make irruption"), but he did not delve into those depths. He resolved to take a "thoroughly 'pragmatic' view of religion" and "judge the religious life by its results exclusively." With these *pragmatic* assumptions about the nature of religion and how to understand it, James explored the varieties of religious experience as he found them, "morbid or healthy," searching for secrets of both normal and abnormal states of mind and ways of life.

Some of James's findings and descriptions have become classics in themselves. His chapters on "The Religion of Healthy-Mindedness" and "The Sick Soul," for instance, memorably portray two types of religious personality. Believers of the first type have "a constitutional incapacity for prolonged suffering" and experience religion as the pursuit of everything good and beneficent, "even the good of this world's life." They also think "evil is a disease" and that "worry over sin is itself an additional form of disease."

The mind-cure movement that James himself turned to for aid in his own emotional trials shared this invincibly healthy-minded disposition. But sympathetic as James was to the religion of healthy-mindedness, he knew from his own darkest days that "the sick soul" lives a deeper life. To the sick soul, he says, "healthy-mindedness pure and simple seems unspeakably blind and shallow," oblivious to the "evil facts" that are "a genuine portion of reality" and that "may after all be the best key to life's significance, and possibly the only openers of our eyes to the deepest levels of truth." What is more, although the life of the sick soul is hard, fraught with despair, "grubbing in rat holes," and beset by visions of evil, it can also bring a second birth in life. James takes up this experience of the "twice-born" in notable chapters on "The Divided Self" and "Conversion."

James knew the experience of a second birth at first hand. But he thought it need not be religious. "To find religion," he remarks, "is only one out of many ways of remedying inner incompleteness" and "discord." In fact, "the new birth may be away from religion into incredulity" or into any new vision and way of life after "a period of storm and stress and inconsistency." Whoever "the new man" becomes, the rebirth is a conversion that changes "the habitual centre" of his or her "personal energy." As mentioned earlier, that amounts to breaking old habits of mind and behavior. Decades later, cofounder of Alcoholics Anonymous Bill Wilson would credit James's account of conversion as a chief inspiration of AA's twelve-step program for converting alcoholics to "kick the habit" and stay sober (James's writings on habit and will also obviously pertain to curing addiction).

James goes from "Conversion" to "Saintliness," which he extols for embodying the "self-surrender"—as in voluntary poverty—of mental discipline and devotion to purpose that are "indispensable to the world's welfare." Again foreshadowing a famous later essay, he finds in the saintly character qualities of the "strenuous life" needed for a "moral equivalent of war." Then he turns to what he elsewhere called "the mother sea and fountain-head of all religions," namely, "the mystical experiences of the individual." For "mystical states" reach into the deepest parts of our being and "offer us *hypotheses*" (as in "The Will to Believe") about "the ideal" that we otherwise could not envision. "The supernaturalism and optimism to which [mystics] would persuade us," James writes, "may be after all the truest of insights into the meaning of this life." That is quite a statement. And it expresses the lasting effect on him of his own glimpse into the mystical powers of mind. Practical-minded as he was, James was always a bit of a mystic, too. That played out more of his radical empiricism.

James completes the book with a paean to religious pluralism that surely catches most readers off guard. Let sects and creeds and religious experiences proliferate, he says, for the varieties of human life require varieties of religious experience. And he goes farther. Defining religion now as "the belief that beyond each man . . . there exists a larger power which is friendly to him and to his ideals,"* he concludes that this power "need not be infinite." It might even be no more than "a larger and more godlike self," and "the universe might conceivably be a collection of such selves" amounting to "a sort of polytheism." Juiced by that heady notion, James declares there should "be different gods, each caring for his part" of the universe—or multiverse. This would be cosmic pluralism for sure. James wraps up by saying that while "the pluralistic hypothesis" cannot guarantee personal salvation as surely as can a monistic philosophy of cosmic unity and necessity, it can supply more possibilities, allowing everyone a chance freely to create a life and to cultivate the will to believe. That is all we need. For "no fact in human nature," he repeats from his essay on determinism, "is more characteristic than its willingness to live on a chance." James could never resist reminding us that in a pluralistic universe of unpredictable, open-ended experience life is pretty much a game of chance.

Like the *Principles of Psychology*, no one could have written *The Varieties of Religious Experience* but William James. It stands as a classic in the study of religion and human nature—and it is a compendium of James's capacious vision of life at age sixty.

In the few years remaining to James after its publication, his reputation soared in America and Europe as he poured ever more of his energies into philosophical pursuits, along with occasional popular lectures and essays. Some of his philosophical writings—notably "Does 'Consciousness' Exist?" and "A World of Pure Experience"—confidently advanced radical empiricism as a philosophy of truth and existence boldly encompassing the entire adventure of human experience while flatly excluding anything outside of this experience. The radicalism of this philosophy had already allied James with, among others, the scientific positivist Ernst Mach, with whom he corresponded and whose stringently empiricist ideas of space and time aided Albert Einstein in devising his special theory of relativity, published in 1905.* But James never published these writings as a book—*Essays in Radical Empiricism* was assembled by others and published after his death. The next book James published was a collection of essays on a subject he had started talking about explicitly only in very recent years: pragmatism. But before that publication, James had a literally earthshaking experience that confirmed many of his intellectual and moral convictions, and that he would put to ingenious philosophical use.

In 1906 James traveled to California to help galvanize the fledgling Philosophy Department of the fifteen-year-old Stanford University. His California days would have given him no more than an academic junket but for what happened in the early morning of April 18. James "felt the bed begin to waggle," he reported, and things all over the room shook to the floor. It was the Great San Francisco Earthquake. And it was *some* experience. James wrote about it in a charming and illuminating little essay called "On Some Mental Effects of the Earthquake."†

The earthquake struck him at once physically, emotionally, and philosophically. Astonishingly, he recalled shortly afterwards, "I felt no trace whatever of fear." To the contrary, he felt "glee" and "pure delight"—as well as "admiration" that the house didn't collapse. Soon he was off to San Francisco to witness the damage there and to examine the human effects. What he saw moved him with amazement at the energies of the survivors, who appeared "busy as ants" amid the desolation as they "doggedly" labored to save lives and salvage the city. A week later he returned to be impressed at the work accomplished and at the wondrously "intact skyscrapers," validating for him the courage and achievements of modern "architects and builders." James was indeed a modern man. In retrospect, two effects of the earthquake reverberated most for him. One was the "improvisation of order out of chaos" by the industrious survivors, demonstrating human resilience and resourcefulness. The other was their "universal equanimity," "steadfastness of tone," and even "cheerfulness," despite the suffering and privation, attesting to the "admirable fortitude" of human beings in a crisis. These experiences gave James new fodder for his philosophy.

That philosophy had always prized will and effort. It had also increasingly valued energy. Now, in the wake of his eye-popping earthquake experience, James fixed his attention on sources of human energy. His presidential address to the American Philosophical Association that December carried the title "The Energies of Men."† It was a pep talk. "We are making use of only a small part of our possible mental and physical resources," he told his audience; "compared to what we ought to be, we are only half-awake." Why? "Habitually narrow actual use." And how do we break those lazy habits? With *will*, of course. "The normal opener of deeper and deeper levels of energy," he said, "is the will." However, the will sometimes needs to be awakened by "excitements, ideas, and efforts." For "the emotions and excitements" of "unusual situations," he explained, are the chief "inciters of the will," prompting it to do its job of attending to one thing instead of another and stirring action. When we experience a jolt of excitement, the will focuses on its cause and gives us a charge of energy that can go on and on.

James mentions wars and shipwrecks as "the great revealers of what men and women are able to do and bear." The San Francisco earthquake was another instance. That geological upheaval, he told his audience, elicited astonishing "stores of bottled up energy and endurance" in the residents of that city. But, he advised, we cannot depend on earthquakes and shipwrecks and the like to release our energies. We need to find other and more manageable means. The first of these is none other than the *habit of effort*. For it opens doors to exertion. As an illustration, James refers to the ascetic exercises of Hindu yoga as exemplified by a friend who had managed to control his physiological processes to a superhuman degree. This friend's new habitual efforts had tapped into extraordinary energies, "waking up deeper levels of will-power than are habitually used"—and he had gained a composure of mind lacking earlier when sunk in neurotic depression. James went on to show how ideas themselves can activate effort and energy. "Ideas set free beliefs," he explained, and then "the beliefs set free our wills." He had in mind here the transfiguring power of "energy-releasing" ideas like "liberty" and "fatherland" and the "unhabitual ideals" he had advocated to make life significant, as well as ideas that inspire conversions and even simple vows of personal loyalty and commitment.\* All rouse energy and channel it into fruitful action.

James concluded by enjoining philosophers and psychologists to study the release of human energies in order to better understand human nature. And he tipped his hat to a "fellow pragmatist in Florence," Giovani Papini, for advancing this through a "new conception of philosophy" that amounted to a *doctrine of action* in the widest sense." Finally, James expressed the hope that his proposal would itself energize his listeners and "unlock unused reservoirs of investigating power" in them and change the course of philosophy and psychology.

If James's enthusiasm here did not spark the crowd to hearty cheers and ignite a rush to labs and libraries to discover the wellsprings of human energy, James had certainly found new sources of energy for himself in the "new conception of philosophy" he shared with the Italian Papini. This was pragmatism. James had been talking and writing about pragmatism by name in passing (as in *Varieties*) since his first mention of the word in a lecture at Berkeley in 1898. But, as we have seen, he had been philosophizing about it without the name since the beginning of his career. Now James viewed pragmatism as nothing less than a revolution in philosophy—"something quite like the Protestant reformation," he exulted to Henry.

Not long after the earthquake, James had published a short article called "G. Papini and the Pragmatist Movement in Italy" that waved the flag of this revolution—and presaged some historical surprises ahead. Papini was a twenty-five-year-old intellectual aflame with Latin fire. Converted to pragmatism by reading some of James's writings on belief, action, results, and so forth, he had met the author at a conference in Rome in 1905. Shortly after that he had published an exuberant article in the journal he edited with fellow hot-bloods, *Leonardo*, spelling out, as James says, "the whole pragmatic scope and program very neatly." Papini had then published an inflammatory book proclaiming the death of traditional philosophy. James loved all of this. And he reveled in the "frolicsomeness and impertinence" of Papini and his comrades, who wrote with "refreshing novelty" and rhetorical flair, unlike the "bald-headed and bald-hearted young aspirants for the Ph.D." in America who "bore one another" to death with their "pedantry and technicality."

James applauded Papini for describing pragmatism as "an *unstiffening* of all our theories and beliefs" and "*a general theory of human action*" that, in Papini's words, called for a "'*quest of instruments to act with*, or, in other words, *the quest of power.*'" James even smiled at Papini's notion that pragmatism so releases human creativity that "man becomes a kind of god"—a thought James himself had toyed with at the end of *Varieties*. And James wrapped up with the flourish that together he and Papini might "make of pragmatism a new militant form of religious or quasi-religious philosophy."

James let his enthusiasm get away from him here again. He could not have foreseen what many readers nowadays know: how Papini's frolicsome promotion of pragmatism as a philosophy of action and a quest for power would play into the martial spirit of pre–World War I Italy and later into the ascendency of Fascism. Papini himself soon turned to Futurism, which disdained the past and idealized war, and he later supported Mussolini, dedicating one of his many books to him. Mussolini himself actually claimed in an interview of 1926 that "the pragmatism of William James was of great use to me in my political career" by fueling an "ardent will to live and fight," stirring "faith in action," and teaching him that action must be judged "by its results." It is unlikely that Mussolini ever read James, but he certainly read Papini and the Italian pragmatists. Had James lived to see any of this, he would surely have jumped up and shouted "No! No! That's not what I meant!"—just as Friedrich Nietzsche would have done, had he seen how his similarly animating words on will and power would be misunderstood and exploited by the Nazis. But ideas can have consequences not imagined by their authors. And there is a piquant irony in James's own ideas of pragmatism having consequences he would not have approved—misguided as those consequences might have been. In truth, pragmatism did not teach Fascism anything. The two only met in the antirationalist currents of early twentieth-century culture. Be that as it may, much as James judged ideas by their results, he would not judge any idea or belief by a single set of results alone. That restriction toughened his pragmatism, as we shall see.

When James gave a series of lectures on pragmatism near the time of the talk on energy—and then published these as a book the next year, when he also retired from teaching—he held his early enthusiasm in check. He led his listeners and readers through his new take on ideas that had been coalescing in him for years around the subjectivity of philosophy, the follies of rationalism and monism and determinism, the persuasiveness of pluralism, the truths of experience, the efficacy of belief, the imperatives of consequences, and more. And he modestly entitled the book *Pragmatism. A New Name for Some Old Ways of Thinking. Popular Lectures on Philosophy*. But it gave James an enduring philosophical identity—along with a taint of infamy among contrary rationalists.

In the chapter "What Pragmatism Means"† James explains that pragmatism (a word and formal doctrine fathered by Charles Sanders Peirce, as James amply acknowledges) is first of all a "*method*" or way of thinking about truth. It is, as James depicts it in one of Papini's metaphors, "like a corridor in a hotel" along which people pass to reach the rooms where they engage in their own activities. Pragmatism "does not stand for any special results" of those activities. It asks only that everyone in the corridor demonstrate "what definite difference it will make to you and me, at definite instants of our life" if this result or that, "this world-formula or that world formula be the true one." If there is no discernible difference in practice, then the ideas are useless. The most useful ideas make a distinct difference, supplying "practical cash-value . . . within the stream of your experience." That cash-value is the currency of useful results.

Here, James says, pragmatism ascends from a method to a "*theory of truth.*" With a nod to fellow pragmatists John Dewey and F. S. C. Schiller, James explains that ideas "*become true*" when, as in science, they accord with actuality. That is the "'instrumental' view of truth." As James says in the chapter on "Pragmatism's Conception of Truth,"† "truth *happens* to an idea. It becomes true, is made true by events." In other words, the cash-value of useful results in experience makes ideas come true. But, as mentioned earlier, this is no simple payoff satisfying single circumstances or myopic interests. The pragmatic truth or cash-value of an idea must pay off within the whole context of our experience. The "only test of probable truth is what . . . fits every part of life best and combines with the collectivity of experience's demands, nothing being omitted." That is one of pragmatism's "tough-minded" rules, as James put it, by contrast to the "tender-minded" standards of rationalism.

James takes pains to apply this rule to religious belief. "*If theological ideas prove to have value for concrete life*" he says, "*they will be true, for pragmatism, in the sense of being good for so much.*" But, like all pragmatic truths, they are limited and provisional, valid until higher truths come along. "*For how much more they are true, will depend entirely on their relations to the other truths that have also to be acknowledged.*" In religion, no less than in other arenas of life, we must stay on the lookout for new truths because "experience, as we know, has ways of *boiling over,* and making us correct our present formulas." The "'absolutely' true" is therefore an illusion, the "ideal vanishing-point towards which we imagine that all of our temporary truths will some day converge."

Pragmatism keeps us aware of this humbling fact, out in "the open air" of "possibilities" that pit us "against dogma" and "the pretense of finality in truth."

This flexible pragmatist theory of truth obviously fit James's own pluralistic vision of life as a welter of experience where we must fight to prevail with will and effort and should extend tolerance to our fellow combatants. In the three years he lived after the publication of *Pragmatism*, James carried on that crusade as usual. He gave a series of lectures at Oxford on philosophical subjects close to his heart that he published under the title *A Pluralistic Universe*† in 1908. These essays revisited with new fervor his familiar arguments against rationalism, idealism, and monism. And, among a few byways, he now made a hero—James openly adopted hero-worship for temperamental and philosophical reasons, sometimes with misplaced generosity—of the French philosopher Henri Bergson. Almost a generation younger than James, Bergson understood more fully than any other philosopher, James says, how "the essence of life is its continuously changing character," and that "what really exists is not things made but things in the making." Such a reality—like James's "stream of consciousness"—cannot be grasped by abstractions but must be experienced directly in all of its existential actuality and incessant flow. Although Bergson was no pragmatist, James found in him a vigorous ally in the war against absolutism and abstract "intellectualism," and they became good friends.

James ended the book with an expression of renewed conviction that we live in an "unfinished pluralistic universe" where "nothing includes everything," where "wild beasts of the philosophic desert" deserve to roam, and where every conviction comes down to "life exceeding logic" as we choose what "*shall be* as if true" for us. Age had done nothing to dim James's philosophical radicalism.

Shortly after sending off *A Pluralistic Universe*, James gathered together a bunch of his published articles and reviews on radical empiricism, pragmatism, and related topics, tossed in a couple of new ones and published them in 1909 as *The Meaning of Truth. A Sequel to Pragmatism.*† It contributed nothing substantial to his philosophy, but it clarified some ideas, if not altogether to his critics' satisfaction—such as his ambiguous notion of how the pragmatic truth of a belief in the mind relates to the actual existence of things in the universe like God— qualified others, and overall thrust them in the face of adversaries (including Bertrand Russell and G. E. Moore) who couldn't understand James's pragmatism and pluralism as philosophy. It shows why James gave headaches to many other philosophers, when he didn't set their hair on fire. They wanted a system from him, tidily knitting everything to everything else and described in conventional philosophical language. But systematic thinking was not really in James's nature, any more than it was in that of, say, Nietzsche's. His mind was too adventurous and scintillating, and his philosophical temperament too fascinated by particularities and open to possibilities. His philosophizing defied system. James waved away most of his critics as ideologically biased old fogeys who couldn't shake ossified habits of mind. But, after settling some of these scores in *The Meaning of Truth*, he started working on a book based on his lectures at Stanford in 1906 that he envisioned as more of a philosophical synthesis than anything he had yet written. He did not live to complete it.

The year 1909 also brought James's historic meeting with Sigmund Freud. This occurred during September at Clark University in western Massachusetts, where G. Stanley Hall was president and had organized an international psychological conference. James attended not to perform but to listen. He heard Freud, on his only visit to this country, introduce America to psychoanalysis with five lectures published in English as *The Origin and Development of Psychoanalysis*. James knew some of Freud's works, as we have seen. Now he responded with both support and criticism. He told Freud's young colleague and future biographer, Ernest Jones, that "the future of psychology belongs to your work." But these words did not endorse psychoanalysis itself. James rather meant Freud's interest, like his own, in "functional psychology," which studied the behavioral functions of mind more than its internal structure. Invoking this term, James wrote to a close professional friend, "I hope Freud and his pupils will push their ideas to their utmost limits, so that we may learn what they are. They can't fail to throw light on human nature." But, he added, "I confess that he [Freud] made on me personally the impression of a man obsessed with fixed ideas. I can make nothing" of "his dream theories, and obviously 'symbolism' is a most dangerous method."

Although Freud and James were fellow explorers of the mental life, they had different perspectives—and temperaments. In Isaiah Berlin's well-known metaphor, James was a fox at home amidst the irreducible multiplicity of experience. Freud was more of a hedgehog who aspired to a comprehensive theory accounting for all human behavior. And, whereas James had strong religious sympathies and a generous intellectual tolerance, Freud derided religion and demanded loyalty among his followers. As to Freud's preoccupation with sexuality, James plainly didn't buy it. The subject of sexuality never held James's attention for long and made only a few brief appearances in *Principles*, more as biology than psychology. We might chalk this relative neglect up to James's American Protestant upbringing. In any case, it did perhaps mark a certain lapse in his explorations of human nature and experience—at least from our post-Freudian perspective.*

Less than a year after the Clark University conference, William James was dead. The end came on August 26, 1910. Freud wrote in *An Autobiographical Study* that he could see James—whom he identified only as "William James the philosopher"—was obviously ill when they met. After they parted on a walk together as James pleaded discomfiting chest pains, Freud was moved by James's Stoic bearing. "I have always wished," he wrote, "that I might be as fearless as he was in the face of approaching death."

That fearlessness and the will, effort, and zest behind it, belonged to James's character and philosophy. He thought they should belong to everyone. Earlier that year he had published an essay on the aggressive energies of human nature and putting them to social use. This became one of his best known—if often misunderstood—writings. It was "The Moral Equivalent of War."

This essay originated as a talk to a university assembly at Stanford in January 1906, three months before the earthquake. It restated James's suspicion that human beings have an innate hunger for violence or something like it and filled out his previous hints on how best to satisfy this hunger. In *Principles* James had remarked that "in many respects man is the most ruthlessly ferocious of beasts," born with instincts to "pugnacity, anger, resentment . . . jealousy and antagonism . . . ready at any moment to burst into flame." Later he had seen these instincts erupting in the barefaced imperialism sweeping the nation and much of the world in the late 1890s. And he had told the World Peace Conference in Boston in 1904, "The plain truth is that people want war. They want it anyhow; for itself." That was an audacious declaration. But James had not, in fact, meant that human beings crave violence and destruction. Instinctually aggressive as they might be, what they really want are "thrills and excitements" to escape the tedium of everyday habits, and "war, they feel, is human nature at its uttermost . . . the final bouquet of life's fireworks." Society, he had said in passing, should somehow meet those needs outside of war. But how? In *Varieties* he had tentatively pointed the way. Although the appetite for war likely arises from "an aboriginal instinct," he had explained, the actual experience of war is "the school of strenuous life and heroism." Because of that, he had advised, "we need to discover . . . the moral equivalent of war" to harness war's strenuousness without violence and "crushing weaker peoples." And he had named the "willed poverty" of saintliness as the model of a truly strenuous peacetime existence.

Now James pulled these strands together. Deploring the physical and emotional horrors of war and the bellicose mood of the age, he nonetheless reminded his listeners and readers of war's appeal and its virtues. And he chided pacifists for ignoring those virtues, such as, "intrepidity, contempt of softness, surrender of private interest, obedience to command," which "are absolute and permanent human goods."* He insisted that a durable peace and a fecund civilization actually depend on such virtues. Civilization should just strive to nurture them for peaceful ends. To do this, James proposed drafting "the whole youthful population" for a few years into "an army" to serve the public welfare. This army would at once produce good works, arouse "the higher ranges of men's spiritual energy," and breed "healthier sympathies and soberer ideas" among citizens who would then "tread the earth more proudly" than before. That strenuous, morally energizing public service—not mere sports or other diversions, as is commonly assumed—was James's "moral equivalent of war." The idea has proven true through the experience of the Peace Corps and other service organizations that channel the energies of the young to worthy social causes.

When James died a few months after publication of this popular essay, he left unfinished his philosophical synthesis. It appeared the next year under the equivocal title *Some Problems of Philosophy. A Beginning of an Introduction to Philosophy.* In a more measured philosophical tone and more technical language than James had previously chosen, its fragmentary chapters reworked a number of James's venerable philosophical arguments under such headings as The Abuse of Concepts, The One and the Many, and The Problem of Novelty, and it appropriately ended with an appendix of James's notes on a cherished theme, labeled by the editors: "Faith and the Right to Believe." But it is telling that James did write a dedication for the book—quoted earlier— honoring Renouvier for the epiphany he had given James about free will. Without that epiphany, William James would not have been the thinker he was.

The last work of William James that he saw published was not so philosophical. And it was pure James. This was an encomium to an eccentric, spirited, and obscure thinker splendidly named Benjamin Paul Blood. It carried a title from James's heart: "A Pluralistic Mystic." A decade older than James, thirsting for life anew each day, gifted with striking literary verve, attracted to mysticism, and a pluralist by nature, Blood was a kindred spirit. He and James had read each other's works and had carried on an animated and admiring correspondence for years. Honoring his offbeat intellectual comrade, James summarized Blood's mystically pluralistic philosophy, lauded his powerful writing, and warmly quoted his vivid image of their nearly common worldview: "Not unfortunately the universe is wild—game flavored as a hawk's wing." James also gave his own version of that worldview: "There is no complete generalization, no total point of view, no all-pervasive unity. . . . Every moment of immediate experience is somewhat absolutely original and novel." And he signed off by saying, "Let my last words . . . be his word:— 'There is no conclusion. . . . There are no fortunes to be told . . . — Farewell!'" (ellipses—ed.)

Those buoyant lines brought James's intellectual career to an end. They also return us to the beginning and to James's vision of life as a "muddle and a struggle with an 'ever not quite' [a phrase James borrowed from Blood] to all formulas, and novelty and possibility forever leaking in." James would have had it no other way. For, in a "pluralistic universe," anything is possible, and if "life be not a fight in which something is gained for the universe by success," what's the purpose of living? Hence James's credo: "Be not afraid of life."

James had learned this "courage to be"—as the existential theologian Paul Tillich named an analogous commitment in a book of that name—from hard experience and intellectual adventures. It became for him an empirical truth that made his own life worth living. It can help anyone in the same way. Not simply as edification of the kind James told Henry that he happily got from "the divine Emerson." More than that, James melded the "tender-minded" virtues of Emerson's moral idealism with the "tough-minded" virtues of radical empiricism—as he says pragmatism does—to meet human experience openly in all of its multiplicity, particularity, and complexity with a spirit of pluralism and tolerance; and to resist the seductions of abstract formulas, ideological self-satisfactions, and mind-numbing habits; and to keep the habits of will and attention and effort alive to the end. This vision of life, together with James's many reasons for embracing it, from his epiphany about will and habit onward, make William James a philosopher for our times unlike any other.

## THE GIST OF JAMES

I have not presumed in this Introduction to track James along every trail of his intellectual life. I have rather traveled some prominent paths through that life leading from the dawn to the dusk of his philosophical vision and aiding our understanding of human experience and how to make the best of it. As a final step to these ends, I offer here a summary—more logical than chronological—of James's vision as presented in this Introduction and in the selections that follow:

Human life as we know it consists of experience. What else can there be? Human experience begins when some stimulus arouses a response in us. The first of these responses comes from instincts. But others come from flashes of attention in our consciousness. Consciousness is not a thing but a function or a process that resembles a stream. That stream carries every experience that happens to us, inside and out, and those experiences all flow together continuously. Consequently, we cannot wholly detach any experience or current in the stream from any other—thoughts from feelings, sensations from memories, certainties from desires, past from present, and so forth. Any of these can attract our attention in consciousness, but none can do it entirely by itself. And many things attract our attention chiefly through the inclinations of our temperaments or our needs and desires. All of this means that every claim to truth and all convictions are awash in the stream of consciousness.

Because human experience is various, particular, interwoven, continuous, and subjective, we can understand it only on its own terms. That means we must think with a courageous openness and clarity of mind unconstrained by blinkered preconceptions, unswayed by a yen for comforting uniformity, and unclouded by the haze of vague abstractions. And we must grasp and express that understanding with the concrete language of experience, unblighted by disembodied, opaque jargon. Such an understanding teaches us that we live in a pluralistic universe of manifold realities, infinite possibilities, and intractable uncertainties. It also reveals that, as far as we know, or can ever know in this world, the human will is free to make choices and to shape human lives. We are free because we feel free and can act as though we are free. That is evidence enough. All we need is a chance. Determinism is merely an abstract theory that belies actual human experience.

Because the world of experience is such an open, undetermined, uncertain place, human life is a struggle. In this struggle, human nature both aids and inhibits us. In the first place, the lives we live take form largely from habits, some of which we do not deliberately choose. We cannot live without habits. They liberate our minds from routine. But some habits do us harm. And they can become so ingrained that they thwart our freedom. The habits of addiction do that. Fortunately, we can break habits and create new ones by acts of will—although breaking bad habits can be harder than creating good ones. The will acts when our minds adopt one idea and reject another; we then do what that idea tells us to do. We develop bad habits when we adopt ideas and actions that work to our detriment. We often do this inadvertently by letting our conscious attention flag. Other times we do it by deliberately indulging in ideas and actions that we think will not become habitual, but they do. We develop good habits when we exercise the "effort of attention" to adopt ideas that work to our benefit, and then we act on those ideas repeatedly. The most important activity of our consciousness is therefore to develop *the habits of will, attention, and effort*, because these habits of mind give us control of our lives.

Probably the most efficacious ideas we can espouse to form good habits and shape our lives well are transcendent ideals born of fervent belief. These ideals can be anything that animates us to act with purpose, but probably the most potent of them is to believe in a benign spiritual realm. In any case, such beliefs become true when we act on them fruitfully. Never mind metaphysics and abstract theories of truth. Ideas are true when they pay off for us in experience. Results in fact, not tidiness in theory, are what matter. That is the pragmatic definition of truth. It holds for ordinary life, primarily the moral life, as well as for science—although science depends on a different breed of facts and technical testing of them. But every pragmatic truth has to work within a wide field of experience, where we have to balance one truth against another, not just in a corner of it. Otherwise we will deceive ourselves with myopic conclusions and self-serving feelings of certainty. By the same token, pragmatic truth is neither universal nor absolute. It is always particular and provisional. It can change when experience requires it, like everything else in human life. That is how science and human beings grow and improve.

Among the limitations of human knowledge is our blindness of what goes on in other peoples' minds and what gives meaning to their lives. Because of this blindness, we should not judge other peoples' lives hastily and should appreciate any experience that lights up their eyes. After all, everyone wants the same thing in life: to have our lives pay off for us. We just pursue this end in disparate ways. So, instead of expecting everyone to submit to a theoretical moral standard of good, let us simply say that the more of peoples' needs and desires that can be satisfied in this world the better. And let us be open to experiments in living that might take us in that direction. The varieties of religious experience are experiments of this kind. We should learn from these, as from all experience, anything we can about human existence.

To live a full human life, we must make the most of human experience. That begins by recognizing the variety of that experience and the subjectivity and complexity of human consciousness, along with the uncertainty of claims to truth (especially moral truth). This recognition teaches us a generous tolerance of human differences, along with resistance to evil. Evil includes the intellectual arrogance, moral fanaticism, intolerant ideologies, and authoritarian domination that defy human freedom and individuality. We should also cultivate those habits of will, attention, and effort that give us the discipline of mind to shape our lives for the better. And we should embrace experience (even suffering) with the zest to take risks, the energy to live strenuously, and the courage never to be afraid of life. Such are the ethics of a pluralistic universe.

# NOTES AND BIBLIOGRAPHY TO THE INTRODUCTION, WITH SUGGESTIONS FOR FURTHER READING

Where a quotation does not appear in these notes, its source is the same as the previous note cited. For the reader's convenience, whenever possible I cite quotations from William James in the two-volume Library of America edition of his *Writings* rather than in the original publications from which the selections below come. I cite *The Principles of Psychology* as PP and *Psychology: Briefer Course* (in *Writings*) as BC. Where a quotation appears in both books, I give the sources for both. I cite *The Will to Believe* as WB. And I cite *Talks to Teachers on Psychology: And to Students on Some of Life's Ideals* as TT. Where quotations from James in the Introduction can be found in the selections of James's writings below I also cite those page numbers in parentheses.

Page

1    "the world," Kallen, 9
     "I doubt whether," Hughes, 112

2    "Be not afraid," "Is Life Worth Living?" WB, in *Writings, 1878–1899*, 503; (281)
     *In the Introduction, I place the symbol† next to titles of James's works included, partially or wholly, in this anthology, unless that inclusion is otherwise indicated in the text.
     "a muddle and a struggle," quoted in Perry, II, 700
     "if this life," "Is Life Worth Living?" 502; (281)
     "Believe that life," Ibid., 503; (281)
     "Do not be afraid," Dostoevsky, *The Brothers Karamazov*, 776

3    *James and Twain dined together several times when their paths crossed in Europe and America. They seem to have enjoyed each other's company, if not fully acknowledging their affinities. After their last meeting in 1907, James wrote to his brother Henry (whose writing Twain disparaged) that Twain was now "only good for monologue in his old age . . . but he is a dear little genius all the same." Letter of 2/14/1907, *The Letters of William James*, II, 264 (cited as *Letters*)

\*\*Sartre gave a nod to James in the novel *Nausea* where he has a "humanist" describe the "voluntary optimism" of James's "Is Life Worth Living?" but then has his pessimistic character Roquentin reject it.

"the gaping contrast," quoted in Perry, II, 127

"hortatory ethics," PP, I, 127; BC, 150; (14)

"little sermons," Santayana, 59

4   \*The attachment went even deeper in his brother Henry, who became an expatriate in England and arguably America's greatest novelist, and whose preferred subject would be the encounter of Americans with Europe. William and Henry's intellectually gifted sister, Alice, also settled in England, where she died prematurely. Two younger, less cerebral, brothers left Europe behind and had checkered careers in America.

"I feel as if the greater part," letter of 11/7/1867, *Letters*, I, 119

6   "All my intellectual life," letter of 12/14/1882, *Letters*, I, 219

\*The two brilliant brothers shared a lifelong bond of fraternal love and sincere admiration, with a mild undercurrent of sibling rivalry, particularly in Henry, fueled by William's readiness to criticize his younger brother, however good-naturedly. For an example of this, see the note to page 17 below.

7   \*The confession, in a letter to the French translator of *Varieties*, Frank Abouzit (6/1/1904), was more clinical than existential. "The document on p. 160," James wrote, "is my own case—acute neurasthenic attack with phobia. I naturally disguised the provenance." Abouzit passed the letter on to James's friend Theodore Flournoy, who quoted it in the French edition of his own book on James (p. 149n), published a year after James's death. It now appears in *The Correspondence of William James*, vol. 10, p. 619.

"state of philosophical pessimism," *The Varieties of Religious Experience* in *Writings, 1902–1910*, 149–50 (cited as *Varieties*); also *Letters* I, 145–47 "a horrible fear," *Varieties*, 150

8   "I feel that we are Nature," letter, c. 3/1869, *Letters*, I, 152–53

"lend life and charm," quoted in Richardson, 293

*Despite his vivacity, James would always take his bleak moods very seriously and record his every agony. He even admitted to occasional hypochondria. His mother and brother Henry thought he sometimes overdid it. Henry wrote to her in 1880: "I can't get rid of the feeling that he takes himself, and his nerves, and his physical condition too hard and too consciously" (quoted in Edel, 419). Incidentally, William also acquired a physical feature that also now seems ill suited to his nature. Both he and Henry grew beards as young men in the manner of the day, but Henry shaved his off at the end of the century, revealing the face we now know, whereas William chose to wear a peculiarly bristly growth to the end, lending his pictures a soberly hirsute nineteenth-century look belying his exuberantly modern spirit.

"Today I about touched bottom," Diary, 2/1/1870, quoted in Allen, *William James*, 164

"useful ends," quoted in Ibid., 165

9   "The question will always," quoted in Richardson, 112

"Minnie, your death," Diary, 3/22/1870, quoted in Allen, *William James*, 167–68

"I think yesterday," *Letters*, I, 147–48

10  *James had previously entertained intimations of the mind's power to thwart despair, but he hadn't been able to make them stick. He had even pulled himself up in 1868 to preach "a new gospel of good cheer" to a disconsolate friend with the words, "I am sure one can by merely thinking" of good things, "limit the power of one's evil moods over one's way of looking at the Kosmos." Letter, 1/1868, *Letters*, I, 128

"reasonable and intelligible," letter 11/2/1872, *Letters*, I, 163

"philosophical manner," *Some Problems in Philosophy, Writings, 1902–1910*, 1066n

"Feeling endlessly," Ibid. and dedication

11 "but especially," letter, 3/18/1873, quoted in Perry, I, 339–40; *Letters*, I, 169–70

"nature in her unfathomable," PP, I, 182

12 "philosophical hypochondria," letter, 8/24/1872, *Letters*, I, 167

"make my *nick*," letter, 1/1868, *Letters*, I, 132

"It is a noble thing," letter, 11/24/1872, *Letters*, I, 167

"the first regular work," Richardson, 147

13 "James's life history," Erikson, 20

14 "There belongs to mind," "Remarks on Spencer's Definition of Mind as Correspondence," in *Writings*, 1878–1899, 908

"whoever studies consciousness," "Are We Automata?" *Essays in Psychology*, 46

"impotently paralytic," Ibid., 61

"pluralistic, restless universe," "The Dilemma of Determinism," *The Will to Believe*, in *Writings*, 1878–1899, 589

15 "the *difference*," Ibid., 576

"follow my own example," Ibid., 566–67

*As it appeared in *The Will to Believe*, this essay united a small part of one article published under this title in mid-1879 (but essentially completed eighteen months earlier) with the bulk of a second written the same year as "Rationality, Activity, and Faith." James included a few pages from the second of these in the chapter "The Perception of Reality" in *Principles* (footnote, II, ch. XXI, 312–15). On the relation of these two essays, see Richardson, 183–85, 200–03, and Gerald E. Myers, "Note on the Texts," William James, *Writings*, 1878–1899, 1173–74.

**That is the subject of H. Stuart Hughes's classic, *Consciousness and Society*, noted earlier. James's many writings on the subjectivity of thought conspicuously anticipated the sociology of science, including such works as Thomas Kuhn's influential *The Structure of Scientific Revolutions*. I might point out that, like Friedrich Nietzsche, Karl Marx belongs among James's fellow pioneers in disclosing the subjective interests that shape thought. But Marx also convinced himself that his own theories transcended those interests to capture the absolute scientific truth of human nature and history. If James had studied Marx, he would have cast him among the self-deceiving materialistic rationalists.

"passion for simplification," "The Sentiment of Rationality," WB, in *Writings*, 1878–1899, 506; (143)

16 "feeling of rationality," Ibid., 504; (141)

"feel at home," Ibid., 515; (149)

"the peace of rationality," Ibid., 512; (146)

"passion for distinguishing," Ibid., 506; (143)

"teeming and dramatic richness," Ibid., 509; (145)

"no abstract concept," Ibid.; (145)

"the entire man," Ibid., 508; (145)

"the awful abstract rigamarole," letter, 12/6/1905, *Letters*, II, 237

17 *As to James's opinion of his brother Henry's literary style, he told Henry in a late letter: "You know how opposed your whole 'third manner' of execution is to the literary ideals which animate my crude and Orson-like breast, mine being to say a thing in one sentence as straight and explicit as it can be made, and then to drop it forever; yours being to avoid naming it straight but by dint of breathing and sighing all round and round it, to arouse in the reader who may have had a similar perception already (Heaven help him if he hasn't!) the illusion of a solid object, made (like the 'ghost' at the Polytechnic) wholly out of impalpable materials, air, and the prismatic interferences of light, ingeniously focused by mirrors upon empty space. But you *do* it, that's the queerness." Letter, 5/4/1907, *Letters*, II, 277

"We cannot live," "The Sentiment of Rationality," 527; (156)

"a certain amount of uncertainty," Ibid., 524; (153)

"in the total game," Ibid., 527; (155)

"the same moral quality," Ibid., 524; (153)

"Naked, [man] is flung," Ibid., 526; (155)

"Again and again," Ibid., 531; (159)

"The truths cannot become," Ibid., 528; (156)

"This world is good," Ibid., 533; (159–60)

"All that the human heart," Ibid., 538; (161)

"all the evidence," Ibid., 536; (160)

"inalienable right," Ibid., 538; (161–62)

18   "a loathsome, distended," letter, 5/9/1890, *Letters*, I, 294

"Psychology is the Science," PP, I, 1

"we may have come by," Ibid., II, 688

"It was a tolerant," Perry, II, 91

"Let psychology," BC, 427

19   "we talk of 'psychology as a natural science'," Ibid., 432

"not a single law," Ibid., 433

"first and foremost," PP, I, 185

"the Psychologist's Fallacy," Ibid., I, 196

"ethical implications," Ibid., I, 120

"This is a work," Santayana, 52

"physiological preliminaries," PP, I, 183

20   "hortatory ethics," PP, I, 127; BC, 150; (92)

"a mere pot boiler," quoted in Perry, II, 90

"practical remarks," letter, 7/24/1890, *Letters*, I, 297

"the *ethical implications*," PP, I, 120

"The laws of Nature," PP, I, 104; BC, 137; (79)

"*Plasticity*," PP, I, 105; BC, 138; (80)

"systems of reflex paths," BC, 140; variation in PP, I, 108; (82)

21   "In habitual action," PP, I, 116; BC 143; (85)

"second nature," PP, I, 120; BC 144; (86)

"*make our nervous system*," PP, I, 122; BC 146; (88)

"walking bundles of habits," PP, I, 127; BC, 150–51; (92)

22   "*Keep the faculty*," PP, I, 126; BC, 150; (92)

"stand like a tower," PP, I, 127; BC, 150; (92)

"faithfully busy each hour," PP, 127; BC, 151; (93)

"it is a matter," Aristotle, *Ethics*, Thompson/Treddnick trans., Bk
        II, sect. I, p. 92

23   "practical aims" Aristotle, *Ethics*, Rackman trans., Bk II, sect. ii,
        p. 75.

"Sow an action," Perry, II, 90

"excessive novel-reading," PP, I, 125; BC, 149; (91)

"if nothing more heroic," PP, I, 126; BC, 149; (92)

"the enormous fly-wheel," PP, I, 121; BC, 145; (87)

"Outside of their own business," PP, II, 402; BC, 378

24  "ideas and habits," *Varieties*, 184

"dead ideas," Ibid., 192

"especially violent," Ibid., 181

"solid meaning of life," "What Makes a Life Significant?," TT,
    in *Writings,* 1878–1899, 878; (299)

"habits of voluntary attention," PP, I, 424; BC, 219

"Genius, in truth," PP, II, 110; BC, 309; (102)

"a lot of inveterate habits," *Pragmatism*, in *Writings*, 1902–1910,
    508; (205)

"Man lives by habits," "Remarks at the Peace Banquet," (*Atlantic
    Monthly*, Dec. 1904, vol. 94, pp. 845–47), in *Memories
    and Studies*, 303.

25  "a 'river' or a 'stream'," PP, I, 239; BC, 159; (105)

"constant change," PP, I, 229; BC, 154; (104)

"Every definite image," PP. I, 255; BC, 164; (106)

"Does consciousness exist?" "Does 'Consciousness' Exist?" in
    *Writings*, 1902–1910,1141–58

26  "the reinstatement of the vague," PP, I, 254; BC, 164; (106)

"reinforcing and inhibiting," PP, I, 228

*"My experience,"* PP, I, 402

"the mystery of interest," Re: p. 15 of Intro.

"only those items," PP, I, 402

"What is called," BC, 170; variation in PP, I, 286

"each of us literally *chooses*," PP, I, 424

*"direct* outward effects," PP, II, 486; BC, 387

"ideo-motor action," PP, II, 522; BC, 393

27  "is a psychic or moral fact," PP, II, 560; BC, 417

"The whole drama," PP, II, 564; BC, 419

*"To think,"* TT, in *Writings*, 1878–1899, 817; (136)

"attention and effort," PP, I, 126; BC, 150; (92)

*"effort of attention,"* PP, II, 562; BC, 418; (118)

"The ethical energy," PP, I, 288; BC, 172; (109)
"*Will you or won't you,*" PP, II, 579; BC, 426; (126)
"strong-willed man," PP, II, 563; BC, 419; (119)
"heroic mind," PP, II, 578; BC, 425; (125)
"effort demanded," PP, II, 579; BC, 426; (126)

28  *I might point out that in his intensive study of James's life and thought, Gerald E. Myers amiably questions the psychological coherence of James's account of will and attention—as have other critics—but concludes: "The chapters on habit, will, and attention in *Principles* offer a sort of manual for improving the psychological and moral dimensions of life." Despite the criticism, James could have lived with that. Myers, 214

"conquistador," quoted in Gay, xvi

**In an Introduction to a new edition of the *Briefer Course* in 1961—at the dawn of a post-behaviorist James revival that continues today—the prominent psychologist Gordon Allport noted the datedness of some of James's science and the shortcomings of a few of his ideas, but summed up his influence in the profession: "the psychological insights of James have the steadiness of a polar star" (Allport, xvi). A generation later, commemorating the centennial of *Principles* in 1990, a group of psychologists looked again at how James's work had stood up. While observing scientific and other limitations of the book, most of the authors illustrated how James nonetheless, as one of them wrote, "clear[ed] the ground for subsequent theorists, researchers, and practitioners" in practically every field of psychology, including behaviorism, which threw out the very concept of consciousness (David E. Leary, "William James on the Self and Personality: Clearing the Ground for Subsequent Theorists, Researchers, and Practitioners," in *Reflections on The Principles of Psychology: William James After a Century*, 101). And another of these authors points out that in the post-behaviorist era, "the more we learn about consciousness, the stronger the stream metaphor becomes"

(Howard R. Pollio, "The Stream of Consciousness Since James," Ibid., 293). Recently, a psychological study of habit confirmed James's legacy in that subject (albeit in prose that would have given James apoplexy) by demonstrating the role of "cues," "contexts," and "goals" in the shaping of habits generally and stressing the necessity of "attention" and "effortful self-control" in breaking bad habits and deliberately forming good ones (Wood and Neal, 843–60, passim). And in a recent popular book called *The Power of Habit* Charles Duhigg reiterates James's theme—without giving James much credit. Over the past couple of decades, the study of attention itself has become a hot topic in neuroscience. "Attention is the holy grail," announced a psychologist in 2010, because "everything that you are conscious of, everything you let in, everything you remember and you forget, depends on it" (David Strayer, quoted in Ritchell, A1). James had said it long ago.

"a masterpiece," Barzun, 34

"especially from the literary," letter, 7/24/1891, *Letters,* I, 314

"wretched twaddle," letter, 10/25/1891, quoted in Perry, II, 126; also letter, 7/21/1898, *Letters,* I, 314

29  "radical empiricism," Preface, WB, in *Writings,* 1878–1899, 447

"The *Right* to Believe," letter, 8/12/1904, *Letters,* II, 207

"Can our will," "The Will to Believe," WB, in *Writings,* 1878–1899, 459; (165)

"*hypothesis*" and "*options,*" Ibid., 457, 458; (163,164)

"*Moral questions,*" Ibid., 472; (172)

"the question," Ibid., 472; (172)

30  "our non-intellectual," Ibid., 464; (169)

"*faith in a fact,*" Ibid., 474; (174)

"the will can change," "The Psychology of Belief," in *Writings,* 1878–1899, 1055. This essay became the chapter "The Perception of Reality" in PP, II, ch. XXI, except for some footnotes and most of the essay's last paragraph, from which the lines quoted here come and which James replaced with a variation in a new section labeled

"Relations of Belief and Will."
"The religious hypothesis," "The Will to Believe," WB, in
    *Writings, 1878–1899*, 474; (176)
"we are better off," Ibid., 475; (176)
"we *act*, taking our lives," Ibid., 478; (179)
"I do not wish," Ibid., 476; (177)
*James's elevation of will over rationality here and elsewhere
    put him not only in the company of his flamboyant
    contemporary Friedrich Nietzsche and other intellectual
    revolutionaries of the day but in a line of thinkers since
    the late eighteenth century who exalted will over reason
    in general. The historian and philosopher Isaiah Berlin
    bemoaned this modern line of thought in classic articles
    on "the Counter-Enlightenment" and "The Apotheosis of
    the Romantic Will"—but Berlin was himself an insistent
    pluralist and overall more of a philosophical ally of James
    than an adversary.
"have a right," "Is Life Worth Living?" *Writings, 1878–1899*,
    495

31  *The idealist Socrates applied this same test of experience to
    his belief in the immortality of the soul. We cannot know
    if the soul is immortal, he conceded to his companions at
    the end of his life, but it is "a belief worth risking, for the
    risk is a noble one" because it helps us "inspire ourselves
    with confidence" (Plato, *Phaedo*, 178). Embracing the will
    to believe and the risks it entails, Socrates became a daring
    pragmatist ages before James—as James acknowledged in
    "What Pragmatism Means."
"not a victory," "Is Life Worth Living?" 500; (279)
"*feels* like a real fight," Ibid., 502; (281)
"The greatest proof," "The Psychology of Belief," 1044; also
    PP, II, 308
"respect one another's," "The Will to Believe," WB, in *Writings,
    1878–1899*, 478; (177)
32  "ethical philosophy dogmatically," "The Moral Philosopher and
    the Moral Life," WB, in *Writings, 1878–1899*, 595; (178)

"*system of truth*," Ibid., 606; (180)

"judgments of good and ill," Ibid., 604; (179)

"Whether a God exist," Ibid., 605; (180)

33 "*The essence of good*," Ibid., 607; (182)

"satisfy at all times," Ibid., 610; (183)

"I for my part," "The Importance of Individuals," in *Writings, 1878–1899*, 651

"by what sort of conduct," "The Moral Philosopher and the Moral Life," in *Writings, 1878–1899*, 612; (184)

"the *highest* ethical life," Ibid., 613; (185)

"be ready to revise," Ibid., 612; (185)

34 "the strenuous mood," Ibid., 615; (187)

"out of the game," Ibid., 616; (188)

"let loose in us," Ibid., 617; (189)

*Along with his hortatory ethics often addressed to the young, the psychological talks to teachers about students and the moralistic talks to students about life displayed James's keen desire to give direction to the younger generation. This exemplified not only James but his times. Adolescence was becoming a pressing social fact and source of psychological interest amid a transforming industrial economy that posed new possibilities and new problems for young people. In 1899 France celebrated those possibilities with a *Fête de l'adolescence* in the Bois de Bologne. The problems gave rise to concerns over the troublesome nature and behavior of adolescents, which James's former student G. Stanley Hall explored at length in his two-volume *Adolescence: Its Psychology and its Relations to Physiology, Anthropology, Sociology, Sex, Crime, Religion, and Education* (1905). James contributed his own share and brand of wisdom to this cultural occupation around the turn of the twentieth century.

"over-tension and jerkiness," "The Gospel of Relaxation," TT, in *Writings, 1878–1899*, 832, 831

"harmony, dignity," Ibid., 834

"to become strenuously," Ibid., 840

"a definite view," Preface, TT, in *Writings, 1878–1899*, 708

35   "the blindness with which," "On a Certain Blindness," Ibid., 841; (190)

"is the root of most human injustices," "What Makes a Life Significant?" Ibid., 861; (258)

"tolerate, respect," "On a Certain Blindness," Ibid., 860; (193)

"the truth is too great," Preface, TT, in *Writings, 1878–1899*, 708

*On the question mark in the title, see "Note on the Texts."

"without a blot," "What Makes a Life Significant?" TT, in *Writings, 1878–1899*, 863; (260)

"the wicked outer world," Ibid., 864; (261)

36   "the flash," letter 7/29/2010, *Letters*, II, 43

"inner meaning," "What Makes a Life Significant?" TT, in *Writings, 1878–1899*, 875; (271)

"Ideals ought to aim," letter, 4/9/1907, *Letters*, II, 270

"the active will," "What Makes a Life Significant?" TT, in *Writings, 1878–1899*, 876; (272)

"pluck," Ibid., 877; (273)

"the particular mood," "The Sentiment of Rationality," WB, in *Writings, 1878–1899*, 521

"new ideals," "What Makes a Life Significant?" TT, in *Writings, 1878–1899*, 879; (275)

"the solid meaning," Ibid., 878; (275)

37   "harmful . . . mental activity," BC, 14

"twilight region," letter, 9/28/1909, *Letters*, II, 327

"buried life," "The Gospel of Relaxation," TT, in *Writings, 1878–1899*, 827

"a 'subliminal' self," "What Psychical Research Has Accomplished," in *Writings, 1878–1899*, 696

38   "I am persuaded," "The Confidences of a 'Psychical Researcher'," in *Writings, 1902–1910*, 1265

"defend . . . 'experience'," letter, 4/12/1900, *Letters*, II, 127

"When I compose," letter, 9/26/1900, *Letters*, II, 136

"your ordinary religious believer," *Varieties*, 15

"neurotic temperament," Ibid., 31
"subject to abnormal," Ibid., 15
"the belief that," Ibid., 55
"subconscious and non-rational," Ibid., 74
39 "an extended subliminal self," letter, 6/16/1901, *Letters*, II, 149
"thoroughly 'pragmatic'," *Varieties*, 463; (196)
"judge the religious life," Ibid., 28
"morbid or healthy," Ibid., 31
"a constitutional incapacity," Ibid., 121
"healthy-mindedness pure and simple," Ibid., 153
"evil facts," ibid., 152
"twice-born," Ibid., 155
"To find religion," Ibid., 163
"the new man," Ibid., 183
40 "self-surrender," Ibid., 296
"indispensable to the world's," Ibid., 340
"strenuous life," Ibid., 332
"moral equivalent of war," Ibid., 334
"the mother sea," letter, 6/16/1901, *Letters*, II, 149
"offer us *hypotheses*," *Varieties*, 386
"the belief that beyond," Ibid., 468; (200)
*In his seminal work on the sociology of religion, *The Elementary Forms of Religious Life* (1915), Emile Durkheim described God very much as James defined religion here. But Durkheim contended that God is nothing more than the power of society that stands above us all, lending a sense of order and security to our lives and being worthy of worship.
"a sort of polytheism," *Varieties*, 468; (200)
"the pluralistic hypothesis," Ibid, 469; (201)
41 *In later years Einstein became quite a monist, searching for a unified field theory to tie the entire universe together from sub-atomic blips to cosmic swirls. Scorning the quizzical theories in sub-atomic quantum physics of Werner Heisenberg and Niels Bohr expressed in "The Uncertainty Principle" and the "Principle of Complementarity,"

Einstein said more than once: "God does not play dice with the universe" (or words to that effect—Isaacson quotes a variation, 335). James rather thought God did just that, and we can imagine him delighting in the radical empiricism and pluralism of quantum theory. Bohr, by the way, told the science historian Thomas Kuhn and others in an interview that he subsequently found James's idea of the stream of consciousness pleasingly compatible with his own paradoxical interpretation of the sub-atomic world.

"felt the bed," "On Some Mental Effects of the Earthquake," *Writings, 1902–1910*, 1215; (228)

42  "I felt no trace," Ibid.; (229)

"busy as ants," Ibid., 1218; (231)

"doggedly," Ibid., 1219; (232)

"intact skyscrapers," Ibid., 1220; (233)

"universal equanimity," Ibid., 1221; (234)

"steadfastness of tone," Ibid., 1222; (235)

"We are making," "The Energies of Men," in W*ritings, 1902–1910*, 1225; (240)

"Habitually narrow," Ibid., 1227; (242)

"The normal opener," Ibid., 1230; (243)

"excitements, ideas," Ibid., 1226; (242)

"the emotions and excitements," Ibid., 1230; (243)

43  "the great revealers," Ibid., 1228; (242)

"waking up," letter, 5/4/1907, *Letters*, II, 277

"Ideas set free," "Energies of Men," in *Writings, 1902–1910*, 1236; (241)

*James's argument here foreshadowed the influential theory of Georges Sorel in *Reflections on Violence* (1908) holding that the emotive ideas of "social myths," not rationality, drive political action. Sorel later adopted portions of James's pragmatism.

"fellow pragmatist," Ibid., 1240; (244)

"unlock unused reservoirs," 1241; (245)

44  "something quite like," letter, 5/4/1907, *Letters*, II, 277

"the whole pragmatic scope," "G. Papini and the Pragmatist

Movement in Italy," *Essays in Philosophy*. Quotations come from pages 145–47.

45   "the pragmatism of William James," quoted in Perry, II, 575
     "*method,*" *Pragmatism, in Writings,* 1901–1910, 506; (203)

46   "like a corridor," Ibid., 510; (206)
     "does not stand," Ibid., 509; (205)
     "what definite difference," Ibid., 508; (204)
     "practical cash-value," Ibid., 509; (205)
     "*theory of truth,*" Ibid., 510; (206)
     "*become true,*" Ibid., 512
     "truth *happens,*" Ibid., 574; (210)
     "only test," Ibid., 522; (208)
     "tough-minded," Ibid., 491
     "*If theological ideas,*" Ibid., 518–19
     "experience, as we know," Ibid., 583; (215)

47   "the open air," Ibid., 509; (205)
     "the essence of life," "Bergson and His Critique of
        Intellectualism," *A Pluralistic Universe*, in *Writings, 1902–1910,* 746
     "what really exists," Ibid., 751
     "unfinished pluralistic universe," Ibid., 780; (221)
     "nothing includes everything," Ibid., 776; (218)
     "wild beasts," Ibid., 780
     "life exceeding logic," Ibid.; (221)

48   "the future of psychology," Jones, II, 57
     "functional psychology," letter, 9/28/1909, *Letters*, II, 328

49   *James apologetically closed his comments on "the *habits*" of
     "abnormal sexual appetites" in the section of *Principles*
     dealing with the "instinct" of "love" by saying, "these
     details are a little unpleasant to discuss," but "it was
     impossible to pass over them unremarked." PP, II, 439
     "William James the philosopher," Freud, *An Autobiographical Study,* 99
     "in many respects," Ibid., II, 409

50   "ready at any moment," Ibid., II, 410
     "the plain truth," "Remarks at the Peace Banquet," *Memories*

# Bibliography for the Introduction

Allen, Gay Wilson. *William James. A Biography.* New York: Viking Press, 1967.

Allport, Gordon W. Introduction. *William James: Psychology, The Briefer Course.* New York: Harper Torchbooks, The Academic Library, Harper and Bros., 1961.

Aristotle. *Ethics.* Translated by J. A. K. Thompson. Revised by Hugh Treddnick. New York: Penguin Books, 1976.

———. *Ethics.* Translated by H. Rackman. Revised edition. Cambridge: Harvard University Press, Loeb Classical Library, 1934.

Barzun, Jacques. *A Stroll with William James.* New York: Harper & Row Publishers, 1983.

Cotkin, George. *William James, Public Philosopher.* Baltimore: Johns Hopkins University Press, 1990.

Dostoevsky, Fyodor. *The Brothers Karamazov.* Translated and annotated by Richard Pevear and Larissa Volokhonsky. New York: Farrar, Straus and Giroux, 1990.

Duhigg, Charles. *The Power of Habit: Why We Do What We Do in Life and Business.* New York: Random House, 2012.

Edel, Leon. *Henry James: The Conquest of London, 1870–1883.* New York: Avon Books, 1962.

Erikson, Erik. *Identity, Youth and Crisis.* New York: W. W. Norton, 1968.

Feinstein, Howard M. *Becoming William James.* Ithaca: Cornell University Press, 1984.

Flournoy, Thèodore. *La Philosophie de William James.* Sainte-Blaise: Foyer Solidariste, 1911.

Freud, Sigmund, *An Autobiographical Study,* Translated by James Strachey, New York: W. W. Norton, 1963

Hughes, H. Stuart. *Consciousness and Society: The Reconstruction of European Thought, 1890–1930.* New York: Random House, Vintage Books, 1958.

Isaacson, Walter. *Einstein: His Life and Universe.* New York: Simon & Schuster, 2007.

James, William. *The Correspondence of William James*. Edited by Ignas
K. Skrupskelis, Elizabeth M. Berkeley, Henry James.
Charlottesville: University Press of Virginia, 1992–2004. Vol.
10.
———. *Essays in Philosophy*. Edited by Fredson Bowers and Ignas K.
Skrupskelis. Cambridge, Mass.: Harvard University Press, 1978.
———. *Essays in Psychology*. Cambridge, Mass.: Harvard University
Press, 1983.
———. *The Letters of William James*. Edited by his son Henry James.
Boston: Little, Brown, and Co., 1926. Two volumes in one.
———. *Memories and Studies*. New York: Longmans, Green, and Co.,
1911.
———. *The Principles of Psychology*. American Science Series—
Advanced Course. New York: Henry Holt & Co. 1890. Two
volumes. (Reprinted as Authorized Edition. New York: Dover
Publications, 1950 [1890]. Two volumes.)
———. *Writings 1878–1899*. Edited by Gerald E. Myers. The Library
of America. New York: Literary Classics of the United States,
Inc., 1992.
———. *Writings 1902–1910*. Edited by Bruce Kuklick. The Library
of America. New York: Literary Classics of the United States,
1987.
Jones, Ernest. *The Life and Work of Sigmund Freud*. New York: Basic
Books, 1955. 2 volumes.
Kallen, Horace M. Introduction. *The Philosophy of William James*.
Selected from His Chief Works with an Introduction by Horace
M. Kallen. New York: Modern Library, 1925.
Matthiessen, F. O. *The James Family: A Group Biography*. New York:
Vintage Books, 1980, 1947.
Menand, Louis. *The Metaphysical Club*. New York: Farrar, Straus &
Giroux, 2001.
Myers, Gerald E. *William James: His Life and Thought*. New Haven:
Yale University Press, 1986.
Oliver, Phil. *William James's "Springs of Delight." The Return to Life*.
Nashville: Vanderbilt University Press, 2001.
Perry, Ralph Barton. *The Thought and Character of William James*.

Boston: Little, Brown and Company, 1935. Two volumes.

Plato, *Phaedo: The Last Days of Socrates.* Translated by Hugh Treddenick. Revised edition. New York: Penguin Books, 1969.

*Reflections on The Principles of Psychology: William James After a Century,* Edited by Michael G. Johnson and Tracy B. Henley. Hillsdale, N.J.: L. Erlbaum Associates, 1990.

Richardson, Robert D. *William James. In the Maelstrom of American Modernism.* Boston: Houghton Mifflin Company, Mariner Books, 2007.

Ritchell, Matt. "*Outdoors and Out of Reach, Studying the Brain.*" *New York Times,* 8/16/1210.

Santayana, George. "*Character and Opinion in the United States.*" *The Genteel Tradition in American Philosophy and Character and Opinion in the United States.* Edited by James Seaton. New Haven: Yale University Press, 2009.

Simon, Linda. *Genuine Reality. A Life of William James.* New York: Harcourt Brace and Company, 1998.

Tursi, Renee. "William James's Narrative of Habit." *Style,* Spring 1999.

Wood, Wendy, and David T. Neal. "A New Look at Habits and the Habit-Goal Interface." *Psychological Review,* 2007, Vol. 114, No. 4, 843–63.

## SUGGESTIONS FOR FURTHER READING

Readers interested in pursuing William James further might want to start with the authoritative current biography *William James in the Maelstrom of American Modernism* by Robert D. Richardson, although the title misleads since there is little if any maelstrom of modernism in the book. And they should at least dip into the monumental and delightfully written documentary biography by James's student and colleague Ralph Barton Perry, *The Thought and Character of William James*. The most probing, persuasive, argumentative, and engaging study of James's thought remains Jacques Barzun's *A Stroll with William James*.

Selections of James's writings have appeared in several anthologies, but none with the thematic focus of *William James on Habit, Will, Truth, and the Meaning of Life*. The fine two-volume Library of America edition of William James, *Writings*, contains most of James's works and a useful chronology and other reference matter, but no introduction. Below I list chronologically anthologies that have substantial introductions:

*The Philosophy of William James*. Selected from His Chief Works. Edited with an Introduction by Horace M. Kallen. New York: Modern Library, 1925.

*The Moral Philosophy of William James*. Edited and with Introduction by John K. Roth. New York: Crowell, 1969.

*The Writings of William James: A Comprehensive Edition*. Edited and with Introduction by John C. McDermott. Chicago: University of Chicago Press, 1977.

*William James: The Essential Writings*. Edited and with Introduction by Bruce Wilshire. Albany: State University of New York, c. 1984.

*The Vision of James*. Edited and with Introduction by Steven Rowe. Rockport, Mass.: Element, c. 1996.

*Pragmatism and Other Writings / William James*. Edited and with Introduction and notes by Giles Gunn. New York: Penguin Books, 2000.

*The Heart of William James*. Edited and with Introduction by Robert D. Richardson. Cambridge, Mass.: Harvard University Press,

2010. [The principal introduction is slender, but Richardson adds handy prefaces to each selection.]

## SELECTIONS

Like the Introduction, the selections that follow span James's intellectual life and trace notable patterns in it without trying to cover it all. Some of the selections consist of short excerpts focused on a single idea. Others are complete chapters or essays. Overall, they compactly show William James talking about the ideas that mattered most to him and that can be especially useful to us.

Those ideas originated in James's singular genius. But they took form only after the epochal days when James discovered the nature of the will and the uses of habit. This discovery resonated throughout his life and works. For this reason, the selections begin with two sections of writings on habit and will—in that sequence from *Principles*—together with some pages on consciousness. I have reprinted James's chapter on habit and portions of those on consciousness and will from *Psychology. American Science Series*—Briefer Course rather than from *The Principles of Psychology* (except for a few passages on habit from *Principles* inserted in brackets and identified) because they deliver the same contents as *Principles* but more efficiently. And I have included the complete chapters on habit and will from *Talks to Teachers on Psychology* because, although these repeat a few passages of *Psychology,* the *Talks* speak to a wider audience, dropping some technicalities and adding some new notions and applications of James's ideas.

After the writings on habit, consciousness, and will come three sections of psychological and philosophical writings arranged in a thematic and loosely chronological order. These begin with a substantial batch on how we think, on the efficacy of belief, and on the making of morality. Next come a few pieces on empiricism, pragmatism, pluralism, and their implications for truth. Last come several popular writings from James's last dozen years or so on energy, ideals, and the conduct of life.

All footnotes are those of William James in the original publications, as are the italics, which he used plentifully, emphatic character that he was. Some of those publications designate footnotes with asterisks; others do it with numbers. For consistency, I have used asterisks. The four dots that appear between some paragraphs indicate an ellipsis of the editor jumping across pages. The ellipses identified with [ed.] signal the editor's breaks within paragraphs or pages. Other ellipses belong to James.

The "Note on the Texts" at the end specifies a few other editorial changes and supplies the sources for all of the selections.

# Part I

# THE POWER OF HABIT

## Habit

**Its Importance for Psychology.**—There remains a condition of general neural activity so important as to deserve a chapter by itself—I refer to the aptitude of the nerve-centres, especially of the hemispheres, for acquiring habits. *An acquired habit, from the physiological point of view, is nothing but a new pathway of discharge formed in the brain, by which certain incoming currents ever after tend to escape.* That is the thesis of this chapter; and we shall see in the later and more psychological chapters that such functions as the association of ideas, perception, memory, reasoning, the education of the will, etc., etc., can best be understood as results of the formation *de novo* of just such pathways of discharge.

[When we look at living creatures from an outward point of view, one of the first things that strike[s] us is that they are bundles of habits. In wild animals, the usual round of daily behavior seems a necessity implanted at birth; in animals domesticated, and especially in man, it seems, to a great extent, to be the result of education. The habits to which there is an innate tendency are called instincts; some of those due to education would by most persons be called acts of reason. It thus appears that habit covers a very large part of life, and that one engaged in studying the objective manifestations of mind is bound at the very outset to define clearly just what its limits are. PP]

**Habit has a physical basis.** The moment one tries to define what habit is, one is led to the fundamental properties of matter. The laws of Nature are nothing but the immutable habits which the different elementary sorts of matter follow in their actions and reactions upon each other. In the organic world, however, the habits are more variable than this. Even instincts vary from one individual to another of a kind; and are modified in the same individual, as we shall later see, to suit the exigencies of the case. On the principles of the atomistic philosophy the habits of an elementary particle of matter cannot change, because the particle is itself an unchangeable thing; but those of a compound mass of matter can change, because they are in the last instance due to the structure of the compound, and either outward forces or inward tensions can, from one hour to another, turn that structure into something different from what it was. That is, they can do so if the body be plastic enough to maintain its integrity, and be not disrupted when its structure yields. The change of structure here spoken of need not involve the outward shape; it may be invisible and molecular, as when a bar of iron becomes magnetic or crystalline through the action of certain outward causes, or india-rubber becomes friable, or plaster "sets." All these changes are rather slow; the material in question opposes a certain resistance to the modifying cause, which it takes time to overcome, but the gradual yielding whereof often saves the material from being disintegrated altogether. When the structure has yielded, the same inertia becomes a condition of its comparative permanence in the new form, and of the new habits the body then manifests. *Plasticity*, then, in the wide sense of the word, means the possession of a structure weak enough to yield to an influence, but strong enough not to yield all at once. Each relatively stable phase of equilibrium in such a structure is marked by what we may call a new set of habits. Organic matter, especially nervous tissue, seems endowed with a very extraordinary degree of plasticity of this sort; so that we may without hesitation lay down as our first proposition the following: that *the phenomena of habit in living beings are due to the plasticity of the organic materials of which their bodies are composed.*

The philosophy of habit is thus, in the first instance, a chapter in physics rather than in physiology or psychology. That it is at bottom a physical principle is admitted by all good recent writers on the subject. They call attention to analogues of acquired habits exhibited by dead matter. Thus, M. Léon Dumont writes:

"Every one knows how a garment, after having been worn a certain time, clings to the shape of the body better than when it was new; there has been a change in the tissue, and this change is a new habit of cohesion. A lock works better after being used some time; at the outset more force was required to overcome certain roughnesses in the mechanism. The overcoming of their resistance is a phenomenon of habituation. It costs less trouble to fold a paper when it has been folded already; . . . and just so the impressions of outer objects fashion for themselves more and more appropriate paths, and these vital phenomena recur under similar excitements from without, when they have been interrupted a certain time."

Not in the nervous system alone. A scar anywhere is a *locus minoris resistentiae*, more liable to be abraded, inflamed, to suffer pain and cold, than are the neighboring parts. A sprained ankle, a dislocated arm, are in danger of being sprained or dislocated again; joints that have once been attacked by rheumatism or gout, mucous membranes that have been the seat of catarrh, are with each fresh recurrence more prone to a relapse, until often the morbid state chronically substitutes itself for the sound one. And in the nervous system itself it is well known how many so-called functional diseases seem to keep themselves going simply because they happen to have once begun; and how the forcible cutting short by medicine of a few attacks is often sufficient to enable the physiological forces to get possession of the field again, and to bring the organs back to functions of health. Epilepsies, neuralgias, convulsive affections of various sorts, insomnias, are so many cases in point. And, to take what are more obviously habits, the success with which a "weaning" treatment can often be applied to the victims of unhealthy indulgence of passion, or of mere complaining or irascible disposition, shows us how much the morbid manifestations themselves were due to the mere inertia of the nervous organs, when once launched on a false career.

[Can we now form a notion of what the inward physical changes may be like, in organs whose habits have thus struck into new paths? In other words, can we say just what mechanical facts the expression "change of habit" covers when it is applied to a nervous system? Certainly we cannot in anything like a minute or definite way. But our usual scientific custom of interpreting hidden molecular events after the analogy of visible massive ones enables us to frame easily an abstract and general scheme of process which the physical changes in question *may* be like. PP]

**Habits are due to pathways through the nerve-centres.** If habits are due to the plasticity of materials to outward agents, we can immediately see to what outward influences, if to any, the brain-matter is plastic. Not to mechanical pressures, not to thermal changes, not to any of the forces to which all the other organs of our body are exposed; for, as we saw on pp. 9–10 [in chapter II, not included here], Nature has so blanketed and wrapped the brain about that the only impressions that can be made upon it are through the blood, on the one hand, and the sensory nerve-roots, on the other; and it is to the infinitely attenuated currents that pour in through these latter channels that the hemispherical cortex shows itself to be so peculiarly susceptible. The currents, once in, must find a way out. In getting out they leave their traces in the paths which they take. The only thing they *can* do, in short, is to deepen old paths or to make new ones; and the whole plasticity of the brain sums itself up in two words when we call it an organ in which currents pouring in from the sense-organs make with extreme facility paths which do not easily disappear. For, of course, a simple habit, like every other nervous event—the habit of snuffling, for example, or of putting one's hands into one's pockets, or if biting one's nails—is, mechanically, nothing but a reflex discharge; and its anatomical substratum must be a path in the system. The most complex habits, as we shall presently see more fully, are, from the same point of view, nothing but *concatenated* discharges in the nerve-centres, due to the presence there of systems of reflex paths, so organized as to wake each other up successively—the impression produced by one muscular contraction serving as a stimulus to provoke the next, until a final impression inhibits the process and closes the chain.

It must be noticed that the growth of structural modification in living matter may be more rapid than in any lifeless mass, because the incessant nutritive renovation of which the living matter is the seat tends often to corroborate and fix the impressed modification, rather than to counteract it by renewing the original constitution of the tissue that has been impressed. Thus, we notice after exercising our muscles or our brain in a new way, that we can do so no longer at that time; but after a day or two of rest, when we resume the discipline, our increase in skill not seldom surprises us. I have often noticed this in learning a tune; and it has led a German author to say that we learn to swim during the winter, and to skate during the summer.

**Practical Effects of Habit.**—First, habit simplifies our movements, makes them accurate, and diminishes fatigue.

Man is born with a tendency to do more things than he has ready-made arrangements for in his nerve-centres. Most of the performances of other animals are automatic. But in him the number of them is so enormous that most of them must be the fruit of painful study. If practice did not make perfect, nor habit economize the expense of nervous and muscular energy, he would be in a sorry plight. As Dr. Maudsley says:*

If an act became no easier after being done several times, if the careful direction of consciousness were necessary to its accomplishment on each occasion, it is evident that the whole activity of a lifetime might be confined to one or two deeds—that no progress could take place in development. A man might be occupied all day in dressing and undressing himself; the attitude of his body would absorb all his attention and energy; the washing of his hands or the fastening of a button would be as difficult to him on each occasion as to the child on its first trial; and he would furthermore be completely exhausted by his exertions. Think of the pains necessary to teach a child to stand, of the many efforts which it must make, and of the ease with which it at last stands, unconscious even of an effort. For while secondary automatic acts are accomplished with comparatively little weariness—in this regard approaching the organic movements, or the original reflex movements—the conscious efforts of the will soon produces exhaustion. A spinal cord without . . . memory would simply be an idiotic spinal cord. . . . It is impossible for an individual to realise how much he owes to its automatic agency until disease has impaired its functions.

Secondly, *habit diminishes the conscious attention with which our acts are performed.*

One may state this abstractly thus: If an act require for its execution a chain, *A, B, C, D, E, F, G,* etc., of successive nervous events, then in the first performances of the action the conscious will must choose

---

* *The Physiology of Mind,* p. 155 [154].

each of these events from a number of wrong alternatives that tend to present themselves; but habit soon brings it about that each event calls up its own appropriate successor without any alternative offering itself, and without any reference to the conscious will, until at last the whole chain, *A, B, C, D, E, F, G*, rattles itself off as soon as *A* occurs, just as if A and the rest of the chain were fused into a continuous stream. Whilst we are learning to walk, to ride, to swim, skate, fence, write, play, or sing, we interrupt ourselves at every step by unnecessary movements and false notes. When we are proficients, on the contrary, the results follow not only with the very minimum of muscular action requisite to bring them forth, but they follow from a single instantaneous "cue." The marksman sees the bird, and, before he knows it, he has aimed and shot. A gleam in his adversary's eye, a momentary pressure from his rapier, and the fencer finds that he has instantly made the right parry and return. A glance at the musical hieroglyphics, and the pianist's fingers have rippled through a shower of notes. And not only is it the right thing at the right time that we thus involuntarily do, but the wrong thing also, if it be an habitual thing. Who is there that has never wound up his watch on taking off his waistcoat in the daytime, or taken his latch-key out on arriving at the door-step of a friend? Persons in going to their bedroom to dress for dinner have been known to take off one garment after another and finally to get into bed, merely because that was the habitual issue of the first few movements when performed at a later hour. We all have a definite routine manner of performing certain daily offices connected with the toilet, with the opening and shutting of familiar cupboards, and the like. But our higher thought-centres know hardly anything about the matter. Few men can tell off-hand which sock, shoe, or trousers-leg they put on first. They must first mentally rehearse the act; and even that is often insufficient—the act must be *performed*. So of the questions, Which valve of the shutters opens first? Which way does my door swing? etc. I cannot *tell* the answer; yet my *hand* never makes a mistake. No one can *describe* the order in which he brushes his hair or teeth; yet it is likely that the order is a pretty fixed one in all of us.

These results may be expressed as follows:

In action grown habitual, what instigates each new muscular

contraction to take place in its appointed order is not a thought or a perception, but the *sensation occasioned by the muscular contraction just finished.* A strictly voluntary act has to be guided by idea, perception, and volition, throughout its whole course. In habitual action, mere sensation is a sufficient guide, and the upper regions of brain and mind are set comparatively free. A diagram will make the matter clear:

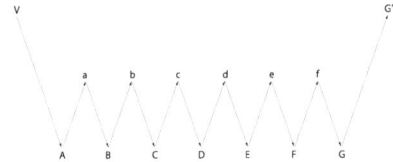

Let *A, B, C, D, E, F, G* represent an habitual chain of muscular contractions, and let *a, b, c, d, e, f* stand for the several sensations which these contractions excite in us when they are successively performed. Such sensations will usually be in the parts moved, but they may also be effects of the movement upon the eye or the ear. Through them, and through them alone, we are made aware whether or not the contraction has occurred. When the series, *A, B, C, D, E, F, G,* is being learned, each of these sensations becomes the object of a separate act of attention by the mind. We test each movement intellectually, to see if it [has] been rightly performed, before advancing to the next. We hesitate, compare, choose, revoke, reject, etc.; and the order by which the next movement is discharged is an express order from the ideational centres after this deliberation has been gone through.

In habitual action, on the contrary, the only impulse which the intellectual centres need send down is that which carries the command to *start.* This is represented in the diagram by *V;* it may be a thought of the first movement or of the last result, or a mere perception of some of the habitual conditions of the chain, the presence, e.g., of the keyboard near the hand. In the present example, no sooner has this conscious thought or volition instigated movement *A,* than *A,* through the sensation *a* of its own occurrence, awakens *B* reflexly; *B* then excites *C* through *b,* and so on till the chain is ended, when the intellect generally takes cognizance of the final result. The intellectual perception at the end is indicated in the diagram by the sensible effect of the movement *G* being represented at *G',* in the ideational centres above the merely sensational line. The sensational impressions, *a,b,c,d,e,f,* are all supposed to have their seat below the ideational level. [That our ideational centres, if involved at all by *a, b, c, d, e, f,* are involved in a minimal degree, is shown by the fact that the attention may be wholly absorbed elsewhere. We may say our prayers, or repeat the alphabet, with our attention far away. PP]

**Habits depend on sensations not attended to.** We have called *a,b,c,d,e,f* by the name of 'sensations.' If sensations, they are sensations to which we are usually inattentive; but that they are more than unconscious nerve-currents seems certain, for they catch our attention if they go wrong. Schneider's account of these sensations deserves to be quoted. In the act of walking, he says, even when our attention is entirely absorbed elsewhere, ["]it is doubtful whether we could preserve equilibrium if no sensation of our body's attitude were there, and doubtful whether we should advance our leg if we had no sensation of its movement as executed, and not even a minimal feeling of impulse to set it down. Knitting appears altogether mechanical, and the knitter keeps up her knitting even while she reads or is engaged in lively talk. But if we ask her how this is possible, she will hardly reply that the knitting goes on of itself. She will rather say that she has a feeling of it, that she feels in her hands that she knits and how she must knit, and that therefore the movements of knitting are called forth and regulated by the sensations associated therewithal, even when the attention is called away. . . ." Again: "When a pupil begins to play on the violin, to keep him from raising his right elbow in playing a book is placed under his right armpit, which he is ordered to hold fast by keeping the upper arm tight against his body. The muscular feelings, and feelings of contact connected with the book, provoke an impulse to press it tight. But often it happens that the beginner, whose attention gets absorbed in the production of the notes, lets drop the book. Later, however, this never happens; the faintest sensations of contact suffice to awaken the impulse to keep it in its place, and the attention may be wholly absorbed by the notes and the fingering with the left hand. *The simultaneous combination of movements is thus in the first instance conditioned by the facility with which in us, alongside of intellectual processes, processes of inattentive feeling may still go on.*"

**Ethical and Pedagogical Importance of the Principle of Habit.**—

"Habit a second nature! Habit is ten times nature," the Duke of Wellington is said to have exclaimed; and the degree to which this is true no one probably can appreciate as well as one who is a veteran soldier himself. The daily drill and the years of discipline end by fashioning a man completely over again, as to most of the possibilities of his conduct.

"There is a story," says Prof. Huxley, "which is credible enough, though it may not be true, of a practical joker, who, seeing a discharged veteran carrying home his dinner, suddenly called out 'Attention!' whereupon the man instantly brought his hands down, and lost his mutton and potatoes in the gutter. The drill had been thorough, and its effects had become embodied in the man's nervous structure."

Riderless cavalry-horses, at many a battle, have been seen to come together and go through their customary evolutions at the sound of the bugle-call. Most domestic beasts seem machines almost pure and simple, undoubtingly, unhesitatingly doing from minute to minute the duties they have been taught, and giving no sign that the possibility of an alternative ever suggests itself to their mind. Men grown old in prison have asked to be readmitted after being once set free. In a railroad accident a menagerie-tiger, whose cage had broken open, is said to have emerged, but presently crept back again, as if too much bewildered by his new responsibilities, so that he was without difficulty secured.

Habit is thus the enormous fly-wheel of society, its most precious conservative agent. It alone is what keeps us all within the bounds of ordinance, and saves the children of fortune from the envious uprisings of the poor. It alone prevents the hardest and most repulsive walks of life from being deserted by those brought up to tread therein. It keeps the fisherman and the deck-hand at sea through the winter; it holds the miner in his darkness, and nails the countryman to his log-cabin and his lonely farm through all the months of snow; it protects us from invasion by the natives of the desert and the frozen zone. It dooms us all to fight out the battle of life upon the lines of our nurture or our early choice, and to make the best of a pursuit that disagrees, because there is no other for which we are fitted, and it is too late to begin again. It keeps different social strata from mixing. Already at the age of twenty-five you see the professional mannerism settling down on the young commercial traveller, on the young doctor, on the young minister, on the young counsellor-at-law. You see the little lines of cleavage running through the character, the tricks of thought, the prejudices, the ways of the 'shop,' in a word, from which the man can by-and-by no more escape than his coat-sleeve can suddenly fall into a new set of folds. On the whole, it is best he should not escape. It is well for the world that in most of us, by the age of thirty, the character has set like plaster, and will never soften again.

If the period between twenty and thirty is the critical one in the formation of intellectual and professional habits, the period below twenty is more important still for the fixing of *personal* habits, properly so called, such as vocalization and pronunciation, gesture, motion, and address. Hardly ever is a language learned after twenty spoken without a foreign accent; hardly ever can a youth transferred to the society of his betters unlearn the nasality and other vices of speech bred in him by the associations of his growing years. Hardly ever, indeed, no matter how much money there be in his pocket, can he even learn to *dress* like a gentleman-born. The merchants offer their wares as eagerly to him as to the veriest 'swell,' but he simply *cannot* buy the right things. An invisible law, as strong as gravitation, keeps him within his orbit, arrayed this year as he was the last; and how his better-clad acquaintances contrive to get the things they wear will be for him a mystery till his dying day.

The great thing, then, in all education, is to *make our nervous system our ally instead of our enemy*. It is to fund and capitalize our acquisitions, and live at ease upon the interest of the fund. *For this we must make automatic and habitual, as early as possible, as many useful actions as we can*, and guard against the growing into ways that are likely to be disadvantageous to us, as we should guard against the plague. The more of the details of our daily life we can hand over to the effortless custody of automatism, the more our higher powers of mind will be set free for their own proper work. There is no more miserable human being than one in whom nothing is habitual but indecision, and for whom the lighting of every cigar, the drinking of every cup, the time of rising and going to bed every day, and the beginning of every bit of work, are subjects of express volitional deliberation. Full half the time of such a man goes to the deciding, or regretting, of matters which ought to be so ingrained in him as practically not to exist for his consciousness at all.

If there be such daily duties not yet ingrained in any one of my readers, let him begin this very hour to set the matter right.

In Professor Bain's chapter on "The Moral Habits" there are some admirable practical remarks laid down. Two great maxims emerge from his treatment. The first is that in the acquisition of a new habit, or the leaving off of an old one, we must take care to *launch ourselves with as strong and decided an initiative as possible.* Accumulate all the possible circumstances which shall re-enforce the right motives; put yourself assiduously in conditions that encourage the new way; make engagements incompatible with the old; take a public pledge, if the case allows; in short, envelop your resolution with every aid you know. This will give your new beginning such a momentum that the temptation to break down will not occur as soon as it otherwise might; and every day during which a breakdown is postponed adds to the chances of its not occurring at all.

The second maxim is: *Never suffer an exception to occur till the new habit is securely rooted in your life.* Each lapse is like the letting fall of a ball of string which one is carefully winding up; a single slip undoes more than a great many turns will wind again. *Continuity* of training is the great means of making the nervous system act infallibly right. As Professor Bain says:

The peculiarity of the moral habits, contra distinguishing them from the intellectual acquisitions, is the presence of two hostile powers, one to be gradually raised into the ascendant over the other. It is necessary, above all things, in such a situation, never to lose a battle. Every gain on the wrong side undoes the effect of many conquests on the right. The essential precaution, therefore, is, so to regulate the two opposing powers that the one may have a series of uninterrupted successes, until repetition has fortified it to such a degree as to enable it to cope with the opposition, under any circumstances. This is the theoretically best career of mental progress.

The need of securing success at the *outset* is imperative. Failure at first is apt to damp the energy of all future attempts, whereas past experiences of success nerve one to future vigor. Goethe says to a man who consulted him about an enterprise but mistrusted his own powers: "Ach! you need only blow on your hands!" And the remark illustrates the effect on Goethe's spirits of his own habitually successful career.

The question of "tapering-off," in abandoning such habits as drink and opium-indulgence comes in here, and is a question about which experts differ within certain limits, and in regard to what may be best for an individual case. In the main, however, all expert opinion would agree that abrupt acquisition of the new habit is the best way, *if there be a real possibility of carrying it out.* We must be careful not to give the will so stiff a task as to insure its defeat at the very outset; but, *provided one can stand it,* a sharp period of suffering, and then a free time, is the best thing to aim at, whether in giving up a habit like that of opium, or in simply changing one's hours of rising or of work. It is surprising how soon a desire will die of inanition if it be *never* fed.

"One must first learn, unmoved, looking neither to the right nor left, to walk firmly on the straight and narrow path, before one can begin 'to make one's self over again.' He who every day makes a fresh resolve is like one who, arriving at the edge of the ditch he is to leap, forever stops and returns for a fresh run. Without *unbroken* advance there is no such thing as *accumulation* of the ethical forces possible, and to make this possible, and to exercise us and habituate us in it, is the sovereign blessing of regular work."*

A third maxim may be added to the preceding pair: *Seize the very first possible opportunity to act on every resolution you make, and on every emotional prompting you may experience in the direction of the habits you aspire to gain.* It is not in the moment of their forming, but in the moment of their producing *motor effects,* that resolves and aspirations communicate the new 'set' to the brain. As the author last quoted remarks:

"The actual presence of the practical opportunity alone furnishes the fulcrum upon which the lever can rest, by means of which the moral will may multiply its strength, and raise itself aloft. He who has no solid ground to press against will never get beyond the stage of empty gesture-making."

No matter how full a reservoir of *maxims* one may possess, and no matter how good one's *sentiments* may be, if one [has] not taken

---

* J. Bahnsen: *Beitrag zu[r] Characterologie* (1867), vol. I, p. 209.

advantage of every concrete opportunity to act, one's character may remain entirely unaffected for the better. With mere good intentions, hell is proverbially paved. And this is an obvious consequence of the principles we have laid down. A "character," as J. S. Mill says, "is a completely fashioned will"; and a will, in the sense in which he means it, is an aggregate of tendencies to act in a firm and prompt and definite way upon all the principal emergencies of life. A tendency to act only becomes effectively ingrained in us in proportion to the uninterrupted frequency with which the actions actually occur, and the brain "grows" to their use. When a resolve or a fine glow of feeling is allowed to evaporate without bearing practical fruit it is worse than a chance lost; it works so as positively to hinder future resolutions and emotions from taking the normal path of discharge. There is no more contemptible type of human character than that of the nerveless sentimentalist and dreamer, who spends his life in a weltering sea of sensibility and emotion, but who never does a manly concrete deed. Rousseau, inflaming all the mothers of France, by his eloquence, to follow Nature and nurse their babies themselves, while he sends his own children to the foundling hospital, is the classical example of what I mean. But every one of us in his measure, whenever, after glowing for an abstractly formulated Good, he practically ignores some actual case, among the squalid "other particulars" of which that same Good lurks disguised, treads straight on Rousseau's path. All Goods are disguised by the vulgarity of their concomitants, in this work-a-day world; but woe to him who can only recognize them when he thinks them in their pure and abstract form! The habit of excessive novel-reading and theatre-going will produce true monsters in this line. The weeping of the Russian lady over the fictitious personages in the play, while her coachman is freezing to death on his seat outside, is the sort of thing that everywhere happens on a less glaring scale. Even the habit of excessive indulgence in music, for those who are neither performers themselves nor musically gifted enough to take it in a purely intellectual way, has probably a relaxing effect upon the character. One becomes filled with emotions which habitually pass without prompting to any deed, and so the inertly sentimental condition is kept up. The remedy would be, never to suffer one's self to have an emotion at a concert, without expressing it afterwards in *some* active way. Let the expression be the least thing in the world—speaking genially to one's grandmother, or giving up one's seat in a horse-car, if nothing more heroic offers—but let it not fail to take place.

These latter cases make us aware that it is not simply *particular lines* of discharge, but also *general forms* of discharge, that seem to be grooved out by habit in the brain. Just as, if we let our emotions evaporate, they get into a way of evaporating; so there is reason to suppose that if we often flinch from making an effort, before we know it the effort-making capacity will be gone; and that, if we suffer the wandering of our attention, presently it will wander all the time. Attention and effort are, as we shall see later, but two names for the same psychic fact. To what brain-processes they correspond we do not know. The strongest reason for believing that they do depend on brain-processes at all, and are not pure acts of the spirit, is just this fact, that they seem in some degree subject to the law of habit, which is a material law. As a final practical maxim, relative to these habits of the will, we may, then, offer something like this: *Keep the faculty of effort alive in you by a little gratuitous exercise every day.* That is, be systematically ascetic or heroic in little unnecessary points, do every day or two something for no other reason than that you would rather not do it, so that when the hour of dire need draws nigh, it may find you not unnerved and untrained to stand the test. Asceticism of this sort is like the insurance which a man pays on his house and goods. The tax does him no good at the time, and possibly may never bring him a return. But if the fire *does* come, his having paid it will be his salvation from ruin. So with the man who has daily inured himself to habits of concentrated attention, energetic volition, and self-denial in unnecessary things. He will stand like a tower when everything rocks around him, and when his softer fellow-mortals are winnowed like chaff in the blast.

The physiological study of mental conditions is thus the most powerful ally of hortatory ethics. The hell to be endured hereafter, of which theology tells, is no worse than the hell we make for ourselves in this world by habitually fashioning our characters in the wrong way. Could the young but realize how soon they will become mere walking bundles of habits, they would give more heed to their conduct while in the plastic state. We are spinning our own fates, good or evil, and never to be undone. Every smallest stroke of virtue or of vice leaves its never so little scar. The drunken Rip Van Winkle, in Jefferson's play, excuses himself for every fresh dereliction by saying, "I won't count this time!" Well! he may not count it, and a kind Heaven may not count it; but it is being counted none the less. Down among his nerve-cells and fibres the molecules are counting it, registering and storing it up to be used against him when the next temptation comes. Nothing we ever do is, in strict scientific literalness, wiped out. Of course this has its good side as well as its bad one. As we become permanent drunkards by so many separate drinks, so we become saints in the moral, and authorities and experts in the practical and scientific spheres, by so many separate acts and hours of work. Let no youth have any anxiety about the upshot of his education, whatever the line of it may be. If he keep faithfully busy each hour of the working day, he may safely leave the final result to itself. He can with perfect certainty count on waking up some fine morning, to find himself one of the competent ones of his generation, in whatever pursuit he may have singled out. Silently, between all the details of his business, the *power of judging* in all that class of matter will have built itself up within him as a possession that will never pass away. Young people should know this truth in advance. The ignorance of it has probably engendered more discouragement and faint-heartedness in youths embarking on arduous careers than all other causes put together.

# The Laws of Habit

It is very important that teachers should realize the importance of habit, and psychology helps us greatly at this point. We speak, it is true, of good habits and of bad habits; but, when people use the word 'habit,' in the majority of instances it is a bad habit which they have in mind. They talk of the smoking-habit and the swearing-habit and the drinking-habit, but not of the abstention-habit or the moderation-habit or the courage-habit. But the fact is that our virtues are habits as much as our vices. All our life, so far as it has definite form, is but a mass of habits—practical, emotional, and intellectual—systematically organized for our weal or woe, and bearing us irresistibly toward our destiny, whatever the latter may be.

Since pupils can understand this at a comparatively early age, and since to understand it contributes in no small measure to their feeling of responsibility, it would be well if the teacher were able himself to talk to them of the philosophy of habit in some such abstract terms as I am now about to talk of it to you.

I believe that we are subject to the law of habit in consequence of the fact that we have bodies. The plasticity of the living matter of our nervous system, in short, is the reason why we do a thing with difficulty the first time, but soon do it more and more easily, and finally, with sufficient practice, do it semi-mechanically, or with hardly any consciousness at all. Our nervous systems have (in Dr. Carpenter's words) *grown* to the way in which they have been exercised, just as a sheet of paper or a coat, once creased or folded, tends to fall forever afterward into the same identical folds.

Habit is thus a second nature, or rather, as the Duke of Wellington said, it is "ten times nature"—at any rate as regards its importance in adult life; for the acquired habits of our training have by that time inhibited or strangled most of the natural impulsive tendencies which were originally there. Ninety-nine hundredths or, possibly, nine hundred and ninety-nine thousandths of our activity is purely automatic and habitual, from our rising in the morning to our lying down each night. Our dressing and undressing, our eating and drinking, our greetings and partings, our hat-raisings and giving way for ladies to precede, nay, even most of the forms of our common speech, are things of a type so fixed by repetition as almost to be classed as reflex actions. To each sort of impression we have an automatic, ready-made response. My very words to you now are an example of what I mean; for having already lectured upon habit and printed a chapter about it in a book, and read the latter when in print, I find my tongue inevitably falling into its old phrases and repeating almost literally what I said before.

So far as we are thus mere bundles of habit, we are stereotyped creatures, imitators and copiers of our past selves. And since this, under any circumstances, is what we always tend to become, it follows first of all that the teacher's prime concern should be to ingrain into the pupil that assortment of habits at shall be most useful to him throughout life. Education is for behavior, and habits are the stuff of which behavior consists.

To quote my earlier book directly, the great thing in all education is to *make our nervous system our ally instead, of our enemy.* It is to fund and capitalize our acquisitions, and live at ease upon the interest of the fund. *For this we must make automatic and habitual, as early as possible, as many useful actions as we can,* and as carefully guard against the growing into ways that are likely to be disadvantageous. The more of the details of our daily life we can hand over to the effortless custody of automatism, the more our higher powers of mind will be set free for their own proper work. There is no more miserable human being than one in whom nothing is habitual but indecision, and for whom the lighting of every cigar, the drinking of every cup, the time of rising and going to bed every day, and the beginning of every bit of work are subjects of express volitional deliberation. Full half the time of such a man goes to the deciding or regretting of matters which ought to be so ingrained in him as practically not to exist for his consciousness at all. If there be such daily duties not yet ingrained in any one of my hearers, let him begin this very hour to set the matter right.

In Professor Bain's chapter on "The Moral Habits" there are some admirable practical remarks laid down. Two great maxims emerge from the treatment. The first is that in the acquisition of a new habit, or the leaving off of an old one, we must take care to *launch ourselves with as strong and decided an initiative as possible.* Accumulate all the possible circumstances which shall reinforce the right motives; put yourself assiduously in conditions that encourage the new way; make engagements incompatible with the old; take a public pledge, if the case allows; in short, envelope your resolution with every aid you know. This will give your new beginning such a momentum that the temptation to break down will not occur as soon as it otherwise might; and every day during which a breakdown is postponed adds to the chances of its not occurring at all.

I remember long ago reading in an Austrian paper the advertisement of a certain Rudolph Somebody, who promised fifty gulden reward to any one who after that date should find him at the wine-shop of Ambrosius So-and-so. "This I do," the advertisement continued, "in consequence of a promise which I have made my wife." With such a wife, and such an understanding of the way in which to start new habits, it would be safe to stake one's money on Rudolph's ultimate success.

The second maxim is, *Never suffer an exception to occur till the new habit is securely rooted in your life.* Each lapse is like the letting fall of a ball of string which one is carefully winding up: a single slip undoes more than a great many turns will wind again. Continuity of training is the great means of making the nervous system act infallibly right. As Professor Bain says:

"The peculiarity of the moral habits, contra-distinguishing them from the intellectual acquisitions, is the presence of two hostile powers, one to be gradually raised into the ascendant over the other. It is necessary above all things, in such a situation, never to lose a battle. Every gain on the wrong side undoes the effect of many conquests on the right. The essential precaution, therefore, is so to regulate the two opposing powers that the one may have a series of uninterrupted successes, until repetition has fortified it to such a degree as to enable it to cope with the opposition, under any circumstances. This is the theoretically best career of mental progress."

A third maxim may be added to the preceding pair: *Seize the very first possible opportunity to act on every resolution you make, and on every emotional prompting you may experience in the direction of the habits you aspire to gain.* It is not in the moment of their forming, but in the moment of their producing motor effects, that resolves and aspirations communicate the new "set" to the brain.

No matter how full a reservoir of maxims one may possess, and no matter how good one's sentiments may be, if one have not taken advantage of every concrete opportunity to act, one's character may remain entirely unaffected for the better. With good intentions, hell proverbially is paved. This is an obvious consequence of the principles I have laid down. A "character," as J. S. Mill says, "is a completely fashioned will," and a will, in the sense in which he means it, is an aggregate of tendencies to act in a firm and prompt and definite way upon all the principal emergencies of life. A tendency to act only becomes effectively ingrained in us in proportion to the uninterrupted frequency with which the actions actually occur, and the brain "grows" to their use. When a resolve or a fine glow of feeling is allowed to evaporate without bearing practical fruit, it is worse than a chance lost: it works so as positively to hinder future resolutions and emotions from taking the normal path of discharge. There is no more contemptible type of human character than that of the nerveless sentimentalist and dreamer, who spends his life in a weltering sea of sensibility, but never does a concrete manly deed.

This leads to a fourth maxim. *Don't preach too much to your pupils or abound in good talk in the abstract.* Lie in wait rather for the practical opportunities, be prompt to seize those as they pass, and thus at one operation get your pupils both to think, to feel, and to do. The strokes of *behavior* are what give the new set to the character, and work the good habits into its organic tissue. Preaching and talking too soon become an ineffectual bore.

There is a passage in Darwin's short autobiography which has been often quoted, and which, for the sake of its bearing on our subject of habit, I must now quote again. Darwin says: "Up to the age of thirty, or beyond it, poetry of many kinds gave me great pleasure; and even as a schoolboy I took intense delight in Shakespeare, especially in the historical plays. I have also said that pictures formerly gave me considerable, and music very great delight. But now for many years I cannot endure to read a line of poetry: I have tried lately to read Shakespeare, and found it so intolerably dull that it nauseated me. I have also almost lost my taste for pictures or music. . . . My mind seems to have become a kind of machine for grinding general laws out of large collections of facts; but why this should have caused the atrophy of that part of the brain alone, on which the higher tastes depend, I cannot conceive. . . . If I had to live my life again, I would have made a rule to read some poetry and listen to some music at least once every week; for perhaps the parts of my brain now atrophied would thus have been kept alive through use. The loss of these tastes is a loss of happiness, and may possibly be injurious to the intellect, and more probably to the moral character, by enfeebling the emotional part of our nature."

We all intend when young to be all that may become a man, before the destroyer cuts us down. We wish and expect to enjoy poetry always, to grow more and more intelligent about pictures and music, to keep in touch with spiritual and religious ideas, and even not to let the greater philosophic thoughts of our time develop quite beyond our view. We mean all this in youth, I say; and yet in how many middle-aged men and women is such an honest and sanguine expectation fulfilled? Surely, in comparatively few; and the laws of habit show us why. Some interest in each of these things arises in everybody at the proper age; but, if not persistently fed with the appropriate matter, instead of growing into a powerful and necessary habit, it atrophies and dies, choked by the rival interests to which the daily food is given. We make ourselves into Darwins in this negative respect by persistently ignoring the essential practical conditions of our case. We say abstractly: "I mean to enjoy poetry, and to absorb a lot of it, of course. I fully intend to keep up my love of music, to read the books that shall give new turns to the thought of my time, to keep my higher spiritual side alive, etc." But we do not attack these things concretely, and we do not begin *today*. We forget that every good that is worth possessing must be paid for in strokes of daily effort. We postpone and postpone, until those smiling possibilities are dead. Whereas ten minutes a day of poetry, of spiritual reading or meditation, and an hour or two a week at music, pictures, or philosophy, provided we began *now* and suffered no remission, would infallibly give us in due time the fulness of all we desire. By neglecting the necessary concrete labor, by sparing ourselves the little daily tax, we are positively digging the graves of our higher possibilities. This is a point concerning which you teachers might well give a little timely information to your older and more aspiring pupils.

According as a function receives daily exercise or not, the man becomes a different kind of being in later life. We have lately had a number of accomplished Hindoo visitors at Cambridge, who talked freely of life and philosophy. More than one of them has confided to me that the sight of our faces, all contracted as they are with the habitual American over-intensity and anxiety of expression, and our ungraceful and distorted attitudes when sitting, made on him a very painful impression. "I do not see," said one, "how it is possible for you to live as you do, without a single minute in your day deliberately given to tranquillity and meditation. It is an invariable part of our Hindoo life to retire for at least half an hour daily into silence, to relax our muscles, govern our breathing, and meditate on eternal things. Every Hindoo child is trained to this from a very early age." The good fruits of such a discipline were obvious in the physical repose and lack of tension, and the wonderful smoothness and calmness of facial expression, and imperturbability of manner of these Orientals. I felt that my countrymen were depriving themselves of an essential grace of character. How many American children ever hear it said, by parent or teacher, that they should moderate their piercing voices, that they should relax their unused muscles, and as far as possible, when sitting, sit quite still? Not one in a thousand, not one in five thousand! Yet, from its reflex influence on the inner mental states, this ceaseless over-tension, over-motion, and over-expression are working on us grievous national harm.

I beg you teachers to think a little seriously of this matter. Perhaps you can help our rising generation of Americans towards the beginning of a better set of personal ideals.*

To go back now to our general maxims, I may at last, as a fifth and final practical maxim about habits, offer something like this: *Keep the faculty of effort alive in you by a little gratuitous exercise every day.* That

---

*See the Address on the Gospel of Relaxation, later in this volume. [Not included in this collection, but see page 34 of the Introduction—ed.]

is, be systematically heroic in little unnecessary points, do every day or two something for no other reason than its difficulty, so that, when the hour of dire need draws nigh, it may find you not unnerved and untrained to stand the test. Asceticism of this sort is like the insurance which a man pays on his house and goods. The tax does him no good at the time, and possibly may never bring him a return. But, if the fire *does* come, his having paid it will be his salvation from ruin. So with the man who has daily inured himself to habits of concentrated attention, energetic volition, and self-denial in unnecessary things. He will stand like a tower when everything rocks around him, and his softer fellow-mortals are winnowed like chaff in the blast.

I have been accused, when talking of the subject of habit, of making old habits appear so strong that the acquiring of new ones, and particularly anything like a sudden reform or conversion, would be made impossible by my doctrine. Of course, this would suffice to condemn the latter; for sudden conversions, however infrequent they may be, unquestionably do occur. But there is no incompatibility between the general laws I have laid down and the most startling sudden alterations in the way of character. New habits *can* be launched, I have expressly said, on condition of there being new stimuli and new excitements. Now life abounds in these, and sometimes they are such critical and revolutionary experiences that they change a man's whole scale of values and system of ideas. In such cases, the old order of his habits will be ruptured; and, if the new motives are lasting, new habits will be formed, and build up in him a new or regenerate "nature."

All this kind of fact I fully allow. But the general laws of habit are no wise altered thereby, and the physiological study of mental conditions still remains on the whole the most powerful ally of hortatory ethics. The hell to be endured hereafter, of which theology tells, is no worse than the hell we make for ourselves in this world by habitually fashioning our characters in the wrong way. Could the young but realize how soon they will become mere walking bundles of habits, they would give more heed to their conduct while in the plastic state. We are spinning our own fates, good or evil, and never to be undone. Every smallest stroke of virtue or of vice leaves its never-so-little scar. The drunken Rip Van Winkle, in Jefferson's play, excuses himself for every fresh dereliction by saying, "I won't count this time!" Well, he may not count it, and a kind Heaven may not count it; but it is being counted none the less. Down among his nerve-cells and fibres the molecules are counting it, registering and storing it up to be used against him when the next temptation comes. Nothing we ever do is, in strict scientific literalness, wiped out.

Of course, this has its good side as well as its bad one. As we become permanent drunkards by so many separate drinks, so we become saints in the moral, and authorities and experts in the practical and scientific spheres, by so many separate acts and hours of work. Let no youth have any anxiety about the upshot of his education, whatever the line of it may be. If he keep faithfully busy each hour of the working day, he may safely leave the final result to itself. He can with perfect certainty count on waking up some fine morning to find himself one of the competent ones of his generation, in whatever pursuit he may have singled out. Silently, between all the details of his business, the *power of judging* in all that class of matter will have built itself up within him as a possession that will never pass away. Young people should know this truth in advance. The ignorance of it has probably engendered more discouragement and faint-heartedness in youths embarking on arduous careers than all other causes put together.

# Genius and Old-fogyism

**Genius and Old-fogyism.**— . . . .[ed.] There is an everlasting struggle in every mind between the tendency to keep unchanged, and the tendency to renovate, its ideas. Our education is a ceaseless compromise between the conservative and the progressive factors. Every new experience must be disposed of under *some* old head. The great point is to find the head which has to be least altered to take it in. Certain Polynesian natives, seeing horses for the first time, called them pigs, that being the nearest head. My child of two played for a week with the first orange that was given him, calling it a "ball." He called the first whole eggs he saw "potatoes," having been accustomed to see his "eggs" broken into his glass, and his potatoes without the skin. A folding pocket-corkscrew he unhesitatingly called "bad-scissors." Hardly any one of us can make new heads easily when fresh experiences come. Most of us grow more and more enslaved to the stock conceptions with which we have once become familiar, and less and less capable of assimilating impressions in any but the old ways. Old-fogyism, in short, is the inevitable terminus to which life sweeps us on. Objects which violate our established habits of "apperception" are simply not taken account of at all; or, if on some occasion we are forced by dint of argument to admit their existence, twenty-four hours later the admission is as if it were not, and every trace of the unassimilable truth has vanished from our thought. Genius, in truth, means little more than the faculty of perceiving in an unhabitual way. . . . [ed.]

# Part II

# CONSCIOUSNESS AND THE HABITS OF WILL

## The Stream of Consciousness

. . . .

**The Fundamental Fact.**—The first and foremost concrete fact which everyone will affirm to belong to his inner experience is the fact that *consciousness of some sort goes on.* *"States of mind" succeed each other in him.* If we could say in English "it thinks," as we say "it rains" or "it blows," we should be stating the fact most simply and with the minimum of assumption. As we cannot, we must simply say that *thought goes on.*

**Four Characters in Consciousness.** — How does it go on? We notice immediately four important characters in the process, of which it shall be the duty of the present chapter to treat in a general way:

1) Every "state" tends to be part of a personal consciousness.

2) Within each personal consciousness states are always changing.

3) Each personal consciousness is sensibly continuous.

4) It is interested in some parts of its object to the exclusion of others, and welcomes or rejects—*chooses* from among them, in a word—all the while.

In considering these four points successively, we shall have to plunge *in medias res* as regards our nomenclature and use psychological terms which can only be adequately defined in later chapters of the book. But everyone knows what the terms mean in a rough way; and it is only in a rough way that we are now to take them. This chapter is like a painter's first charcoal sketch upon his canvas, in which no niceties appear.

When I say *every "state"* or *"thought" is part of a personal consciousness,* "personal consciousness" is one of the terms in question. Its meaning we know so long as no one asks us to define it, but to give an accurate account of it is the most difficult of philosophic tasks. This task we must confront in the next chapter; here a preliminary word will suffice.

In this room—this lecture-room, say—there are a multitude of thoughts, yours and mine, some of which cohere mutually, and some not. They are as little each-for-itself and reciprocally independent as they are all-belonging-together. They are neither: no one of them is separate, but each belongs with certain others and with none beside. My thought belongs with *my* other thoughts, and your thought with *your* other thoughts. Whether anywhere in the room there be a *mere* thought, which is nobody's thought, we have no means of ascertaining, for we have no experience of its like. The only states of consciousness that we naturally deal with are found in personal consciousnesses, minds, selves, concrete particular I's and you's.

Each of these minds keeps its own thoughts to itself. There is no giving or bartering between them. No thought even comes into direct *sight* of a thought in another personal consciousness than its own. Absolute insulation, irreducible pluralism, is the law. It seems as if the elementary psychic fact were not *thought* or *this thought* or *that thought*, but *my thought*, every thought being *owned*. Neither contemporaneity, nor proximity in space, nor similarity of quality and content are able to fuse thoughts together which are sundered by this barrier of belonging to different personal minds. The breaches between such thoughts are the most absolute breaches in nature. Everyone will recognize this to be true, so long as the existence of *something* corresponding to the term "personal mind" is all that is insisted on, without any particular view of its nature being implied. On these terms the personal self rather than the thought might be treated as the immediate datum in psychology. The universal conscious fact is not "feelings and thoughts exist," but "I think" and "I feel." No psychology, at any rate, can question the *existence* of personal selves. Thoughts connected as we feel them to be connected are *what we mean* by personal selves. The worst a psychology can do is so to interpret the nature of these selves as to rob them of their *worth*.

**Consciousness is in constant change.** I do not mean by this to say that no one state of mind has any duration—even if true, that would be hard to establish. What I wish to lay stress on is this, that *no state once gone can recur and be identical with what it was before.* Now we are seeing, now hearing; now reasoning, now willing; now recollecting, now expecting; now loving, now hating; and in a hundred other ways we know our minds to be alternately engaged. But all these are complex states, it may be said, produced by combination of simpler ones;—do not the simpler ones follow a different law? Are not the *sensations* which we get from the same object, for example, always the same? Does not the same piano key, struck with the same force, make us hear in the same way? Does not the same grass give us the same feeling of green, the same sky the same feeling of blue, and do we not get the same olfactory sensation no matter how many times we put our nose to the same flask of cologne? It seems a piece of metaphysical sophistry to suggest that we do not; and yet a close attention to the matter shows that *there is no proof that an incoming current ever gives us just the same bodily sensation twice.*

*What is got twice is the same* OBJECT. We hear the same *note* over and over again; we see the same *quality* of green, or smell the same objective perfume, or experience the same *species* of pain. The realities, concrete and abstract, physical and ideal, whose permanent existence we believe in, seems to be constantly coming up again before our thought, and lead us, in our carelessness, to suppose that our "ideas" of them are the same ideas. When we come, some time later, to the chapter on Perception, we shall see how inveterate is our habit of simply using our sensible impressions as stepping-stones to pass over to the recognition of the realities whose presence they reveal.

. . . .

Consciousness, then, does not appear to itself chopped up in bits. Such words as "chain" or "train" do not describe it fitly as it presents itself in the first instance. It is nothing jointed; it flows. A "river" or a "stream" are the metaphors by which it is most naturally described. *In talking of it hereafter, let us call it the stream of thought, of consciousness, or of subjective life.*

. . . .

When we take a general view of the wonderful stream of our

consciousness, what strikes us first is the different pace of its parts. Like a bird's life, it seems to be an alternation of flights and perchings. The rhythm of language expresses this, where every thought is expressed in a sentence, and every sentence closed by a period. The resting-places are usually occupied by sensorial imaginations of some sort, whose peculiarity is that they can be held before the mind for an indefinite time, and contemplated without changing; the places of flight are filled with thoughts of relations, static or dynamic, that for the most part obtain between the matters contemplated in the periods of comparative rest.

. . . .

It is, the reader will see, the reinstatement of the vague and inarticulate to its proper place in our mental life which I am so anxious to press on the attention . . . . [ed.] What must be admitted is that the definite images of traditional psychology form but the very smallest part of our minds as they actually live. The traditional psychology talks like one who should say a river consists of nothing but pailsful, spoonsful, quartpotsful, barrelsful, and other moulded forms of water. Even were the pails and the pots all actually standing in the stream, still between them the free water would continue to flow. It is just this free water of consciousness that psychologists resolutely overlook. Every definite image in the mind is steeped and dyed in the free water that flows round it. With it goes the sense of its relations, near and remote, the dying echo of whence it came to us, the dawning sense of whither it is to lead. The significance, the value, of the image is all in this halo or penumbra that surrounds and escorts it—or rather that is fused into one with it and has become bone of its bone and flesh of its flesh; leaving it, it is true, an image of the same *thing* it was before, but making it an image of that thing newly taken and freshly understood.

*Let us call the consciousness of this halo of relations around the image by the name of "psychic overtone" or "fringe."*

. . . .

The last peculiarity to which attention is to be drawn in this first rough description of thought's stream is that—

**Consciousness is always interested more in one part of its object than in another, and welcomes and rejects, or chooses, all the while it thinks.**

The phenomena of selective attention and of deliberative will are of course patent examples of this choosing activity. But few of us are aware how incessantly it is at work in operations not ordinarily called by these names. Accentuation and Emphasis are present in every perception we have. We find it quite impossible to disperse our attention impartially over a number of impressions. A monotonous succession of sonorous strokes is broken up into rhythms, now of one sort, now of another, by the different accent which we place on different strokes. The simplest of these rhythms is the double one, tick-tóck, tick-tóck, tick-tóck. Dots dispersed on a surface are perceived in rows and groups. Lines separate into diverse figures. The ubiquity of the distinctions, *this* and *that*, *here* and *there*, *now* and *then*, in our minds is the result of our laying the same selective emphasis on parts of place and time.

But we do far more than emphasize things, and unite some, and keep others apart. We actually *ignore* most of the things before us. Let me briefly show how this goes on.

To begin at the bottom, what are our very senses themselves, as we saw on pp. 10–12 [in chapter II, not included here], but organs of selection? Out of the infinite chaos of movements, of which physics teaches us that the outer world consists, each sense-organ picks out those which fall within certain limits of velocity. To these it responds, but ignores the rest as completely as if they did not exist. Out of what is in itself an undistinguishable, swarming *continuum,* devoid of distinction or emphasis, our senses make for us, by attending to this motion and ignoring that, a world full of contrasts, of sharp accents, of abrupt changes, of picturesque light and shade.

If the sensations we receive from a given organ have their causes thus picked out for us by the conformation of the organ's termination, Attention, on the other hand, out of all the sensations yielded, picks out certain ones as worthy of its notice and suppresses all the rest. We notice only those sensations which are signs to us of *things* which happen practically or aesthetically to interest us, to which we therefore give substantive names, and which we exalt to this exclusive status of independence and dignity. But in itself, apart from my interest, a particular dust-wreath on a windy day is just as much of an individual *thing,* and just as much or as little deserves an individual name, as my own body does.

And then, among the sensations we get from each separate thing, what happens? The mind selects again. It chooses certain of the sensations to represent the thing most *truly,* and considers the rest as its appearances, modified by the conditions of the moment. Thus my table-top is named *square,* after but one of an infinite number of retinal sensations which it yields, the rest of them being sensations of two acute and two obtuse angles; but I call the latter *perspective* views, and the four right angles the *true* form of the table, and erect the attribute squareness into the table's essence, for aesthetic reasons of my own. In like manner, the real form of the circle is deemed to be the sensation it gives when the line of vision is perpendicular to its centre—all its other sensations are *signs* of this sensation. The real sound of the cannon is the sensation it makes when the ear is close by. The real color of the brick is the sensation it gives when the eye looks squarely at it from a near point, out of the sunshine and yet not in the gloom; under other circumstances it gives us other color-sensations which are but signs of this—we then see it looks pinker or bluer than it really is. The reader knows no object which he does not represent to himself by preference as in some typical attitude, of some normal size, at some characteristic distance, of some standard tint, etc., etc. But all these essential characteristics, which together form for us the genuine objectivity of the thing and are contrasted with what we call the subjective sensations it may yield us at a given moment, are mere sensations like the latter. The mind chooses to suit itself, and decides what particular sensation shall be held more real and valid than all the rest.

Next, in a world of objects thus individualized by our mind's selective industry, what is called our "experience" is almost entirely determined by our habits of attention. A thing may be present to a man a hundred times, but if he persistently fails to notice it, it cannot be said to enter into his experience. We are all seeing flies, moths, and beetles by the thousand, but to whom, save an entomologist, do they say anything distinct? On the other hand, a thing met only once in a lifetime may leave an indelible experience in the memory. Let four men make a tour in Europe. One will bring home only picturesque impressions—costumes and colors, parks and views and works of architecture, pictures and statues. To another all this will be non-existent; and distances and prices, populations and drainage-arrangements, door- and window-fastenings, and other useful statistics will take their place. A third will give a rich account of the theatres, restaurants, and public halls and naught beside; whilst the fourth will perhaps have been so wrapped in his own subjective broodings as to be able to tell little more than a few names of places through which he passed. Each has selected, out of the same mass of presented objects, those which suited his private interest and has made his experience thereby. . . . [ed.]

Ascending still higher, we reach the plane of Ethics, where choice reigns notoriously supreme. An act has no ethical quality whatever unless it be chosen out of several all equally possible. To sustain the arguments for the good course and keep them ever before us, to stifle our longing for more flowery ways, to keep the foot unflinchingly on the arduous path, these are characteristic ethical energies. But more than these; for these but deal with the means of compassing interests already felt by the man to be supreme. The ethical energy *par excellence* has to go farther and choose which *interest* out of several, equally coercive, shall become supreme. The issue here is of the utmost pregnancy, for it decides a man's entire career. When he debates, Shall I commit this crime? choose that profession? accept that office, or marry this fortune? —his choice really lies between one of several equally possible future Characters. What he shall *become* is fixed by the conduct of this moment. . . . [ed.] The problem with the man is less what act he shall now resolve to do than what being he shall now choose to become.

Taking human experience in a general way, the choosings of different men are to a great extent the same. The race as a whole largely agrees as to what it shall notice and name; and among the noticed parts we select in much the same way for accentuation and preference, or subordination and dislike. There is, however, one entirely extraordinary case in which no two men ever are known to choose alike. One great splitting of the whole universe into two halves is made by each of us; and for each of us almost all of the interest attaches to one of the halves; but we all draw the line of division between them in a different place. When I say that we all call the two halves by the same names, and that those names are "*me*" and "*not-me*" respectively, it will at once be seen what I mean. The altogether unique kind of interest which each human mind feels in those parts of creation which it can call *me* or *mine* may be a moral riddle, but it is a fundamental psychological fact. No mind can take the same interest in his neighbor's *me* as in his own. The neighbor's me falls together with all the rest of things in one foreign mass against which his own me stands out in startling relief. Even the trodden worm, as Lotze somewhere says, contrasts his own suffering self with the whole remaining universe, though he have no clear conception either of himself or of what the universe may be. He is for me a mere part of the world; for him it is I who am the mere part. Each of us dichotomizes the Kosmos in a different place. . . . [ed.]

## Attention and Free Will

**Attention and Free Will.**— I have spoken as if our attention were wholly determined by neural conditions. I believe that the array of *things* we can attend to is so determined. No object can *catch* our attention except by the neural machinery. But the *amount* of the attention which an object receives after it has caught our mental eye is another question. It often takes effort to keep the mind upon it. We feel that we can make more or less of the effort as we choose. If this feeling be not deceptive, if our effort be a spiritual force, and an indeterminate one, then of course it contributes coequally with the cerebral conditions to the result. Though it *introduce* no new idea, it will deepen and prolong the stay in consciousness of innumerable ideas which else would fade more quickly away. The delay thus gained might not be more than a second in duration—but that second may be *critical*; for in the constant rising and falling of considerations in the mind, where two associated systems of them are nearly in equilibrium it is often a matter of but a second more or less of attention at the outset, whether one system shall gain force to occupy the field and develop itself, and exclude the other, or be excluded itself by the other. When developed, it may make us act; and that act may seal our doom. When we come to the chapter on the Will, we shall see that the whole drama of the voluntary life hinges on the amount of attention, slightly more or slightly less, which rival motor ideas may receive. But the whole feeling of reality, the whole sting and excitement of our voluntary life, depends on our sense that in it things are *really being decided* from one moment to another, and that it is not the dull rattling off of a chain that was forged innumerable ages ago. This appearance, which makes life and history tingle with such a tragic zest, *may* not be an illusion. Effort may be an original force and not a mere effect, and it may be indeterminate in amount. The last word of sober insight here is ignorance, for the forces engaged are too delicate ever to me measured in detail. Psychology, however, as a would-be "Science," must, like every other Science, *postulate* complete determinism in its facts, and abstract consequently from the effects of free will, even if such a force exist. I shall do so in this book like other psychologists; well knowing, however, that such a procedure, although a methodical device justified by the subjective need of arranging the facts in a simple and "scientific" form, does not settle the ultimate truth of the free-will question one way or the other.

# Will

**Voluntary Acts.**—Desire, wish, will, are states of mind which everyone knows, and which no definition can make plainer. We desire to feel, to have, to do, all sorts of things which at the moment are not felt, had, or done. If with the desire there goes a sense that attainment is not possible, we simply *wish*; but if we believe that the end is in our power, we *will* that the desired feeling, having, or doing shall be real; and real it presently becomes, either immediately upon the willing or after certain preliminaries have been fulfilled.

The only ends which follow *immediately* upon our willing seem to be movements of our own bodies. Whatever *feelings* and *havings* we may will to get come in as results of preliminary movements which we make for the purpose. This fact is too familiar to need illustration; so that we may start with the proposition that the only *direct* outward effects of our will are bodily movements. The mechanism of production of these voluntary movements is what befalls us to study now.

**They are secondary performances.** The movements we have studied hitherto have been automatic and reflex, and (on the first occasion of their performance, at any rate) unforeseen by the agent. The movements to the study of which we now address ourselves, being desired and intended beforehand, are of course done with full prevision of what they are to be. It follows from this that *voluntary movements must be secondary, not primary, functions of our organism.* This is the first point to understand in the psychology of Volition. Reflex, instinctive, and emotional movements are all primary performances. The nerve-centres are so organized that certain stimuli pull the trigger of certain explosive parts; and a creature going through one of these explosions for the first time undergoes an entirely novel experience. . . . [ed.] We learn all our possibilities by the way of experience. When a particular movement, having once occurred in a random, reflex, or involuntary way, has left an image of itself in the memory, then the movement can be desired again, and deliberately willed. But it is impossible to see how it could be willed before.

*A supply of ideas of the various movements that are possible, left in the memory by experiences of their involuntary performance, is thus the first prerequisite of the voluntary life.*

. . . .

The existence of the effort as a phenomenal fact in our consciousness cannot of course be doubted or denied. Its significance, on the other hand, is a matter about which the gravest difference of opinion prevails. Questions as momentous as that of the very existence of spiritual causality, as vast as that of universal predestination or free-will, depend on its interpretation. It therefore becomes essential that we study with some care the conditions under which the feeling of volitional effort is found.

**The Feeling of Effort.**—When I said, awhile back, that *consciousness* (or the neural process which goes with it) *is in its very nature impulsive*, I should have added the proviso that *it must be sufficiently intense*. Now there are remarkable differences in the power of different sorts of consciousness to excite movement. The intensity of some feelings is practically apt to be below the discharging point, whilst that of others is apt to be above it. By practically apt, I mean apt under ordinary circumstances. These circumstances may be habitual inhibitions, like that comfortable feeling of the *dolce far niente* which gives to each and all of us a certain dose of laziness only to be overcome by the acuteness of the impulsive spur; or they may consist in the native inertia, or internal resistance, of the motor centres themselves, making explosion impossible until a certain inward tension has been reached and over-passed. These conditions may vary from one person to another, and in the same person from time to time. The neural inertia may wax or wane, and the habitual inhibitions dwindle or augment. The intensity of particular thought-processes and stimulations may also change independently, and particular paths of association grow more pervious or less so. There thus result great possibilities of alteration in the actual impulsive efficacy of particular motives compared with others. It is where the normally less efficacious motive becomes more efficacious, and the normally more efficacious one less so, that actions ordinarily effortless, or abstinences ordinarily easy, either become impossible, or are effected (if at all) by the expenditure of effort.

. . . .

**Effort feels like an original force.** We now see at one view when it is that effort complicates volition. It does so whenever a rarer and more ideal impulse is called upon to neutralize others of a more instinctive and habitual kind; it does so whenever strongly explosive tendencies are checked, or strongly obstructive conditions overcome. The *âme bien née*, the child of the sunshine, at whose birth the fairies made their gifts, does not need much of it in his life. The hero and the neurotic subject, on the other hand, do. Now our spontaneous way of conceiving the effort, under all these circumstances, is as an active force adding its strength to that of the motives which ultimately prevail. When outer forces impinge upon a body, we say that the resultant motion is in the line of least resistance, or of greatest traction. But it is a curious fact that our spontaneous language never speaks of volition with effort in this way. Of course if we proceed *a priori* and define the line of least resistance as the line that is followed, the physical law must also hold good in the mental sphere. But we *feel*, in all hard cases of volition, as if the line taken, when the rarer and more ideal motives prevail, were the line of greater resistance, and as if the line of coarser motivation were the more pervious and easy one, even at the very moment when we refuse to follow it. He who under the surgeon's knife represses cries of pain, or he who exposes himself to social obloquy for duty's sake, feels as if he were following the line of greatest temporary resistance. He speaks of conquering and overcoming his impulses and temptations.

But the sluggard, the drunkard, the coward, never talk of their conduct in that way, or say they resist their energy, overcome their sobriety, conquer their courage, and so forth. If in general we class all springs of action as propensities on the one hand and ideals on the other, the sensualist never says of his behavior that it results from a victory over his ideals, but the moralist always speaks of his as a victory over his propensities. The sensualist uses terms of inactivity, says he forgets his ideals, is deaf to duty, and so forth; which terms seem to imply that the ideal motives *per se* can be annulled without energy or effort, and that the strongest mere traction lies in the line of the propensities. The ideal impulse appears, in comparison with this, a still small voice which must be artificially reinforced to prevail. Effort is what reinforces it, making things seem as if, while the force of propensity were essentially a fixed quantity, the ideal force might be of various amount. But what determines the amount of the effort when, by its aid, an ideal motive becomes victorious over a great sensual resistance? The very greatness of the resistance itself. If the sensual propensity is small, the effort is small. The latter is *made great* by the presence of a great antagonist to overcome. And if a brief definition of ideal or moral action were required, none could be given which would better fit the appearances than this: *It is action in the line of the greatest resistance.*

. . . .

**What holds attention determines action.** If one must have a single name for the condition upon which the impulsive and inhibitive quality of objects depends, one had better call it their *interest.* "The interesting" is a title which covers not only the pleasant and the painful, but also the morbidly fascinating, the tediously haunting, and even the simply habitual, inasmuch as the attention usually travels on habitual lines, and what-we-attend-to and what-interests-us are synonymous terms. It seems as if we ought to look for the secret of an idea's impulsiveness, not in any peculiar relations which it may have with paths of motor discharge—for *all* ideas have relations with some such paths—but rather in a preliminary phenomenon, the *urgency, namely, with which it is able to compel attention and dominate in consciousness.* Let it once so dominate, let no other ideas succeed in displacing it, and whatever motor effects belong to it by nature will inevitably occur—its impulsion, in short, will be given to boot, and will manifest itself as a matter of course. This is what we have seen in instinct, in emotion, in common ideo-motor action, in hypnotic suggestion, in morbid impulsion, and in *voluntas invita*—the impelling idea is simply the one which possesses the attention. It is the same where pleasure and pain are the motor spurs—they drive other thoughts from consciousness at the same time that they instigate their own characteristic "volitional" effects. And this is also what happens at the moment of the *fiat*, in all the five types of "decision" which we have described. In short, one does not see any case in which the steadfast occupancy of consciousness does not appear to be the prime condition of impulsive power. It is still more obviously the prime condition of inhibitive power. What checks our impulses is the mere thinking of reasons to the contrary—it is their bare presence to the mind which gives the veto, and makes acts, otherwise seductive, impossible to perform. If we could only *forget* our scruples, our doubts, our fears, what exultant energy we should for a while display!

**Will is a relation between the mind and its "ideas."** In closing in, therefore, after all these preliminaries, upon the more *intimate* nature of the volitional process, we find ourselves driven more and more exclusively to consider the conditions which make ideas prevail in the mind. With the prevalence, once there as a fact, of the motive idea, the *psychology* of volition properly stops. The movements which ensue are exclusively physiological phenomena, following according to physiological laws upon the neural events to which the idea corresponds. The *willing* terminates with the prevalence of the idea; and whether the act then follows or not is a matter quite immaterial, so far as the willing itself goes. I will to write, and the act follows. I will to sneeze, and it does not. I will that the distant table slide over the floor towards me; it also does not. My willing representation can no more instigate my sneezing-centre than it can instigate the table to activity. But in both cases it is as true and good willing as it was when I willed to write. In a word, volition is a psychic or moral fact pure and simple, and is absolutely completed when the stable state of the idea is there. The supervention of motion is a supernumerary phenomenon depending on executive ganglia whose function lies outside the mind. If the ganglia work duly, the act occurs perfectly. If they work, but work wrongly, we have St. Vitus's dance, locomotor ataxy, motor aphasia, or minor degrees of awkwardness. If they don't work at all, the act fails altogether, and we say the man is paralyzed. He may make a tremendous effort, and contract the other muscles of the body, but the paralyzed limb fails to move. In all these cases, however, the volition considered as a psychic process is intact.

**Volitional effort is effort of attention.** We thus find that *we reach the heart of our inquiry into volition when we ask by what process it is that the thought of any given action comes to prevail stably in the mind.* Where thoughts prevail without effort, we have sufficiently studied in the several chapters on Sensation, Association, and Attention, the laws of their advent before consciousness and of their stay. We shall not go over that ground again, for we know that interest and association are the words, let their worth be what it may, on which our explanations must perforce rely. Where, on the other hand, the prevalence of the thought is accompanied by the phenomenon of effort, the case is much less clear. Already in the chapter on Attention we postponed the final consideration of voluntary attention with effort to a later place. We have now brought things to a point at which we see that attention with effort is all that any case of volition implies. *The essential achievement of the will, in short, when it is most "voluntary" is to attend to a difficult object and hold it fast before the mind.* The so-doing is the *fiat*; and it is a mere physiological incident that when the object is thus attended to, immediate motor consequences should ensue.

*Effort of attention is thus the essential phenomenon of will.*\* Every reader must know by his own experience that this is so, for every reader must have felt some fiery passion's grasp. What constitutes the difficulty for a man laboring under an unwise passion of acting as if the passion were wise? Certainly there is no physical difficulty. It is as easy physically to avoid a fight as to begin one, to pocket one's money as to squander it on one's cupidities, to walk away from as towards a coquette's door. The difficulty is mental: it is that of getting the idea of the wise action to stay before our mind at all. When any strong emotional state whatever is upon us, the tendency is for no images but such as are congruous with it to come up. If others by chance offer themselves, they are instantly smothered and crowded out. If we be joyous, we cannot keep thinking of those uncertainties and risks of failure which abound upon our path; if lugubrious, we cannot think of new triumphs, travels, loves, and joys; nor if vengeful, of our oppressor's community of nature with ourselves. The cooling advice which we get from others when the fever-fit is on us is the most jarring and exasperating thing in life. Reply we cannot, so

---

\*This *volitional* effort pure and simple must be carefully distinguished from the *muscular* effort with which it is usually confounded. The latter consists of all those peripheral feelings to which a muscular "exertion" may give rise. These feelings, whenever they are massive and the body is not "fresh," are rather disagreeable, especially when accompanied by stopped breath, congested head, bruised skin of fingers, toes, or shoulders, and strained joints. And it is only as *thus* disagreeable that the mind must make its *volitional* effort in stably representing their reality and consequently bringing it about. That they happen to be made real by muscular activity is a purely accidental circumstance. There are instances where the fiat demands great volitional effort though the muscular activity be insignificant, e.g., the getting out of bed and bathing one's self on a cold morning. Again, a soldier standing still to be fired at expects disagreeable sensations from his muscular passivity. The action of his will, in sustaining the expectation, is identical with that required for a painful muscular effort. What is hard for both is *facing an idea as real.*

we get angry; for by a sort of self-preserving instinct which our passion has, it feels that these chill objects, if they once but gain a lodgment, will work and work until they have frozen the very vital spark from out of all our mood and brought our airy castles in ruin to the ground. Such is the inevitable effect of reasonable ideas over others—*if they can once get a quiet hearing*; and passion's cue accordingly is always and everywhere to prevent their still small voice from being heard it all. "Let me not think of that! Don't speak to me of that!" This is the sudden cry of all those who in a passion perceive some sobering considerations about to check them in mid-career. There is something so icy in this cold-water bath, something which seems so hostile to the movement of our life, so purely negative, in Reason, when she lays her corpse-like finger on our heart and says "Halt! give up! leave off! go back! sit down!" that it is no wonder that to most men the steadying influence seems, for the time being, a very minister of death.

The strong-willed man, however, is the man who hears the still small voice unflinchingly, and who, when the death-bringing consideration comes, looks at its face, consents to its presence, clings to it, affirms it, and holds it fast, in spite of the host of exciting mental images which rise in revolt against it and would expel it from the mind. Sustained in this way by a resolute effort of attention, the difficult object erelong begins to call up its own congeners and associates and ends by changing the disposition of the man's consciousness altogether. And with his consciousness his action changes, for the new object, once stably in possession of the field of his thoughts, infallibly produces its own motor effects. The difficulty lies in the gaining possession of that field. Though the spontaneous drift of thought is all the other way, the attention must be kept strained on that one object until at last it *grows*, so as to maintain itself before the mind with ease. This strain of the attention is the fundamental act of will. And the will's work is in most cases practically ended when the bare presence to our thought of the naturally unwelcome object has been secured. For the mysterious tie between the thought and the motor centres next comes into play, and, in a way which we cannot even guess at, the obedience of the bodily organs follows as a matter of course.

In all this one sees how the immediate point of application of the volitional effort lies exclusively in the mental world. The whole drama is a mental drama. The whole difficulty is a mental difficulty, a difficulty with an ideal object of our thought. It is, in one word, an *idea* to which our will applies itself, an idea which if we let it go would slip away, but which we will not let go. *Consent to the idea's undivided presence, this is effort's sole achievement.* Its only function is to get this feeling of consent into the mind. And for this there is but one way. The idea to be consented to must be kept from flickering and going out. It must be held steadily before the mind until it *fills* the mind. Such filling of the mind by an idea, with its congruous associates, *is* consent to the idea and to the fact which the idea represents. If the idea be that, or include that, of a bodily movement of our own, then we call the consent thus laboriously gained a motor volition. For Nature here "backs" us instantaneously and follows up our inward willingness by outward changes on her own part. She does this in no other instance. Pity she should not have been more generous, nor made a world whose other parts were as immediately subject to our will!

On page 430 [not included here], in describing the "reasonable type" of decision, it was said that it usually came when the right conception of the case was found. Where, however, the right conception is an anti-impulsive one, the whole intellectual ingenuity of the man usually goes to work to crowd it out of sight, and to find for the emergency names by the help of which the dispositions of the moment may sound sanctified, and sloth or passion may reign unchecked. How many excuses does the drunkard find when each new temptation comes! It is a new brand of liquor which the interests of intellectual culture in such matters oblige him to test; moreover it is poured out and it is sin to waste it; also others are drinking and it would be churlishness to refuse. Or it is but to enable him to sleep, or just to get through this job of work; or it isn't drinking, it is because he feels so cold; or it is Christmas-day; or it is a means of stimulating him to make a more powerful resolution in favor of abstinence than any he has hitherto made; or it is just this once, and once doesn't count, etc., etc., *ad libitum*—it is, in fact, anything you like except *being a drunkard. That* is the conception that will not stay before the poor soul's attention. But if he once gets able to pick out that way of conceiving, from all the other possible ways of conceiving the various opportunities which occur, if through thick and thin he holds to it that this is being a drunkard and is nothing else, he is not likely to remain one long. The effort by which he succeeds in keeping the right *name* unwaveringly present to his mind proves to be his saving moral act.

Everywhere, then, the function of the effort is the same: to keep affirming and adopting a thought which, if left to itself, would slip away. It may be cold and flat when the spontaneous mental drift is towards excitement, or great and arduous when the spontaneous drift is towards repose. In the one case the effort has to inhibit an explosive, in the other to arouse an obstructed will. The exhausted sailor on a wreck has a will which is obstructed. One of his ideas is that of his sore hands, of the nameless exhaustion of his whole frame which the act of farther pumping involves, and of the deliciousness of sinking into sleep. The other is that of the hungry sea ingulfing him. "Rather the aching toil!" he says; and it becomes reality then, in spite of the inhibiting influence of the relatively luxurious sensations which he gets from lying still. Often again it may be the thought of sleep and what leads to it which is the hard one to keep before the mind. If a patient afflicted with insomnia can only control the whirling chase of his ideas so far as to think of *nothing at all* (which can be done), or so far as to imagine one letter after another of a verse of Scripture or poetry spelt slowly and monotonously out, it is almost certain that here, too, specific bodily effects will follow, and that sleep will come. The trouble is to keep the mind upon a train of objects naturally so insipid. *To sustain a representation, to think*, is, in short, the only moral act, for the impulsive and the obstructed, for sane and lunatics alike. Most maniacs know their thoughts to be crazy, but find them too pressing to be withstood. Compared with them the sane truths are so deadly sober, so cadaverous, that the lunatic cannot bear to look them in the face and say, "Let these alone be my reality!" But with sufficient effort, as Dr. Wigan says, "Such a man can for a time *wind himself up*, as it were, and determine that the notions of the disordered brain shall not be manifested. Many instances are on record similar to that told by Pinel, where an inmate of the Bicêtre, having stood a long cross-examination, and given every mark of restored reason, signed his name to the paper authorizing his discharge as "Jesus Christ," and then went off into all the vagaries connected with that delusion. In the phraseology of the gentleman whose case is related in an early part of this [Wigan's] work he had "held himself tight" during the examination in order to attain his object; this once accomplished, he "let himself down" again, and, if even *conscious* of his delusion, could not control it. I have observed with such persons that it requires a considerable time to wind themselves up to the pitch of complete self-control, and that the effort is a painful tension of the mind. . . . When thrown off their guard by any accidental remark or worn out by the length of the examination, they *let themselves go*, and cannot gather themselves up again without preparation."

To sum it all up in a word, *the terminus of the psychological process in volition, the point to which the will is directly applied, is always an idea.* There are at all times some ideas from which we shy away like frightened horses the moment we get a glimpse of their forbidding profile upon the threshold of our thought. *The only resistance which our will can possibly experience is the resistance which such an idea offers to being attended to at all.* To attend to it is the volitional act, and the only inward volitional act which we ever perform.

**The Question of "Free-will."**—As was remarked on p. 443, [p. 115 here, first paragraph of "Effort feels like an original force"] in the experience of effort we feel as if we might make more or less than we actually at any moment are making.

The effort appears, in other words, not as a fixed reaction on our part which the object that resists us necessarily calls forth, but as what the mathematicians call an "independent variable" amongst the fixed data of the case, our motives, character, etc. If it be really so, if the amount of our effort is not a determinate function of those other data, then, in common parlance, *our wills are free.* If, on the contrary, the amount of effort be a fixed function, so that whatever object at any time fills our consciousness was from eternity bound to fill it then and there, and compel from us the exact effort, neither more nor less, which we bestow upon it—then our wills are not free, and all our acts are foreordained. *The question of fact in the free-will controversy is thus extremely simple. It relates solely to the amount of effort of attention which we can at any time put forth.* Are the duration and intensity of this effort fixed functions of the object, or are they not? Now, as I just said, it seems as if we might exert more or less in any given case. When a man has let his thoughts go for days and weeks until at last they culminate in some particularly dirty or cowardly or cruel act, it is hard to persuade him, in the midst of his remorse, that he might not have reined them in; hard to make him believe that this whole goodly universe (which his act so jars upon) required and exacted it of him at that fatal moment, and from eternity made aught else impossible. But, on the other hand, there is the certainty that all his *effortless* volitions are resultants of interests and associations whose strength and sequence are mechanically determined by the structure of that physical mass, his brain; and the general continuity of things and the monistic conception of the world may lead one irresistibly to postulate that a little fact like effort can form no real exception to the overwhelming reign of deterministic law. Even in effortless volition we have the consciousness of the alternative being also possible. This is surely a delusion here; why is it not a delusion everywhere?

*The fact is that the question of free-will is insoluble on strictly psychologic grounds.* After a certain amount of effort of attention has been given to an idea, it is manifestly impossible to tell whether either more or less of it *might* have been given or not. To tell that, we should have to ascend to the antecedents of the effort, and defining them with mathematical exactitude, prove, by laws of which we have not at present even an inkling, that the only amount of sequent effort which could *possibly* comport with them was the precise amount that actually came. Such measurements, whether of psychic or of neural quantities, and such deductive reasonings as this method of proof implies, will surely be forever beyond human reach. No serious psychologist or physiologist will venture even to suggest a notion of how they might be practically made. Had one no motives drawn from elsewhere to make one partial to either solution, one might easily leave the matter undecided. But a psychologist cannot be expected to be thus impartial, having a great motive in favor of determinism. He wants to build a *Science*; and a Science is a system of fixed relations. Wherever there are independent variables, there Science stops. So far, then, as our volitions may be independent variables, a scientific psychology must ignore that fact, and treat of them only so far as they are fixed functions. In other words, she must deal with the *general laws* of volition exclusively; with the impulsive and inhibitory character of ideas; with the nature of their appeals to the attention; with the conditions under which effort may arise, etc.; but not with the precise amounts of effort, for these, if our wills be free, are impossible to compute. She thus abstracts from free-will, without necessarily denying its existence. Practically, however, such abstraction is not distinguished from rejection; and most actual psychologists have no hesitation in denying that free-will exists.

For ourselves, we can hand the free-will controversy over to meta-physics. Psychology will surely never grow refined enough to discover, in the case of any individual's decision, a discrepancy between her scientific calculations and the fact. Her prevision will never foretell, whether the effort be completely predestinate or not, the way in which each individual emergency is resolved. Psychology will be psychology, and Science science, as much as ever (as much and no more) in this world, whether free-will be true in it or not.

We can thus ignore the free-will question in psychology. As we said on p. 452 [p. 119 here, para beginning with "The strong-willed man"], the operation of free effort, if it existed, could only be to hold some one ideal object, or part of an object, a little longer or a little more intensely before the mind. Amongst the alternatives which present themselves as *genuine possibles*, it would thus make one effective. And although such quickening of one idea might be morally and historically momentous, yet, if considered *dynamically*, it would be an operation amongst those physiological infinitesimals which an actual science must forever neglect.

**Ethical Importance of the Phenomenon of Effort.**—But whilst eliminating the question about the amount of our effort as one which psychology will never have a practical call to decide, I must say one word about the extraordinarily intimate and important character which the phenomenon of effort assumes in our own eyes as individual men. Of course we measure ourselves by many standards. Our strength and our intelligence, our wealth and even our good luck, are things which warm our heart and make us feel ourselves a match for life. But deeper than all such things, and able to suffice unto itself without them, is the sense of the amount of effort which we can put forth. Those are, after all, but effects, products, and reflections of the outer world within. But the effort seems to belong to an altogether different realm, as if it were the substantive thing which we *are*, and those were but externals which we *carry*. If the "searching of our heart and reins" be the purpose of this human drama, then what is sought seems to be what effort we can make. He who can make none is but a shadow; he who can make much is a hero. The huge world that girdles us about puts all sorts of questions to us, and tests us in all sorts of ways. Some of the tests we meet by actions that are easy, and some of the questions we answer in articulately formulated words. But the deepest question that is ever asked admits of no reply but the dumb turning of the will and tightening of our heart-strings as we say, "*Yes, I will even have it so!*" When a dreadful object is presented, or when life as a whole turns up its dark abysses to our view, then the worthless ones among us lose their hold on the situation altogether, and either escape from its difficulties by averting their attention, or if they cannot do that, collapse into yielding masses of plaintiveness and fear. The effort required for facing and consenting to such objects is beyond their power to make. But the heroic mind does differently. To it, too, the objects are sinister and dreadful, unwelcome, incompatible with wished-for things. But it can face them if necessary, without for that losing its hold upon the rest of life. The world thus finds in the heroic man its worthy match and mate; and the effort which he is able to put forth to hold himself erect and keep his heart unshaken is the direct measure of his worth and function in the game of human life. He can *stand* this Universe. He can meet it and keep up his faith in it in presence of those same features which lay his weaker brethren low. He can still find a zest in it, not by "ostrich-like forgetfulness," but by pure inward willingness to face it with those deterrent objects there. And hereby he makes himself one of the masters and the lords of life. He must be counted with henceforth; he forms a part of human destiny. Neither in the theoretic nor in the practical sphere do we care for, or go for help to, those who have no head for risks, or sense for living on the perilous edge. Our religious life lies more, our practical life lies less, than it used to, on the perilous edge. But just as our courage is so often a reflex of another's courage, so our faith is apt to be a faith in someone else's faith. We draw new life from the heroic example. The prophet has drunk more deeply than anyone of the cup of bitterness, but his countenance is so unshaken and he speaks such mighty words of cheer that his will becomes our will, and our life is kindled at his own.

Thus not only our morality but our religion, so far as the latter is deliberate, depend on the effort which we can make. "*Will you or won't you have it so?*" is the most probing question we are ever asked; we are asked it every hour of the day, and about the largest as well as the smallest, the most theoretical as well as the most practical, things. We answer by *consents or non-consents* and not by words. What wonder that these dumb responses should seem our deepest organs of communication with the nature of things! What wonder if the effort demanded by them be the measure of our worth as men! What wonder if the amount which we accord of it were the one strictly underived and original contribution which we make to the world!

# The Will

Since mentality terminates naturally in outward conduct, the final chapter in psychology has to be the chapter on the will. But the word "will" can be used in a broader and in a narrower sense. In the broader sense, it designates our entire capacity for impulsive and active life, including our instinctive reactions and those forms of behavior that have become secondarily automatic and semi-unconscious through frequent repetition. In the narrower sense, acts of will are such acts only as cannot be inattentively performed. A distinct idea of what they are, and a deliberate fiat on the mind's part, must precede their execution.

Such acts are often characterized by hesitation, and accompanied by a feeling, altogether peculiar, of resolve, a feeling which may or may not carry with it a further feeling of effort. In my earlier talks, I said so much of our impulsive tendencies that I will restrict myself in what follows to volition in this narrower sense of the term.

All our deeds were considered by the early psychologists to be due to a peculiar faculty called the will, without whose fiat action could not occur. Thoughts and impressions, being intrinsically inactive, were supposed to produce conduct only through the intermediation of this superior agent. Until they twitched its coat-tails, so to speak, no outward behavior could occur. This doctrine was long ago exploded by the discovery of the phenomena of reflex action, in which sensible impressions, as you know, produce movement immediately and of themselves. The doctrine may also be considered exploded as far as ideas go.

The fact is that there is no sort of consciousness whatever, be it sensation, feeling, or idea, which does not directly and of itself tend to discharge into some motor effect. The motor effect need not always be an outward stroke of behavior. It may be only an alteration of the heart-beats or breathing, or a modification in the distribution of blood, such as blushing or turning pale; or else a secretion of tears, or what not. But, in any case, it is there in some shape when any consciousness is there; and a belief as fundamental as any in modern psychology is the belief at last attained that conscious processes of any sort, conscious processes merely as such, *must* pass over into motion, open or concealed.

The least complicated case of this tendency is the case of a mind possessed by only a single idea. If that idea be of an object connected with a native impulse, the impulse will immediately proceed to discharge. If it be the idea of a movement, the movement will occur. Such a case of action from a single idea has been distinguished from more complex cases by the name of "ideo-motor" action, meaning action without express decision or effort. Most of the habitual actions to which we are trained are of this ideo-motor sort. We perceive, for instance, that the door is open, and we rise and shut it; we perceive some raisins in a dish before us, and extend our hand and carry one of them to our mouth without interrupting the conversation; or, when lying in bed, we suddenly think that we shall be late for breakfast, and instantly we get up with no particular exertion or resolve. All the ingrained procedures by which life is carried on—the manners and customs, dressing and undressing, acts of salutation, etc.—are executed in this semi-automatic way unhesitatingly and efficiently, the very outermost margin of consciousness seeming to be concerned in them, while the focus may be occupied with widely different things.

But now turn to a more complicated case. Suppose two thoughts to be in the mind together, of which one, A, taken alone, would discharge itself in a certain action, but of which the other, B, suggests an action of a different sort, or a consequence of the first action calculated to make us shrink. The psychologists now say that the second idea, B, will probably arrest or *inhibit* the motor effects of the first idea, A. One word, then, about "inhibition" in general, to make this particular case more clear.

One of the most interesting discoveries of physiology was the discovery, made simultaneously in France and Germany fifty years ago, that nerve currents do not only start muscles into action, but may check action already going on or keep it from occurring as it otherwise might. *Nerves of arrest* were thus distinguished alongside of motor nerves. The pneumogastric nerve, for example, if stimulated, arrests the movements of the heart: the splanchnic nerve arrests those of the intestines, if already begun. But it soon appeared that this was too narrow a way of looking at the matter, and that arrest is not so much the specific function of certain nerves as a general function which any part of the nervous system may exert upon other parts under the appropriate conditions. The higher centres, for example, seem to exert a constant inhibitive influence on the excitability of those below. The reflexes of an animal with its hemispheres wholly or in part removed become exaggerated. You all know that common reflex in dogs, whereby, if you scratch the animal's side, the corresponding hind leg will begin to make scratching movements, usually in the air. Now in dogs with mutilated hemispheres this scratching reflex is so incessant that, as Goltz first described them, the hair gets all worn off their sides. In idiots, the functions of the hemispheres being largely in abeyance, the lower impulses, not inhibited, as they would be in normal human beings, often express themselves in most odious ways. You know also how any higher emotional tendency will quench a lower one. Fear arrests appetite, maternal love annuls fear, respect checks sensuality, and the like; and in the more subtle manifestations of the moral life, whenever an ideal stirring is suddenly quickened into intensity, it is as if the whole scale of values of our motives changed its equilibrium. The force of old temptations vanishes, and what a moment ago was impossible is now not only possible, but easy, because of their inhibition. This has been well called the "expulsive power of the higher emotion."

It is easy to apply this notion of inhibition to the case of our ideational processes. I am lying in bed, for example, and think it is time to get up; but alongside of this thought there is present to my mind a realization of the extreme coldness of the morning and the pleasantness of the warm bed. In such a situation the motor consequences of the first idea are blocked; and I may remain for half an hour or more with the two ideas oscillating before me in a kind of deadlock, which is what we call the state of hesitation or deliberation. In a case like this the deliberation can be resolved and the decision reached in either of two ways:—

(1) I may forget for a moment the thermometric conditions, and then the idea of getting up will immediately discharge into act: I shall suddenly find that I have got up—or

(2) Still mindful of the freezing temperature, the thought of the duty of rising may become so pungent that it determines action in spite of inhibition. In the latter case, I have a sense of energetic moral effort, and consider that I have done a virtuous act.

All cases of wilful action properly so called, of choice after hesitation and deliberation, may be conceived after one of these latter patterns. So you see that volition, in the narrower sense, takes place only when there are a number of conflicting systems of ideas, and depends on our having a complex field of consciousness. The interesting thing to note is the extreme delicacy of the inhibitive machinery. A strong and urgent motor idea in the focus may be neutralized and made inoperative by the presence of the very faintest contradictory idea in the margin. For instance, I hold out my forefinger, and with closed eyes try to realize as vividly as possible that I hold a revolver in my hand and am pulling the trigger. I can even now fairly feel my finger quivering with the tendency to contract; and, if it were hitched to a recording apparatus, it would certainly betray its state of tension by registering incipient movements. Yet it does not actually crook, and the movement of pulling the trigger is not performed. Why not? Simply because, all concentrated though I am upon the idea of the movement, I nevertheless also realize the total conditions of the experiment, and in the back of my mind, so to speak, or in its fringe and margin, have the simultaneous idea that the movement is not to take place. The mere presence of that marginal intention, without effort, urgency, or emphasis, or any special reinforcement from my attention, suffices to the inhibitive effect.

And this is why so few of the ideas that flit through our minds do, in point of fact, produce their motor consequences. Life would be a curse and a care for us if every fleeting fancy were to do so. Abstractly, the law of ideo-motor action is true; but in the concrete our fields of consciousness are always so complex that the inhibiting margin keeps the centre inoperative most of the time. In all this, you see, I speak as if ideas by their mere presence or absence determined behavior, and as if between the ideas themselves on the one hand and the conduct on the other there were no room for any third intermediate principle of activity, like that called "the will."

If you are struck by the materialistic or fatalistic doctrines which seem to follow this conception, I beg you to suspend your judgment for a moment, as I shall soon have something more to say about the matter. But, meanwhile yielding one's self to the mechanical conception of the psychophysical organism, nothing is easier than to indulge in a picture of the fatalistic character of human life. Man's conduct appears as the mere resultant of all his various impulsions and inhibitions. One object, by its presence, makes us act: another object checks our action. Feelings aroused and ideas suggested by objects sway us one way and another: emotions complicate the game by their mutual inhibitive effects, the higher abolishing the lower or perhaps being itself swept away. The life in all this becomes prudential and moral; but the psychologic agents in the drama may be described, you see, as nothing but the "ideas" themselves—ideas for the whole system of which what we call the "soul" or "character" or "will" of the person is nothing but a collective name. As Hume said, the ideas are themselves the actors, the stage, the theatre, the spectators, and the play. This is the so-called "associationist" psychology, brought down to its radical expression: it is useless to ignore its power as a conception. Like all conceptions, when they become clear and lively enough, this conception has a strong tendency to impose itself upon belief; and psychologists trained on biological lines usually adopt it as the last word of science on the subject. No one can have an adequate notion of modern psychological theory unless he has at some time apprehended this view in the full force of its simplicity.

Let us humor it for a while, for it has advantages in the way of exposition.

*Voluntary action, then, is at all times a resultant of the compounding of our impulsions with our inhibitions.*

From this it immediately follows that there will be two types of will, in one of which impulsions will predominate, in the other inhibitions. We may speak of them, if you like, as the precipitate and the obstructed will, respectively. When fully pronounced, they are familiar to everybody. The extreme example of the precipitate will is the maniac: his ideas discharge into action so rapidly, his associative processes are so extravagantly lively, that inhibitions have no time to arrive, and he says and does whatever pops into his head without a moment of hesitation. Certain melancholiacs furnish the extreme example of the over-inhibited type. Their minds are cramped in a fixed emotion of fear or helplessness, their ideas confined to the one thought that for them life is impossible. So they show a condition of perfect "abulia," or inability to will or act. They cannot change their posture or speech or execute the simplest command.

The different races of men show different temperaments in this regard. The Southern races are commonly accounted the more impulsive and precipitate: the English race, especially our New England branch of it, is supposed to be all sicklied over with repressive forms of self-consciousness, and condemned to express itself through a jungle of scruples and checks.

The highest form of character, however, abstractly considered, must be full of scruples and inhibitions. But action, in such a character, far from being paralyzed, will succeed in energetically keeping on its way, sometimes overpowering the resistances, sometimes steering along the line where they lie thinnest.

Just as our extensor muscles act most truly when a simultaneous contraction of the flexors guides and steadies them; so the mind of him whose fields of consciousness are complex, and who, with the reasons for the action, sees the reasons against it, and yet, instead of being palsied, acts in the way that takes the whole field into consideration—so, I say, is such a mind the ideal sort of mind that we should seek to reproduce in our pupils. Purely impulsive action, or action that proceeds to extremities regardless of consequences, on the other hand, is the easiest action in the world, and the lowest in type. Any one can show energy, when made quite reckless. An Oriental despot requires but little ability: as long as he lives, he succeeds, for he has absolutely his own way; and, when the world can no longer endure the horror of him, he is assassinated. But not to proceed immediately to extremities, to be still able to act energetically under an array of inhibitions—that indeed is rare and difficult. Cavour, when urged to proclaim martial law in 1859, refused to do so, saying: "Any one can govern in that way. I will be constitutional." Your parliamentary rulers, your Lincoln, your Gladstone, are the strongest type of man, because they accomplish results under the most intricate possible conditions. We think of Napoleon Bonaparte as a colossal monster of will-power, and truly enough he was so. But, from the point of view of the psychological machinery, it would be hard to say whether he or Gladstone was the larger volitional quantity; for Napoleon disregarded all the usual inhibitions, and

Gladstone, passionate as he was, scrupulously considered them in his statesmanship.

A familiar example of the paralyzing power of scruples is the inhibitive effect of conscientiousness upon conversation. Nowhere does conversation seem to have flourished as brilliantly as in France during the last century. But, if we read old French memoirs, we see how many brakes of scrupulosity which tie our tongues to-day were then removed. Where mendacity, treachery, obscenity, and malignity find unhampered expression, talk can be brilliant indeed. But its flame waxes dim where the mind is stitched all over with conscientious fear of violating the moral and social proprieties.

The teacher often is confronted in the schoolroom with an abnormal type of will, which we may call the "balky will." Certain children, if they do not succeed in doing a thing immediately, remain completely inhibited in regard to it: it becomes literally impossible for them to understand it if it be an intellectual problem, or to do it if it be an outward operation, as long as this particular inhibited condition lasts. Such children are usually treated as sinful, and are punished; or else the teacher pits his or her will against the child's will, considering that the latter must be "broken." "Break your child's will, in order that it may not perish," wrote John Wesley. "Break its will as soon as it can speak plainly—or even before it can speak at all. It should be forced to do as it is told, even if you have to whip it ten times running. Break its will, in order that its soul may live." Such will-breaking is always a scene with a great deal of nervous wear and tear on both sides, a bad state of feeling left behind it, and the victory not always with the would-be will-breaker.

When a situation of the kind is once fairly developed, and the child is all tense and excited inwardly, nineteen times out of twenty it is best for the teacher to apperceive the case as one of neural pathology rather than as one of moral culpability. So long as the inhibiting sense of impossibility remains in the child's mind, he will continue unable to get beyond the obstacle. The aim of the teacher should then be to make him simply forget. Drop the subject for the time, divert the mind to something else: then, leading the pupil back by some circuitous line of association, spring it on him again before he has time to recognize it, and as likely as not he will go over it now without any difficulty. It is in no other way that we overcome balkiness in a horse: we divert his attention, do something to his nose or ear, lead him round in a circle, and thus get him over a place where flogging would only have made him more invincible. A tactful teacher will never let these strained situations come up at all.

You perceive now, my friends, what your general or abstract duty is as teachers. Although you have to generate in your pupils a large stock of ideas, any one of which may be inhibitory, yet you must also see to it that no habitual hesitancy or paralysis of the will ensues, and that the pupil still retains his power of vigorous action. Psychology can state your problem in these terms, but you see how impotent she is to furnish the elements of its practical solution. When all is said and done, and your best efforts are made, it will probably remain true that the result will depend more on a certain native tone or temper in the pupil's psychological constitution than on anything else. Some persons appear to have a naturally poor focalization of the field of consciousness; and in such persons actions hang slack, and inhibitions seem to exert peculiarly easy sway.

But let us now close in a little more closely on this matter of the education of the will. Your task is to build up a *character* in your pupils; and a character, as I have so often said, consists in an organized set of habits of reaction. Now of what do such habits of reaction themselves consist? They consist of tendencies to act characteristically when certain ideas possess us, and to refrain characteristically when possessed by other ideas.

Our volitional habits depend, then, first, on what the stock of ideas is which we have; and, second, on the habitual coupling of the several ideas with action or inaction respectively. How is it when an alternative is presented to you for choice, and you are uncertain what you ought to do? You first hesitate, and then you deliberate. And in what does your deliberation consist? It consists in trying to apperceive the case successively by a number of different ideas, which seem to fit it more or less, until at last you hit on one which seems to fit it exactly. If that be an idea which is a customary forerunner of action in you, which enters into one of your maxims of positive behavior, your hesitation ceases, and you act immediately. If, on the other hand, it be an idea which carries inaction as its habitual result, if it ally itself with *prohibition*, then you unhesitatingly refrain. The problem is, you see, to find the right idea or conception for the case. This search for the right conception may take days or weeks.

I spoke as if the action were easy when the conception once is found. Often it is so, but it may be otherwise; and, when it is otherwise, we find ourselves at the very centre of a moral situation, into which I should now like you to look with me a little nearer.

The proper conception, the true head of classification, may be hard to attain; or it may be one with which we have contracted no settled habits of action. Or, again, the action to which it would prompt may be dangerous and difficult; or else inaction may appear deadly cold and negative when our impulsive feeling is hot. In either of these latter cases it is hard to hold the right idea steadily enough before the attention to let it exert its adequate effects. Whether it be stimulative or inhibitive, it is *too reasonable* for us; and the more instinctive passional propensity then tends to extrude it from our consideration. We shy away from the thought of it. It twinkles and goes out the moment it appears in the margin of our consciousness; and we need a resolute effort of voluntary attention to drag it into the focus of the field, and to keep it there long enough for its associative and motor effects to be exerted. Every one knows only too well how the mind flinches from looking at considerations hostile to the reigning mood of feeling.

Once brought, however, in this way to the centre of the field of consciousness, and held there, the reasonable idea will exert these effects inevitably; for the laws of connection between our consciousness and our nervous system provide for the action then taking place. Our moral effort, properly so called, terminates in our holding fast to the appropriate idea.

If, then, you are asked, "*In what does a moral act consist* when reduced to its simplest and most elementary form?" you can make only one reply. You can say that *it consists in the effort of attention by which we hold fast to an idea* which but for that effort of attention would be driven out of the mind by the other psychological tendencies that are there. *To think*, in short, is the secret of will, just as it is the secret of memory.

This comes out very clearly in the kind of excuse which we most frequently hear from persons who find themselves confronted by the sinfulness or harmfulness of some part of their behavior. "I never *thought*," they say. "I never *thought* how mean the action was, I never *thought* of these abominable consequences." And what do we retort when they say this? We say: "Why *didn't* you think? What were you there for but to think?" And we read them a moral lecture on their irreflectiveness.

The hackneyed example of moral deliberation is the case of an habitual drunkard under temptation. He has made a resolve to reform, but he is now solicited again by the bottle. His moral triumph or failure literally consists in his finding the right *name* for the case. If he says that it is a case of not wasting good liquor already poured out, or a case of not being churlish and unsociable when in the midst of friends, or a case of learning something at last about a brand of whiskey which he never met before, or a case of celebrating a public holiday, or a case of stimulating himself to a more energetic resolve in favor of abstinence than any he has ever yet made, then he is lost. His choice of the wrong name seals his doom. But if, in spite of all the plausible good names with which his thirsty fancy so copiously furnishes him, he unwaveringly clings to the truer bad name, and apperceives the case as that of "being a drunkard, being a drunkard, being a drunkard," his feet are planted on the road to salvation. He saves himself by thinking rightly.

Thus are your pupils to be saved: first, by the stock of ideas with which you furnish them; second, by the amount of voluntary attention that they can exert in holding to the right ones, however unpalatable; and, third, by the several habits of acting definitely on these latter to which they have been successfully trained.

In all this the power of voluntarily attending is the point of the whole procedure. Just as a balance turns on its knife-edges, so on it our moral destiny turns. You remember that, when we were talking of the subject of attention, we discovered how much more intermittent and brief our acts of voluntary attention are than is commonly supposed. If they were all summed together, the time that they occupy would cover an almost incredibly small portion of our lives. But I also said, you will remember, that their brevity was not in proportion to their significance, and that I should return to the subject again. So I return to it now. It is not the mere size of a thing which constitutes its importance: it is its position in the organism to which it belongs. Our acts of voluntary attention, brief and fitful as they are, are nevertheless momentous and critical, determining us, as they do, to higher or lower destinies. The exercise of voluntary attention in the schoolroom must therefore be counted one of the most important points of training that take place there; and the first-rate teacher, by the keenness of the remoter interests which he is able to awaken, will provide abundant opportunities for its occurrence. I hope that you appreciate this now without any further explanation.

I have been accused of holding up before you, in the course of these talks, a mechanical and even a materialistic view of the mind. I have called it an organism and a machine. I have spoken of its reaction on the environment as the essential thing about it; and I have referred this, either openly or implicitly, to the construction of the nervous system. I have, in consequence, received notes from some of you, begging me to be more explicit on this point; and to let you know frankly whether I am a complete materialist, or not.

Now in these lectures I wish to be strictly practical and useful, and to keep free from all speculative complications. Nevertheless, I do not wish to leave any ambiguity about my own position; and I will therefore say, in order to avoid all misunderstanding, that in no sense do I count myself a materialist. I cannot see how such a thing as our consciousness can possibly be *produced* by a nervous machinery, though I can perfectly well see how, if "ideas" do accompany the workings of the machinery, the *order* of the ideas might very well follow exactly the *order* of the machine's operations. Our habitual associations of ideas, trains of thought, and sequences of action, might thus be consequences of the succession of currents in our nervous systems. And the possible stock of ideas which a man's free spirit would have to choose from might depend exclusively on the native and acquired powers of his brain. If this were all, we might indeed adopt the fatalist conception which I sketched for you but a short while ago. Our ideas would be determined by brain currents, and these by purely mechanical laws.

But, after what we have just seen—namely, the part played by voluntary attention in volition—a belief in free will and purely spiritual causation is still open to us. The duration and amount of this attention seem within certain limits indeterminate. We *feel* as if we could make it really more or less, and as if our free action in this regard were a genuine critical point in nature—a point on which our destiny and that of others might hinge. The whole question of free will concentrates itself, then, at this same small point: "Is or is not the appearance of indetermination at this point an illusion?"

It is plain that such a question can be decided only by general analogies, and not by accurate observations. The free-willist believes the appearance to be a reality: the determinist believes that it is an illusion. I myself hold with the free-willists—not because I cannot conceive the fatalist theory clearly, or because I fail to understand its plausibility, but simply because, if free will *were* true, it would be absurd to have the belief in it fatally forced on our acceptance. Considering the inner fitness of things, one would rather think that the very first act of a will endowed with freedom should be to sustain the belief in the freedom itself. I accordingly believe freely in my freedom; I do so with the best of scientific consciences, knowing that the predetermination of the amount of my effort of attention can never receive objective proof, and hoping that, whether you follow my example in this respect or not, it will at least make you see that such psychological and psychophysical theories as I hold do not necessarily force a man to become a fatalist or a materialist.

Let me say one more final word now about the will, and therewith conclude both that important subject and these lectures.

There are two types of will. There are also two types of inhibition. We may call them inhibition by repression or by negation, and inhibition by substitution, respectively. The difference between them is that, in the case of inhibition by repression, both the inhibited idea and the inhibiting idea, the impulsive idea and the idea that negates it, remain along with each other in consciousness, producing a certain inward strain or tension there: whereas, in inhibition by substitution, the inhibiting idea supersedes altogether the idea which it inhibits, and the latter quickly vanishes from the field.

For instance, your pupils are wandering in mind, are listening to a sound outside the window, which presently grows interesting enough to claim all their attention. You can call the latter back again by bellowing at them not to listen to those sounds, but to keep their minds on their books or on what you are saying. And, by thus keeping them conscious that your eye is sternly on them, you may produce a good effect. But it will be a wasteful effect and an inferior effect; for the moment you relax your supervision the attractive disturbance, always there soliciting their curiosity, will overpower them, and they will be just as they were before: whereas, if, without saying anything about the street disturbances, you open a counter-attraction by starting some very interesting talk or demonstration yourself, they will altogether forget the distracting incident, and without any effort follow you along. There are many interests that can never be inhibited by the way of negation. To a man in love, for example, it is literally impossible, by any effort of will, to annul his passion. But let "some new planet swim into his ken," and the former idol will immediately cease to engross his mind.

It is clear that in general we ought, whenever we can, to employ the method of inhibition by substitution. He whose life is based upon the word "no," who tells the truth because a lie is wicked, and who has constantly to grapple with his envious and cowardly and mean propensities, is in an inferior situation in every respect to what he would be if the love of truth and magnanimity positively possessed him from the outset, and he felt no inferior temptations. Your born gentleman is certainly, for this world's purposes, a more valuable being than your "Crump, with his grunting resistance to his native devils," even though in God's sight the latter may, as the Catholic theologians say, be rolling up great stores of "merit."

Spinoza long ago wrote in his *Ethics* that anything that a man can avoid under the notion that it is bad he may also avoid under the notion that something else is good. He who habitually acts *sub specie mali*, under the negative notion, the notion of the bad, is called a slave by Spinoza. To him who acts habitually under the notion of good he gives the name of freeman. See to it now, I beg you, that you make freemen of your pupils by habituating them to act, whenever possible, under the notion of a good. Get them habitually to tell the truth, not so much through showing them the wickedness of lying as by arousing their enthusiasm for honor and veracity. Wean them from their native cruelty by imparting to "them some of your own positive sympathy with an animal's inner springs of joy. And, in the lessons which you may be legally obliged to conduct upon the bad effects of alcohol, lay less stress than the books do on the drunkard's stomach, kidneys, nerves, and social miseries, and more on the blessings of having an organism kept in lifelong possession of its full youthful elasticity by a sweet, sound blood, to which stimulants and narcotics are unknown, and to which the morning sun and air and dew will daily come as sufficiently powerful intoxicants.

. . . .

# Part III

# THE EFFICACY OF BELIEF AND CLUES TO MORALITY

## The Sentiment of Rationality*

What is the task which philosophers set themselves to perform; and why do they philosophize at all? Almost every one will immediately reply: They desire to attain a conception of the frame of things which shall on the whole be more rational than that somewhat chaotic view which every one by nature carries about with him under his hat. But suppose this rational conception attained, how is the philosopher to recognize it for what it is, and not let it slip through ignorance? The only answer can be that he will recognize its rationality as he recognizes everything else, by certain subjective marks with which it affects him. When he gets the marks, he may know that he has got the rationality.

What, then, are the marks? A strong feeling of ease, peace, rest, is one of them. The transition from a state of puzzle and perplexity to rational comprehension is full of lively relief and pleasure.

But this relief seems to be a negative rather than a positive character. Shall we then say that the feeling of rationality is constituted merely by the absence of any feeling of irrationality? I think there are very good grounds for upholding such a view. All feeling whatever, in the light of certain recent psychological speculations, seems to depend for its physical condition not on simple discharge of nerve-currents, but on their discharge under arrest, impediment, or resistance. Just as we feel no particular pleasure when we breathe freely, but a very intense feeling of distress when the respiratory motions are prevented—so any unobstructed tendency to action discharges itself without the production of much cogitative accompaniment, and any perfectly fluent course of thought awakens but little feeling; but when the movement is inhibited,

---

*This essay as far as page 75 [page 147 in this collection] consists of extracts from an article printed in *Mind* for July, 1879. Thereafter it is a reprint of an address to the Harvard Philosophical Club, delivered in 1880, and published in the *Princeton Review*, July, 1882.

or when the thought meets with difficulties, we experience distress. It is only when the distress is upon us that we can be said to strive, to crave, or to aspire. When enjoying plenary freedom either in the way of motion or of thought, we are in a sort of anaesthetic state in which we might say with Walt Whitman, if we cared to say anything about ourselves at such times, "I am sufficient as I am." This feeling of the sufficiency of the present moment, of its absoluteness— this absence of all need to explain it, account for it, or justify it—is what I call the Sentiment of Rationality. As soon, in short, as we are enabled from any cause whatever to think with perfect fluency, the thing we think of seems to us *pro tanto* rational.

Whatever modes of conceiving the cosmos facilitate this fluency, produce the sentiment of rationality. Conceived in such modes, being vouches for itself and needs no further philosophic formulation. But this fluency may be obtained in various ways; and first I will take up the theoretic way.

The facts of the world in their sensible diversity are always before us, but our theoretic need is that they should be conceived in a way that reduces their manifoldness to simplicity. Our pleasure at finding that a chaos of facts is the expression of a single underlying fact is like the relief of the musician at resolving a confused mass of sound into melodic or harmonic order. The simplified result is handled with far less mental effort than the original data; and a philosophic conception of nature is thus in no metaphorical sense a labor-saving contrivance. The passion for parsimony, for economy of means in thought, is the philosophic passion *par excellence*; and any character or aspect of the world's phenomena which gathers up their diversity into monotony will gratify that passion, and in the philosopher's mind stand for that essence of things compared with which all their other determinations may by him be overlooked.

More universality or extensiveness is, then, one mark which the philosopher's conceptions must possess. Unless they apply to an enormous number of cases they will not bring him relief. The knowledge of things by their causes, which is often given as a definition of rational knowledge, is useless to him unless the causes converge to a minimum number, while still producing the maximum number of effects. The more multiple then are the instances, the more flowingly does his mind rove from fact to fact. The phenomenal transitions are no real transitions; each item is the same old friend with a slightly altered dress.

Who does not feel the charm of thinking that the moon and the apple are, as far as their relation to the earth goes, identical; of knowing respiration and combustion to be one; of understanding that the balloon rises by the same law whereby the stone sinks; of feeling that the warmth in one's palm when one rubs one's sleeve is identical with the motion which the friction checks; of recognizing the difference between beast and fish to be only a higher degree of that between human father and son; of believing our strength when we climb the mountain or fell the tree to be no other than the strength of the sun's rays which made the corn grow out of which we got our morning meal?

But alongside of this passion for simplification there exists a sister passion, which in some minds—though they perhaps form the minority—is its rival. This is the passion for distinguishing; it is the impulse to be *acquainted* with the parts rather than to comprehend the whole. Loyalty to clearness and integrity of perception, dislike of blurred outlines, of vague identifications, are its characteristics. It loves to recognize particulars in their full completeness and the more of these it can carry the happier it is. It prefers any amount of incoherence, abruptness, and fragmentariness (so long as the literal details of the separate facts are saved) to an abstract way of conceiving things that, while it simplifies them, dissolves away at the same time their concrete fulness. Clearness and simplicity thus set up rival claims, and make a real dilemma for the thinker.

A man's philosophic attitude is determined by the balance in him of these two cravings. No system, of philosophy can hope to be universally accepted among men which grossly violates either need, or entirely subordinates the one to the other. The fate of Spinoza, with his barren union of all things in one substance, on the one hand; that of Hume, with his equally barren "looseness and separateness" of everything, on the other—neither philosopher owning any strict and systematic disciples to-day, each being to posterity a warning as well as a stimulus—show us that the only possible philosophy must be a compromise between an abstract monotony and a concrete heterogeneity. But the only way to mediate between diversity and unity is to class the diverse items as cases of a common essence which you discover in them. Classification of things into extensive "kinds" is thus the first step; and classification of their relations and conduct into extensive "laws" is the last step, in their philosophic unification. A completed theoretic philosophy can thus never be anything more than a completed classification of the world's ingredients; and its results must always be abstract, since the basis of every classification is the abstract essence embedded in the living fact—the rest of the living fact being for the time ignored by the classifier. This means that none of our explanations are complete. They subsume things under heads wider or more familiar; but the last heads, whether of things or of their connections, are mere abstract genera, data which we just find in things and write down.

When, for example, we think that we have rationally explained the connection of the facts $A$ and $B$ by classing both under their common attribute $x$, it is obvious that we have really explained only so much of these items as is $x$. To explain the connection of choke-damp and suffocation by the lack of oxygen is to leave untouched all the other peculiarities both of choke-damp and of suffocation—such as convulsions and agony on the one hand, density and explosibility on the other. In a word, so far as $A$ and $B$ contain $l$, $m$, $n$, and $o$, $p$, $q$, respectively, in addition to $x$, they are not explained by $x$. Each additional particularity makes its distinct appeal. A single explanation of a fact only explains it from a single point of view. The entire fact is not accounted for until each and all of its characters have been classed with their likes elsewhere. To apply this now to the case of the universe, we see that the explanation of the world by molecular movements explains it only so far as it actually is such movements. To invoke the "Unknowable" explains only so much as is unknowable, "Thought" only so much as is thought, "God" only so much as is God. *Which* thought? *Which* God?—are questions that have to be answered by bringing in again the residual data from which the general term was abstracted. All those data that cannot be analytically identified with the attribute invoked as universal principle, remain as independent kinds or natures, associated empirically with the said attribute but devoid of rational kinship with it.

Hence the unsatisfactoriness of all our speculations. On the one hand, so far as they retain any multiplicity in their terms, they fail to get us out of the empirical sand-heap world; on the other, so far as they eliminate multiplicity the practical man despises their empty barrenness. The most they can say is that the elements of the world are such and such, and that each is identical with itself wherever found; but the question Where is it found? the practical man is left to answer by his own wit. Which, of all the essences, shall here and now be held the essence of this concrete thing, the fundamental philosophy never attempts to decide. We are thus led to the conclusion that the simple classification of things is, on the one hand, the best possible theoretic philosophy, but is, on the other, a most miserable and inadequate substitute for the fulness of the truth. It is a monstrous abridgment of life, which, like all abridgments got by the absolute loss and casting out of real matter. This is why so few human beings truly care for philosophy. The particular determinations which she ignores are the real matter exciting needs, quite as potent and authoritative as hers. What does the moral enthusiast care for philosophical ethics? Why does the *Aesthetik* of every German philosopher appear to the artist an abomination of desolation?

Grau, theurer Freund, ist alle Theorie
Und grün des Lebens goldner Baum.

The entire man, who feels all needs by turns, will take nothing as an equivalent for life but the fulness of living itself. Since the essences of things are as a matter of fact disseminated through the whole extent of time and space, it is in their spread-outness and alternation that he will enjoy them. When weary of the concrete clash and dust and pettiness, he will refresh himself by a bath in the eternal springs, or fortify himself by a look at the immutable natures. But he will only be a visitor, not a dweller in the region; he will never carry the philosophic yoke upon his shoulders, and when tired of the gray monotony of her problems and insipid spaciousness of her results, will always escape gleefully into the teeming and dramatic richness of the concrete world.

So our study turns back here to its beginning. Every way of classifying a thing is but a way of handling it for some particular purpose. Conceptions, "kinds," are teleological instruments. No abstract concept can be a valid substitute for a concrete reality except with reference to a particular interest in the conceiver. The interest of theoretic rationality, the relief of identification, is but one of a thousand human purposes. When others rear their heads, it must pack up its little bundle and retire till its turn recurs. The exaggerated dignity and value that philosophers have claimed for their solutions is thus greatly reduced. The only virtue their theoretic conception need have is simplicity, and a simple conception is an equivalent for the world only so far as the world is simple—the world meanwhile, whatever simplicity it may harbor, being also a mightily complex affair. Enough simplicity remains, however, and enough urgency in our craving to reach it, to make the theoretic function one of the most invincible of human impulses. The quest of the fewest elements of things is an ideal that some will follow, as long as there are men to think at all.

. . . .

The peace of rationality may be sought through ecstasy when logic fails. To religious persons of every shade of doctrine moments come when the world, as it is, seems so divinely orderly, and the acceptance of it by the heart so rapturously complete, that intellectual questions vanish; nay, the intellect itself is hushed to sleep—as Wordsworth says, "thought is not; in enjoyment it expires." Ontological emotion so fills the soul that ontological speculation can no longer overlap it and put her girdle of interrogation-marks round existence. Even the least religious of men must have felt with Walt Whitman, when loafing on the grass on some transparent summer morning, that "swiftly arose and spread round him the peace and knowledge that pass all the argument of the earth." At such moments of energetic living we feel as if there were something diseased and contemptible, yea vile, in theoretic grubbing and brooding. In the eye of healthy sense the philosopher is at best a learned fool.

Since the heart can thus wall out the ultimate irrationality which the head ascertains, the erection of its procedure into a systematized method would be a philosophic achievement of first-rate importance. But as used by mystics hitherto it has lacked universality, being available for few persons and at few times, and even in these being apt to be followed by fits of reaction and dryness; and if men should agree that the mystical method is a subterfuge without logical pertinency, a plaster but no cure, and that the idea of non-entity can never be exorcised, empiricism will be the ultimate philosophy. Existence then will be a brute fact to which as a whole the emotion of ontologic wonder shall rightfully cleave, but remain eternally unsatisfied. Then wonderfulness or mysteriousness will be an essential attribute of the nature of things, and the exhibition and emphasizing of it will continue to be an ingredient in the philosophic industry of the race. Every generation will produce its Job, its Hamlet, its Faust, or its Sartor Resartus.

With this we seem to have considered the possibility of purely theoretic rationality. But we saw at the outset that rationality meant only unimpeded mental action. Impediments that arise in the theoretic sphere might perhaps be avoided if the stream of mental action should leave that sphere betimes and pass into the practical. Let us therefore inquire what constitutes the feeling of rationality in its *practical* aspect. If thought is not to stand forever pointing at the universe in wonder, if its movement is to be diverted from the issueless channel of purely theoretic contemplation, let us ask what conception of the universe will awaken active impulses capable of effecting this diversion. A definition of the world which will give back to the mind the free motion which has been blocked in the purely contemplative path may so far make the world seem rational again.

Well, of two conceptions equally fit to satisfy the logical demand, that one which awakens the active impulses, or satisfies other aesthetic demands better than the other, will be accounted the more rational conception, and will deservedly prevail.

There is nothing improbable in the supposition that an analysis of the world may yield a number of formulas, all consistent with the facts. In physical science different formulae may explain the phenomena equally well —the one-fluid and the two-fluid theories of electricity, for example. Why may it not be so with the world? Why may there not be different points of view for surveying it, within each of which all data harmonize, and which the observer may therefore either choose between, or simply cumulate one upon another? A Beethoven string-quartet is truly, as some one has said, a scraping of horses' tails on cats' bowels, and may be exhaustively described in such terms; but the application of this description in no way precludes the simultaneous applicability of an entirely different description. Just so a thoroughgoing interpretation of the world in terms of mechanical sequence is compatible with its being interpreted teleologically, for the mechanism itself may be designed.

If, then, there were several systems excogitated, equally satisfying to our purely logical needs, they would still have to be passed in review, and approved or rejected by our aesthetic and practical nature. Can we define the tests of rationality which these parts of our nature would use?

Philosophers long ago observed the remarkable fact that mere familiarity with things is able to produce a feeling of their rationality. The empiricist school has been so much struck by this circumstance as to have laid it down that the feeling of rationality and the feeling of familiarity are one and the same thing, and that no other kind of rationality than this exists. The daily contemplation of phenomena juxtaposed in a certain order begets an acceptance of their connection, as absolute as the repose engendered by theoretic insight into their coherence. To explain a thing is to pass easily back to its antecedents; to know it is easily to foresee its consequents. Custom, which lets us do both, is thus the source of whatever rationality the thing may gain in our thought.

In the broad sense in which rationality was defined at the outset of this essay, it is perfectly apparent that custom must be one of its factors. We said that any perfectly fluent and easy thought was devoid of the sentiment of irrationality. Inasmuch then as custom acquaints us with all the relations of a thing, it teaches us to pass fluently from that thing to others, and *pro tanto* tinges it with the rational character.

Now, there is one particular relation of greater practical importance than all the rest—I mean the relation of a thing to its future consequences. So long as an object is unusual, our expectations are baffled; they are fully determined as soon as it becomes familiar. I therefore propose this as the first practical requisite which a philosophic conception must satisfy: *It must, in a general way at least, banish uncertainty from the future.* The permanent presence of the sense of futurity in the mind has been strangely ignored by most writers, but the fact is that our consciousness at a given moment is never free from the ingredient of expectancy. Every one knows how when a painful thing has to be undergone in the near future, the vague feeling that it is impending penetrates all our thought with uneasiness and subtly vitiates our mood even when it does not control our attention; it keeps us from being at rest, at home in the given present. The same is true when a great happiness awaits us. But when the future is neutral and perfectly certain, "we do not mind it," as we say, but give an undisturbed attention to the actual. Let now this haunting sense of futurity be thrown off its bearings or left without an object, and immediately uneasiness takes possession of the mind. But in every novel or unclassified experience this is just what occurs; we do not know what will come next; and novelty *per se* becomes a mental irritant, while custom *per se* is a mental sedative, merely because the one baffles while the other settles our expectations.

Every reader must feel the truth of this. What is meant by coming "to feel at home" in a new place, or with new people? It is simply that, at first, when we take up our quarters in a new room, we do not know what draughts may blow in upon our back, what doors may open, what forms may enter, what interesting objects may be found in cupboards and corners. When after a few days we have learned the range of all these possibilities, the feeling of strangeness disappears. And so it does with people, when we have got past the point of expecting any essentially new manifestations from their character.

The utility of this emotional effect of expectation is perfectly obvious; "natural selection," in fact, was bound to bring it about sooner or later. It is of the utmost practical importance to an animal that he should have prevision of the qualities of the objects that surround him, and especially that he should not come to rest in presence of circumstances that might be fraught cither with peril or advantage—go to sleep, for example, on the brink of precipices, in the dens of enemies, or view with indifference some new-appearing object that might, if chased, prove an important addition to the larder. Novelty *ought* to irritate him. All curiosity has thus a practical genesis. . . . [ed.]

To turn back now to philosophy. An ultimate datum, even though it be logically unrationalized, will, if its quality is such as to define expectancy, be peacefully accepted by the mind; while if it leave the least opportunity for ambiguity in the future, it will to that extent cause mental uneasiness if not distress. Now, in the ultimate explanations of the universe which the craving for rationality has elicited from the human mind, the demands of expectancy to be satisfied have always played a fundamental part.

. . . .

If we survey the field of history and ask what feature all great periods of revival, of expansion of the human mind, display in common, we shall find, I think, simply this: that each and all of them have said to the human being, "The inmost nature of the reality is congenial to *powers* which you possess." In what did the emancipating message of primitive Christianity consist but in the announcement that God recognizes those weak and tender impulses which paganism had so rudely overlooked? Take repentance: the man who can do nothing rightly can at least repent of his failures. But for paganism this faculty of repentance was a pure supernumerary, a straggler too late for the fair. Christianity took it, and made it the one power within us which appealed straight to the heart of God. And after the night of the middle ages had so long branded with obloquy even the generous impulses of the flesh, and defined the reality to be such that only slavish natures could commune with it, in what did the *sursum corda* of the platonizing renaissance lie but in the proclamation that the archetype of verity in things laid claim on the widest activity of our whole aesthetic being? What were Luther's mission and Wesley's but appeals to powers which even the meanest of men might carry with them—faith and self-despair—but which were personal, requiring no priestly intermediation, and which brought their owner face to face with God? What caused the wildfire influence of Rousseau but the assurance he gave that man's nature was in harmony with the nature of things, if only the paralyzing corruptions of custom would stand from between? How did Kant and Fichte, Goethe and Schiller, inspire their time with cheer, except by saying, "Use all your powers; that is the only obedience the universe exacts"? And Carlyle with his gospel of work, of fact, of veracity, how does he move us except by saying that the universe imposes no tasks upon us but such as the most humble can perform? Emerson's creed that everything that ever was or will be is here in the enveloping now; that man has but to obey himself—"He who will rest in what he is, is a part of destiny"—is in like manner nothing but an exorcism of all scepticism as to the pertinency of one's natural faculties.

In a word, "Son of Man, *stand upon thy feet* and I will speak unto thee!" is the only revelation of truth to which the solving epochs have helped the disciple. But that has been enough to satisfy the greater part of his rational need. *In se* and *per se* the universal essence has hardly been more defined by any of these formulas than by the agnostic $x$; but the mere assurance that my powers, such as they are, are not irrelevant to it, but pertinent; that it speaks to them and will in some way recognize their reply; that I can be a match for it if I will, and not a footless waif—suffices to make it rational to my feeling in the sense given above. Nothing could be more absurd than to hope for the definitive triumph of any philosophy which should refuse to legitimate, and to legitimate in an emphatic manner, the more powerful of our emotional and practical tendencies. Fatalism, whose solving word in all crises of behavior is "all striving is vain," will never reign supreme, for the impulse to take life strivingly is indestructible in the race. Moral creeds which speak to that impulse will be widely successful in spite of inconsistency, vagueness, and shadowy determination of expectancy. Man needs a rule for his will, and will invent one if one be not given him.

But now observe a most important consequence. Men's active impulses are so differently mixed that a philosophy fit in this respect for Bismarck will almost certainly be unfit for a valetudinarian poet. In other words, although one can lay down in advance the rule that a philosophy which utterly denies all fundamental ground for seriousness, for effort, for hope, which says the nature of things is radically alien to human nature, can never succeed—one cannot in advance say what particular dose of hope, or of gnosticism of the nature of things, the definitely successful philosophy shall contain. In short, it is almost certain that personal temperament will here make itself felt, and that although all men will insist on being spoken to by the universe in some way, few will insist on being spoken to in just the same way. We have here, in short, the sphere of what Matthew Arnold likes to call *Aberglaube,* legitimate, inexpugnable, yet doomed to eternal variations and disputes.

Take idealism and materialism as examples of what I mean, and suppose for a moment that both give a conception of equal theoretic clearness and consistency, and that both determine our expectations equally well. Idealism will be chosen by a man of one emotional constitution, materialism by another. At this very day all sentimental natures, fond of conciliation and intimacy, tend to an idealistic faith. Why? Because idealism gives to the nature of things such kinship with our personal selves. Our own thoughts are what we are most at home with, what we are least afraid of. To say then that the universe essentially is thought, is to say that I myself, potentially at least, am all. There is no radically alien corner, but an all-pervading *intimacy*. Now, in certain sensitively egotistic minds this conception of reality is sure to put on a narrow, close, sick-room air. Everything sentimental and priggish will be consecrated by it. That element in reality which every strong man of common-sense willingly feels there because it calls forth powers that he owns—the rough, harsh, sea-wave, north-wind element, the denier of persons, the democratizer—is banished because it jars too much on the desire for communion. Now, it is the enjoyment of this element that throws many men upon the materialistic or agnostic hypothesis, as a polemic reaction against the contrary extreme. They sicken at a life wholly constituted of intimacy. There is an overpowering desire at moments to escape personality, to revel in the action of forces that have no respect for our ego, to let the tides flow, even though they flow over us. The strife of these two kinds of mental temper will, I think, always be seen in philosophy. Some men will keep insisting on the reason, the atonement, that lies in the heart of things, and that we can act *with*; others, on the opacity of brute fact that we must react *against*.

Now, there is one element of our active nature which the Christian religion has emphatically recognized, but which philosophers as a rule have with great insincerity tried to huddle out of sight in their pretension to found systems of absolute certainty. I mean the element of faith. Faith means belief in something concerning which doubt is still theoretically possible; and as the test of belief is willingness to act, one may say that faith is the readiness to act in a cause the prosperous issue of which is not certified to us in advance. It is in fact the same moral quality which we call courage in practical affairs; and there will be a very widespread tendency in men of vigorous nature to enjoy a certain amount of uncertainty in their philosophic creed, just as risk lends a zest to worldly activity. Absolutely certified philosophies seeking the *inconcussum* are fruits of mental natures in which the passion for identity (which we saw to be but one factor of the rational appetite) plays an abnormally exclusive part. In the average man, on the contrary, the power to trust, to risk a little beyond the literal evidence, is an essential function. Any mode of conceiving the universe which makes an appeal to this generous power, and makes the man seem as if he were individually helping to create the actuality of the truth whose metaphysical reality he is willing to assume, will be sure to be responded to by large numbers.

The necessity of faith as an ingredient in our mental attitude is strongly insisted on by the scientific philosophers of the present day; but by a singularly arbitrary caprice they say that it is only legitimate when used in the interests of one particular proposition—the proposition, namely, that the course of nature is uniform. That nature will follow to-morrow the same laws that she follows to-day is, they all admit, a truth which no man can *know*; but in the interests of cognition as well as of action we must postulate or assume it. As Helmholtz says: "Hier gilt nur der eine Rath: vertraue und handle!" And Professor Bain urges: "Our only error is in proposing to give any reason or justification of the postulate, or to treat it as otherwise than begged at the very outset."

With regard to all other possible truths, however, a number of our most influential contemporaries think that an attitude of faith is not only illogical but shameful. Faith in a religious dogma for which there is no outward proof, but which we are tempted to postulate for our emotional interests, just as we postulate the uniformity of nature for our intellectual interests, is branded by Professor Huxley as "the lowest depth of immorality." Citations of this kind from leaders of the modern *Aufklärung* might be multiplied almost indefinitely. Take Professor Clifford's article on the "Ethics of Belief." He calls it "guilt" and "sin" to believe even the truth without "scientific evidence." But what is the use of being a genius, unless *with the same scientific evidence* as other men, one can reach more truth than they? Why does Clifford fearlessly proclaim his belief in the conscious-automaton theory, although the "proofs" before him are the same which make Mr. Lewes reject it? Why does he believe in primordial units of "mind-stuff" on evidence which would seem quite worthless to Professor Bain? Simply because, like every human being of the slightest mental originality, he is peculiarly sensitive to evidence that bears in some one direction. It is utterly hopeless to try to exorcise such sensitiveness by calling it the disturbing subjective factor, and branding it as the root of all evil. "Subjective" be it called! and "disturbing" to those whom it foils! But if it helps those who, as Cicero says, "*vim naturae magis sentiunt,*" it is good and not evil. Pretend what we may, the whole man within us is at work when we form our philosophical opinions. Intellect, will, taste, and passion co-operate just as they do in practical affairs; and lucky it is if the passion be not something as petty as a love of personal conquest over the philosopher across the way. The absurd abstraction of an intellect verbally formulating all its evidence and carefully estimating the probability thereof by a vulgar fraction by the size of whose denominator and numerator alone it is swayed, is ideally as inept as it is actually impossible. It is almost incredible that men who are themselves working philosophers should pretend that any philosophy can be, or ever has been, constructed without the help of personal preference, belief, or divination. How have they succeeded in so stultifying their sense for the living facts of human nature as not to perceive that every philosopher, or man of science either, whose initiative counts for anything in the evolution of thought, has taken his stand on a sort of dumb conviction that the truth must lie in one direction rather than another, and a sort of preliminary assurance that his notion can be made to work; and has borne his best fruit in trying to make it work? These mental instincts in different men are the spontaneous variations upon which the intellectual struggle for existence is based. The fittest conceptions survive, and with them the names of their champions shining to all futurity.

The coil is about us, struggle as we may. The only escape from faith is mental nullity. What we enjoy most in a Huxley or a Clifford is not the professor with his learning, but the human personality ready to go in for what it feels to be right, in spite of all appearances. The concrete man has but one interest—to be right. That for him is the art of all arts, and all means are fair which help him to it. Naked he is flung into the world, and between him and nature there are no rules of civilized warfare. The rules of the scientific game, burdens of proof, presumptions, *experimenta, crucis,* complete inductions, and the like, are only binding on those who enter that game. As a matter of fact we all more or less do enter it, because it helps us to our end. But if the means presume to frustrate the end and call us cheats for being right in advance of their slow aid, by guesswork or by hook or crook, what shall we say of them? Were all of Clifford's works, except the "Ethics of Belief," forgotten, he might well figure in future treatises on psychology in place of the somewhat threadbare instance of the miser who has been led by the association of ideas to prefer his gold to all the goods he might buy therewith.

In short, if I am born with such a superior general reaction to evidence that I can guess right and act accordingly, and gain all that comes of right action, while my less gifted neighbor (paralyzed by his scruples and waiting for more evidence which he dares not anticipate, much as he longs to) still stands shivering on the brink, by what law shall I be forbidden to reap the advantages of my superior native sensitiveness? Of course I yield to my belief in such a case as this or distrust it, alike at my peril, just as I do in any of the great practical decisions of life. If my inborn faculties are good, I am a prophet; if poor, I am a failure: nature spews me out of her mouth, and there is an end of me. In the total game of life we stake our persons all the while; and if in its theoretic part our persons will help us to a conclusion, surely we should also stake them there, however inarticulate they may be.*

But in being myself so very articulate in proving what to all readers with a sense for reality will seem a platitude, am I not wasting words?

---

*At most, the command laid upon us by science to believe nothing not yet verified by the senses is a prudential rule intended to maximize our right thinking and minimize our errors *in the long run.* In the particular instance we must frequently lose truth by obeying it; but on the whole we are safer if we follow it consistently, for we are sure to cover our losses with our gains. It is like those gambling and insurance rules based on probability, in which we secure ourselves against losses in detail by hedging on the total run. But this hedging philosophy requires that long run should be there; and this makes it inapplicable to the question of religious faith as the latter comes home to the individual man. He plays the game of life not to escape losses, for he brings nothing with him to lose; he plays it for gains; and it is now or never with him, for the long run which exists indeed for humanity, is not there for him. Let him doubt, believe, or deny, he runs his risk, and has the natural right to choose which one it shall be.

We cannot live or think at all without some degree of faith. Faith is synonymous with working hypothesis. The only difference is that while some hypotheses can be refuted in five minutes, others may defy ages. A chemist who conjectures that a certain wall-paper contains arsenic, and has faith enough to lead him to take the trouble to put some of it into a hydrogen bottle, finds out by the results of his action whether he was right or wrong. But theories like that of Darwin, or that of the kinetic constitution of matter, may exhaust the labors of generations in their corroboration, each tester of their truth proceeding in this simple way—that he acts as if it were true, and expects the result to disappoint him if his assumption is false. The longer disappointment is delayed, the stronger grows his faith in his theory.

Now, in such questions as God, immortality, absolute morality, and free-will, no non-papal believer at the present day pretends his faith to be of an essentially different complexion; he can always doubt his creed. But his intimate persuasion is that the odds in its favor are strong enough to warrant him in acting all along on the assumption of its truth. His corroboration or repudiation by the nature of things may be deferred until the day of judgment. The uttermost he now means is something like this: "I *expect* then to triumph with tenfold glory; but if it should turn out, as indeed it may, that I have spent my days in a fool's paradise, why, better have been the dupe of *such* a dreamland than the cunning reader of a world like that which then beyond all doubt unmasks itself to view." In short, we *go in* against materialism very much as we should *go in*, had we a chance, against the second French empire or the Church of Rome, or any other system of things toward which our repugnance is vast enough to determine energetic action, but too vague to issue in distinct argumentation. Our reasons are ludicrously incommensurate with the volume of our feeling, yet on the latter we unhesitatingly act.

Now, I wish to show what to my knowledge has never been clearly pointed out, that belief (as measured by action) not only does and must continually outstrip scientific evidence, but that there is a certain class of truths of whose reality belief is a factor as well as a confessor; and that as regards this class of truths faith is not only licit and pertinent, but essential and indispensable. The truths cannot become true till our faith has made them so.

Suppose, for example, that I am climbing in the Alps, and have had the ill-luck to work myself into a position from which the only escape is by a terrible leap. Being without similar experience, I have no evidence of my ability to perform it successfully; but hope and confidence in myself make me sure I shall not miss my aim, and nerve my feet to execute what without those subjective emotions would perhaps have been impossible. But suppose that, on the contrary, the emotions of fear and mistrust preponderate; or suppose that, having just read the "Ethics of Belief," I feel it would be sinful to act upon an assumption unverified by previous experience—why, then I shall hesitate so long that at last, exhausted and trembling, and launching myself in a moment of despair, I miss my foothold and roll into the abyss. In this case (and it is one of an immense class) the part of wisdom clearly is to believe what one desires; for the belief is one of the indispensable preliminary conditions of the realization of its object. *There are then cases where faith creates its own verification.* Believe, and you shall be right, for you shall save yourself; doubt, and you shall again be right, for you shall perish. The only difference is that to believe is greatly to your advantage.

The future movements of the stars or the facts of past history are determined now once for all, whether I like them or not. They are given irrespective of my wishes, and in all that concerns truths like these subjective preference should have no part; it can only obscure the judgment. But in every fact into which there enters an element of personal contribution on my part, as soon as this personal contribution demands a certain degree of subjective energy which, in its turn, calls for a certain amount of faith in the result—so that, after all, the future fact is conditioned by my present faith in it—how trebly asinine would it be for me to deny myself the use of the subjective method, the method of belief based on desire!

In every proposition whose bearing is universal (and such are all the propositions of philosophy), the acts of the subject and their consequences throughout eternity should be included in the formula. If $M$ represent the entire world *minus* the reaction of the thinker upon it, and if $M + x$ represent the absolutely total matter of philosophic propositions ($x$ standing for the thinker's reaction and its results)— what would be a universal truth if the term $x$ were of one complexion, might become egregious error if *x* altered its character. Let it not be said that *x* is too infinitesimal a component to change the character of the immense whole in which it lies imbedded. Everything depends on the point of view of the philosophic proposition in question. If we have to define the universe from the point of view of sensibility, the critical material for our judgment lies in the animal kingdom, insignificant as that is, quantitatively considered. The moral definition of the world may depend on phenomena more restricted still in range. In short, many a long phrase may have its sense reversed by the addition of three letters, *n-o-t*; many a monstrous mass have its unstable equilibrium discharged one way or the other by a feather weight that falls.

Let us make this clear by a few examples. The philosophy of evolution offers us to-day a new criterion to serve as an ethical test between right and wrong. Previous criteria, it says, being subjective, have left us still floundering in variations of opinion and the *status belli*. Here is a criterion which is objective and fixed: *That is to be called good which is destined to prevail or survive.* But we immediately see that this standard can only remain objective by leaving myself and my conduct out. If what prevails and survives does so by my help, and cannot do so without that help; if something else will prevail in case I alter my conduct—how can I possibly now, conscious of alternative courses of action open before me, either of which I may suppose capable of altering the path of events, decide which course to take by asking what path events will follow? If they follow my direction, evidently my direction cannot wait on them. The only possible manner in which an evolutionist can use his standard is the obsequious method of forecasting the course society would take *but for him*, and then putting an extinguisher on all personal idiosyncrasies of desire and interest, and with bated breath and tiptoe tread following as straight as may be at the tail, and bringing up the rear of everything. Some pious creatures may find a pleasure in this; but not only does it violate our general wish to lead and not to follow (a wish which is surely not immoral if we but lead aright), but if it be treated as every ethical principle must be treated—namely, as a rule good for all men alike—its general observance would lead to its practical refutation by bringing about a general deadlock. Each good man hanging back and waiting for orders from the rest, absolute stagnation would ensue.

Happy, then, if a few unrighteous ones contribute an initiative which sets things moving again!

All this is no caricature. That the course of destiny may be altered by individuals no wise evolutionist ought to doubt. Everything for him has small beginnings, has a bud which may be "nipped," and nipped by a feeble force. Human races and tendencies follow the law, and have also small beginnings. The best, according to evolution, is that which has the biggest endings. Now, if a present race of men, enlightened in the evolutionary philosophy, and able to forecast the future, were able to discern in a tribe arising near them the potentiality of future supremacy; were able to see that their own race would eventually be wiped out of existence by the new-comers if the expansion of these were left unmolested—these present sages would have two courses open to them, either perfectly in harmony with the evolutionary test: Strangle the new race *now,* and ours survives; help the new race, and *it* survives. In both cases the action is right as measured by the evolutionary standard—it is action for the winning side.

Thus the evolutionist foundation of ethics is purely objective only to the herd of nullities whose votes count for zero in the march of events. But for others, leaders of opinion or potentates, and in general those to whose actions position or genius gives a far-reaching import, and to the rest of us, each in his measure—whenever we espouse a cause we contribute to the determination of the evolutionary standard of right. The truly wise disciple of this school will then admit faith as an ultimate ethical factor. Any philosophy which makes such questions as, What is the ideal type of humanity? What shall be reckoned virtues? What conduct is good? depend on the question, What is going to succeed?—must needs fall back on personal belief as one of the ultimate conditions of the truth. For again and again success depends on energy of act; energy again depends on faith that we shall not fail; and that faith in turn on the faith that we are right—which faith thus verifies itself.

. . . .

But the highest good can be achieved only by our getting our proper life; and that can come about only by help of a moral energy born of the faith that in some way or other we shall succeed in getting it if we try pertinaciously enough. This world *is* good, we must say, since it is what we make it—and we shall make it good. . . . [ed.] The belief creates its verification. The thought becomes literally father to the fact, as the wish was father to the thought.

Let us now turn to the radical question of life—the question whether this be at bottom a moral or an unmoral universe—and see whether the method of faith may legitimately have a place there.

. . . .

. . . [ed.] [But] in a question of this scope, the experience of the entire human race must make the verification, and that all the evidence will not be "in" till the final integration of things, when the last man has had his say and contributed his share to the still unfinished *x*.

. . . .

. . .[ed.] The world may in fact be likened unto a lock, whose inward nature, moral or unmoral, will never reveal itself to our simply expectant gaze. The positivists, forbidding us to make any assumptions regarding it, condemn us to eternal ignorance, for the "evidence" which they wait for can never come so long as we are passive. But nature has put into our hands two keys, by which we may test the lock. If we try the moral key *and it fits*, it is a moral lock. If we try the unmoral key and it fits, it is an unmoral lock. I cannot possibly conceive of any other sort of "evidence" or "proof" than this. It is quite true that the co-operation of generations is needed to educe it. But in these matters the solidarity (so called) of the human race is a patent fact. The essential thing to notice is that our active preference is a legitimate part of the game— that it is our plain business as men to try one of the keys, and the one in which we most confide. If then the proof exist not till I have acted, and I must needs in acting run the risk of being wrong, how can the popular science professors be right in objurgating in me as infamous a "credulity" which the strict logic of the situation requires? If this really be a moral universe; if by my acts I be a factor of its destinies; if to believe where I may doubt be itself a moral act analogous to voting for a side not yet sure to win—by what right shall they close in upon me and steadily negate the deepest conceivable function of my being by their preposterous command that I shall stir neither hand nor foot, but remain balancing myself in eternal and insoluble doubt? Why, doubt itself is a decision of the widest practical reach, if only because we may miss by doubting what goods we might be gaining by espousing the winning side. But more than that! it is often practically impossible to distinguish doubt from dogmatic negation. If I refuse to stop a murder because I am in doubt whether it be not justifiable homicide, I am virtually abetting the crime. If I refuse to bale out a boat because I am in doubt whether my efforts will keep her afloat, I am really helping to sink her. If in the mountain precipice I doubt my right to risk a leap, I actively connive at my destruction. He who commands himself not to be credulous of God, of duty, of freedom, of immortality, may again and again be indistinguishable from him who dogmatically denies them. Scepticism in moral matters is an active ally of immorality. Who is not for is against. The universe will have no neutrals in these questions. In theory as in practice, dodge or hedge, or talk as we like about a wise scepticism, we are really doing volunteer military service for one side or the other.

Yet obvious as this necessity practically is, thousands of innocent magazine readers lie paralyzed and terrified in the network of shallow negations which the leaders of opinion have thrown over their souls. All they need to be free and hearty again in the exercise of their birthright is that these fastidious vetoes should be swept away. All that the human heart wants is its chance. It will willingly forego certainty in universal matters if only it can be allowed to feel that in them it has that same inalienable right to run risks, which no one dreams of refusing to it in the pettiest practical affairs. And if I, in these last pages, like the mouse in the fable, have gnawed a few of the strings of the sophistical net that has been binding down its lion-strength, I shall be more than rewarded for my pains.

To sum up: No philosophy will permanently be deemed rational by all men which (in addition to meeting logical demands) does not to some degree pretend to determine expectancy, and in a still greater degree make a direct appeal to all those powers of our nature which we hold in highest esteem. Faith, being one of these powers, will always remain a factor not to be banished from philosophic constructions, the more so since in many ways it brings forth its own verification. In these points, then, it is hopeless to look for literal agreement among, mankind.

The ultimate philosophy, we may therefore conclude, must not be too strait-laced in form, must not in all its parts divide heresy from orthodoxy by too sharp a line. There must be left over and above the propositions to be subscribed, *ubique, semper, et ab omnibus*, another realm into which the stifled soul may escape from pedantic scruples and indulge its own faith at its own risks; and all that can here be done will be to mark out distinctly the questions which fall within faith's sphere.

# THE WILL TO BELIEVE[*]

In the recently published *Life* by Leslie Stephen of his brother, Fitz-james, there is an account of a school to which the latter went when he was a boy. The teacher, a certain Mr. Guest, used to converse with his pupils in this wise: "Gurney, what is the difference between justification and sanctification?—Stephen, prove the Omnipotence of God!" etc. In the midst of our Harvard freethinking and indifference we are prone to imagine that here at your good old orthodox College conversation continues to be somewhat upon this order; and to show you that we at Harvard have not lost all interest in these vital subjects, I have brought with me to-night something like a sermon on justification by faith to read to you—I mean an essay in justification *of* faith, a defence of our right to adopt a believing attitude in religious matters, in spite of the fact that our merely logical intellect may not have been coerced. "The Will to Believe," accordingly, is the title of my paper.

I have long defended to my own students the lawfulness of voluntarily adopted faith; but as soon as they have got well imbued with the logical spirit, they have as a rule refused to admit my contention to be lawful philosophically, even though in point of fact they were personally all the time chock-full of some faith or other themselves. I am all the while, however, so profoundly convinced that my own position is correct, that your invitation has seemed to me a good occasion to make my statements more clear. Perhaps your minds will be more open than those with which I have hitherto had to deal. I will be as little technical as I can, though I must begin by setting up some technical distinctions that will help us in the end.

# I

Let us give the name of *hypothesis* to anything that may be proposed to our belief; and just as the electricians speak of live and dead wires, let us speak of any hypothesis as either *live* or *dead*. A live hypothesis is one which appeals as a real possibility to him to whom it is proposed. If I ask

[*]An Address to the Philosophical Clubs of Yale and Brown Universities. Published in the *New World*, June 1896.

you to believe in the Mahdi, the notion makes no electric connection with your nature—it refuses to scintillate with any credibility at all. As an hypothesis it is completely dead. To an Arab, however (even if he be not one of the Mahdi's followers), the hypothesis is among the mind's possibilities: it is alive. This shows that deadness and liveness in an hypothesis are not intrinsic properties, but relations to the individual thinker. They are measured by his willingness to act. The maximum of liveness in an hypothesis means willingness to act irrevocably. Practically, that means belief; but there is some believing tendency wherever there is willingness to act at all.

Next, let us call the decision between two hypotheses an *option*. Options may be of several kinds. They may be—1, *living* or *dead*; 2, *forced* or *avoidable*; 3, *momentous* or *trivial*; and for our purposes we may call an option a *genuine* option when it is of the forced, living and momentous kind.

1. A living option is one in which both hypotheses are live ones. If I say to you: "Be a theosophist or be a Mohammedan," it is probably a dead option, because for you neither hypothesis is likely to be alive. But if I say: "Be an agnostic or be a Christian," it is otherwise: trained as you are, each hypothesis makes some appeal, however small, to your belief.

2. Next, if I say to you: "Choose between going out with your umbrella or without it," I do not offer you a genuine option, for it is not forced. You can easily avoid it by not going out at all. Similarly, if I say, "Either love me or hate me," "Either call my theory true or call it false," your option is avoidable. You may remain indifferent to me, neither loving nor hating, and you may decline to offer any judgment as to my theory. But if I say, "Either accept this truth or go without it," I put on you a forced option, for there is no standing place outside of the alternative. Every dilemma based on a complete logical disjunction, with no possibility of not choosing, is an option of this forced kind.

3. Finally, if I were Dr. Nansen and proposed to you to join my North Pole expedition, your option would be momentous; for this would probably be your only similar opportunity, and your choice now would either exclude you from the North Pole sort of immortality altogether or put at least the chance of it into your hands. He who refuses to embrace a unique opportunity loses the prize as surely as if he

tried and failed. *Per contra*, the option is trivial when the opportunity is not unique, when the stake is insignificant, or when the decision is reversible if it later prove unwise. Such trivial options abound in the scientific life. A chemist finds an hypothesis live enough to spend a year in its verification: he believes in it to that extent. But if his experiments prove inconclusive either way, he is quit for his loss of time, no vital harm being done.

It will facilitate our discussion if we keep all these distinctions well in mind.

# II

The next matter to consider is the actual psychology of human opinion. When we look at certain facts, it seems as if our passional and volitional nature lay at the root of all our convictions. When we look at others, it seems as if they could do nothing when the intellect had once said its say. Let us take the latter facts up first.

Does it not seem preposterous on the very face of it to talk of our opinions being modifiable at will? Can our will either help or hinder our intellect in its perceptions of truth? Can we, by just willing it, believe that Abraham Lincoln's existence is a myth, and that the portraits of him in *McClure's Magazine* are all of someone else? Can we, by any effort of our will, or by any strength of wish that it were true, believe ourselves well and about when we are roaring with rheumatism in bed, or feel certain that the sum of the two one-dollar bills in our pocket must be a hundred dollars? We can say any of these things, but we are absolutely impotent to believe them; and of just such things is the whole fabric of the truths that we do believe in made up—matters of fact, immediate or remote, as Hume said, and relations between ideas, which are either there or not there for us if we see them so, and which if not there cannot be put there by any action of our own.

In Pascal's *Thoughts* there is a celebrated passage known in literature as Pascal's wager. In it he tries to force us into Christianity by reasoning as if our concern with truth resembled our concern with the stakes in a game of chance. Translated freely his words are these: You must either believe or not believe that God is—which will you do? Your human reason cannot say. A game is going on between you and the nature of things which at the day of judgment will bring out either heads or tails. Weigh what your gains and your losses would be if you should stake all you have on heads, or God's existence: if you win in such case, you gain eternal beatitude; if you lose, you lose nothing at all. If there were an infinity of chances, and only one for God in this wager, still you ought to stake your all on God; for though you surely risk a finite loss by this procedure, any finite loss is reasonable, even a certain one is reasonable, if there is but the possibility of infinite gain. Go, then, and take holy water, and have masses said; belief will come and stupefy your scruples—*Cela vous fera croire et vous abêtira*. Why should you not? At bottom, what have you to lose? You probably feel that when religious faith expresses itself thus, in the language of the gaming table, it is put to its last trumps. Surely Pascal's own personal belief in masses and holy water had far other springs; and this celebrated page of his is but an argument for others, a last desperate snatch at a weapon against the hardness of the unbelieving heart. We feel that a faith in masses and holy water adopted wilfully after such a mechanical calculation would lack the inner soul of faith's reality; and if we were ourselves in the place of the Deity, we should probably take particular pleasure in cutting off believers of this pattern from their infinite reward. It is evident that unless there be some pre-existing tendency to believe in masses and holy water, the option offered to the will by Pascal is not a living option. Certainly no Turk ever took to masses and holy water on its account; and even to us Protestants these means of salvation seem such foregone impossibilities that Pascal's logic, invoked for them specifically, leaves us unmoved. As well might the Mahdi write to us, saying, "I am the Expected One whom God has created in his effulgence. You shall be infinitely happy if you confess me; otherwise you shall be cut off from the light of the sun. Weigh, then, your infinite gain if I am genuine against your finite sacrifice if I am not!" His logic would be that of Pascal; but he would vainly use it on us, for the hypothesis he offers us is dead. No tendency to act on it exists in us to any degree.

The talk of believing by our volition seems, then, from one point of view, simply silly. From another point of view it is worse than silly, it is vile. When one turns to the magnificent edifice of the physical sciences, and sees how it was reared; what thousands of disinterested moral lives of men lie buried in its mere foundations; what patience and postponement, what choking down of preference, what submission to the icy laws of outer fact are wrought into its very stones and mortar; how absolutely impersonal it stands in its vast augustness—then how besotted and contemptible seems every little sentimentalist who comes blowing his voluntary smoke-wreaths, and pretending to decide things from out of his private dream! Can we wonder if those bred in the rugged and manly school of science should feel like spewing such subjectivism out of their mouths? The whole system of loyalties which grow up in the schools of science go dead against its toleration; so that it is only natural that those who have caught the scientific fever should pass over to the opposite extreme, and write sometimes as if the incorruptibly truthful intellect ought positively to prefer bitterness and unacceptableness to the heart in its cup.

It fortifies my soul to know
That, though I perish, Truth is so —

sings Clough, while Huxley exclaims: "My only consolation lies in the reflection that, however bad our posterity may become, so far as they hold by the plain rule of not pretending to believe what they have no reason to believe, because it may be to their advantage so to pretend [the word "pretend" is surely here redundant], they will not have reached the lowest depth of immorality." And that delicious *enfant terrible* Clifford writes: "Belief is desecrated when given to unproved and unquestioned statements for the solace and private pleasure of the believer. . . . Whoso would deserve well of his fellows in this matter will guard the purity of his belief with a very fanaticism of jealous care, lest at any time it should rest on an unworthy object, and catch a stain which can never be wiped away . . . If [a] belief has been accepted on insufficient evidence [even though the belief be true, as Clifford on the same page explains] the pleasure is a stolen one. . . . It is sinful because it is stolen in defiance of our duty to mankind. That duty is to guard ourselves from such beliefs as from a pestilence which may shortly master our own body and then spread to the rest of the town. . . . It is wrong always, everywhere, and for every one, to believe anything upon insufficient evidence." [Words in brackets above are WJ's—ed.]

# III

All this strikes one as healthy, even when expressed, as by Clifford, with somewhat too much of robustious pathos in the voice. Free-will and simple wishing do seem, in the matter of our credences, to be only fifth wheels to the coach. Yet if any one should thereupon assume that intellectual insight is what remains after wish and will and sentimental preference have taken wing, or that pure reason is what then settles our opinions, he would fly quite as directly in the teeth of the facts.

It is only our already dead hypotheses that our willing nature is unable to bring to life again. But what has made them dead for us is for the most part a previous action of our willing nature of an antagonistic kind. When I say "willing nature," I do not mean only such deliberate volitions as may have set up habits of belief that we cannot now escape from—I mean all such factors of belief as fear and hope, prejudice and passion, imitation and partisanship, the circumpressure of our caste and set. As a matter of fact we find ourselves believing, we hardly know how or why. Mr. Balfour gives the name of "authority" to all those influences, born of the intellectual climate, that make hypotheses possible or impossible for us, alive or dead. Here in this room, we all of us believe in molecules and the conservation of energy, in democracy and necessary progress, in Protestant Christianity and the duty of fighting for "the doctrine of the immortal Monroe," all for no reasons worthy of the name. We see into these matters with no more inner clearness, and probably with much less, than any disbeliever in them might possess. His unconventionality would probably have some grounds to show for its conclusions; but for us, not insight, but the *prestige* of the opinions, is what makes the spark shoot from them and light up our sleeping magazines of faith. Our reason is quite satisfied, in nine hundred and ninety-nine cases out of every thousand of us, if it can find a few arguments that will do to recite in case our credulity is criticized by someone else. Our faith is faith in someone else's faith, and in the greatest matters this is most the case. Our belief in truth itself, for instance, that there is a truth, and that our minds and it are made for each other—what is it but a passionate affirmation of desire, in which our social system backs us up? We want to have a truth; we want to believe that our experiments and studies and discussions must put us in a continually better and better position towards it; and on this line we agree to fight out our thinking lives. But if a pyrrhonistic sceptic asks us *how we know* all this, can our logic find a reply? No! certainly it cannot. It is just one volition against another— we willing to go in for life upon a trust or assumption which he, for his part, does not care to make.*

As a rule we disbelieve all facts and theories for which we have no use. Clifford's cosmic emotions find no use for Christian feelings. Huxley belabors the bishops because there is no use for sacerdotalism in his scheme of life. Newman, on the contrary, goes over to Romanism, and finds all sorts of reasons good for staying there, because a priestly system is for him an organic need and delight. Why do so few "scientists" even look at the evidence for telepathy, so called? Because they think, as a leading biologist, now dead, once said to me, that even if such a thing were true, scientists ought to band together to keep it suppressed and concealed. It would undo the uniformity of Nature and all sorts of other things without which scientists cannot carry on their pursuits. But if this very man had been shown something which as a scientist he might *do* with telepathy, he might not only have examined the evidence, but even have found it good enough. This very law which the logicians would impose upon us—if I may give the name of logicians to those who would rule out our willing nature here—is based on nothing but their own natural wish to exclude all elements for which they, in their professional quality of logicians, can find no use.

Evidently, then, our non-intellectual nature does influence our convictions. There are passional tendencies and volitions which run before and others which come after belief, and it is only the latter that are too late for the fair; and they are not too late when the previous passional work has been already in their own direction. Pascal's argument, instead of being powerless, then seems a regular clincher, and is the last stroke needed to make our faith in masses and holy water complete. The state of things is evidently far from simple; and pure insight and logic, whatever they might do ideally, are not the only things that really do produce our creeds.

. . . .

---

*Compare the admirable page 310 in S. H. Hodgson's *Time and Space*, London, 1865.

# VIII

And now, after all this introduction, let us go straight at our question. I have said, and now repeat it, that not only as a matter of fact do we find our passional nature influencing us in our opinions, but that there are some options between opinions in which this influence must be regarded both as an inevitable and as a lawful determinant of our choice.

I fear here that some of you my hearers will begin to scent danger, and lend an inhospitable ear. Two first steps of passion you have indeed had to admit as necessary—we must think so as to avoid dupery, and we must think so as to gain truth; but the surest path to those ideal consummations, you will probably consider, is from now onwards to take no further passional step.

Well, of course, I agree as far as the facts will allow. Wherever the option between losing truth and gaining it is not momentous, we can throw the chance of *gaining truth* away, and at any rate save ourselves from any chance of *believing falsehood*, by not making up our minds at all till objective evidence has come. In scientific questions, this is almost always the case; and even in human affairs in general, the need of acting is seldom so urgent that a false belief to act on is better than no belief at all. Law courts, indeed, have to decide on the best evidence attainable for the moment, because a judge's duty is to make law as well as to ascertain it, and (as a learned judge once said to me) few cases are worth spending much time over: the great thing is to have them decided on *any* acceptable principle, and got out of the way. But in our dealings with objective nature we obviously are recorders, not makers, of the truth; and decisions for the mere sake of deciding promptly and getting on to the next business would be wholly out of place. Throughout the breadth of physical nature facts are what they are quite independently of us, and seldom is there any such hurry about them that the risks of being duped by believing a premature theory need be faced. The questions here are always trivial options, the hypotheses are hardly living (at any rate not living for us spectators), the choice between believing truth or falsehood is seldom forced. The attitude of sceptical balance is therefore the absolutely wise one if we would escape mistakes. What difference, indeed, does it make to most of us whether we have or have not a theory of the Röntgen rays, whether we believe or not in mind-stuff, or have a conviction about the causality of conscious states? It makes no difference. Such options are not forced on us. On every account it is better not to make them, but still keep weighing reasons *pro et contra* with an indifferent hand.

I speak, of course, here of the purely judging mind. For purposes of discovery such indifference is to be less highly recommended, and science would be far less advanced than she is if the passionate desires of individuals to get their own faiths confirmed had been kept out of the game. See for example the sagacity which Spencer and Weismann now display. On the other hand, if you want an absolute duffer in an investigation, you must, after all, take the man who has no interest whatever in its results: he is the warranted incapable, the positive fool. The most useful investigator, because the most sensitive observer, is always he whose eager interest in one side of the question is balanced by an equally keen nervousness lest he become deceived.* Science has organized this nervousness into a regular *technique*, her so-called method of verification; and she has fallen so deeply in love with the method that one may even say she has ceased to care for truth by itself at all. It is only truth as technically verified that interests her. The truth of truths might come in merely affirmative form, and she would decline to touch it. Such truth as that, she might repeat with Clifford, would be stolen in defiance of her duty to mankind. Human passions, however, are stronger than technical rules. "Le coeur a ses raisons," as Pascal says, "que la raison ne connaît point"; and however indifferent to all but the bare rules of the game the umpire, the abstract intellect, may be, the concrete players who furnish him the materials to judge of are usually, each one of them, in love with some pet "live hypothesis" of his own. Let us agree, however, that wherever there is no forced option, the dispassionately judicial intellect with no pet hypothesis, saving us, as it does, from dupery at any rate, ought to be our ideal.

The question next arises: Are there not somewhere forced options in our speculative questions, and can we (as men who may be interested at

---

*Compare Wilfred Ward's Essay, "The Wish to Believe," in his *Witness to the Unseen*. Macmillan & Co., 1893.

least as much in positively gaining truth as in merely escaping dupery) always wait with impunity till the coercive evidence shall have arrived? It seems *a priori* improbable that the truth should be so nicely adjusted to our needs and powers as that. In the great boarding-house of nature, the cakes and the butter and the syrup seldom come out so even and leave the plates so clean. Indeed, we should view them with scientific suspicion if they did.

# IX

*Moral questions* immediately present themselves as questions whose solution cannot wait for sensible proof. A moral question is a question not of what sensibly exists, but of what is good, or would be good if it did exist. Science can tell us what exists; but to compare the *worths*, both of what exists and of what does not exist, we must consult not science, but what Pascal calls our heart. Science herself consults her heart when she lays it down that the infinite ascertainment of fact and correction of false belief are the supreme goods for man. Challenge the statement, and science can only repeat it oracularly, or else prove it by showing that such ascertainment and correction bring man all sorts of other goods which man's heart in turn declares. The question of having moral beliefs at all or not having them is decided by our will. Are our moral preferences true or false, or are they only odd biological phenomena, making things good or bad for *us*, but in themselves indifferent? How can your pure intellect decide? If your heart does not *want* a world of moral reality, your head will assuredly never make you believe in one. Mephistophelian scepticism, indeed, will satisfy the head's play-instincts much better than any rigorous idealism can. Some men (even at the student age) are so naturally cool-hearted that the moralistic hypothesis never has for them any pungent life, and in their supercilious presence the hot young moralist always feels strangely ill at ease. The appearance of knowingness is on their side, of *naïveté* and gullibility on his. Yet, in the inarticulate heart of him, he clings to it that he is not a dupe, and that there is a realm in which (as Emerson says) all their wit and intellectual superiority is no better than the cunning of a fox. Moral scepticism can no more be refuted or proved by logic than intellectual scepticism can. When we stick to it that there *is* truth (be it of either kind), we do so with our whole nature, and resolve to stand or fall by the results. The sceptic with his whole nature adopts the doubting attitude; but which of us is the wiser, Omniscience only knows.

Turn now from these wide questions of good to a certain class of questions of fact, questions concerning personal relations, states of mind between one man and another. *Do you like me or not?*—for example. Whether you do or not depends, in countless instances, on whether I meet you half-way, am willing to assume that you must like me, and show you trust and expectation. The previous faith on my part in your liking's existence is in such cases what makes your liking come. But if I stand aloof, and refuse to budge an inch until I have objective evidence, until you shall have done something apt, as the absolutists say, *ad extorquendum assensum meum,* ten to one your liking never comes. How many women's hearts are vanquished by the mere sanguine insistence of some man that they *must* love him! he will not consent to the hypothesis that they cannot. The desire for a certain kind of truth here brings about that special truth's existence; and so it is in innumerable cases of other sorts. Who gains promotions, boons, appointments, but the man in whose life they are seen to play the part of live hypotheses, who discounts them, sacrifices other things for their sake before they have come, and takes risks for them in advance? His faith acts on the powers above him as a claim, and creates its own verification.

A social organism of any sort whatever, large or small, is what it is because each member proceeds to his own duty with a trust that the other members will simultaneously do theirs. Wherever a desired result is achieved by the co-operation of many independent persons, its existence as a fact is a pure consequence of the precursive faith in one another of those immediately concerned. A government, an army, a commercial system, a ship, a college, an athletic team, all exist on this condition, without which not only is nothing achieved, but nothing is even attempted. A whole train of passengers (individually brave enough) will be looted by a few highwaymen, simply because the latter can count on one another, while each passenger fears that if he makes a movement of resistance, he will be shot before any one else backs him up. If we believed that the whole car-full would rise at once with us, we should each severally rise, and train-robbing would never even be attempted. There are, then, cases where a fact cannot come at all unless a preliminary faith exists in its coming. *And where faith in a fact can help create the fact*, that would be an insane logic which should say that faith running ahead of scientific evidence is the "lowest kind of immorality" into which a thinking being can fall. Yet such is the logic by which our scientific absolutists pretend to regulate our lives!

# X

In truths dependent on our personal action, then, faith based on desire is certainly a lawful and possibly an indispensable thing.

But now, it will be said, these are all childish human cases, and have nothing to do with great cosmical matters, like the question of religious faith. Let us then pass on to that. Religions differ so much in their accidents that in discussing the religious question we must make it very generic and broad. What then do we now mean by the religious hypothesis? Science says things are; morality says some things are better than other things; and religion says essentially two things.

First, she says that the best things are the more eternal things, the overlapping things, the things in the universe that throw the last stone, so to speak, and say the final word. "Perfection is eternal"—this phrase of Charles Secrétan seems a good way of putting this first affirmation of religion, an affirmation which obviously cannot yet be verified scientifically at all.

The second affirmation of religion is that we are better off even now if we believe her first affirmation to be true.

Now, let us consider what the logical elements of this situation are *in case the religious hypothesis in both its branches be really true.* (Of course, we must admit that possibility at the outset. If we are to discuss the question at all, it must involve a living option. If for any of you religion be a hypothesis that cannot, by any living possibility be true, then you need go no farther. I speak to the "saving remnant" alone.) So proceeding, we see, first that religion offers itself as a *momentous* option. We are supposed to gain, even now, by our belief, and to lose by our non-belief, a certain vital good. Secondly, religion is a *forced* option, so far as that good goes. We cannot escape the issue by remaining sceptical and waiting for more light, because, although we do avoid error in that way *if religion be untrue*, we lose the good, *if it be true*, just as certainly as if we positively chose to disbelieve. It is as if a man should hesitate indefinitely to ask a certain woman to marry him because he was not perfectly sure that she would prove an angel after he brought her home. Would he not cut himself off from that particular angel-possibility as decisively as if he went and married some one else? Scepticism, then, is not avoidance of option; it is option of a certain particular kind of risk. *Better risk loss of truth than chance of error* —that is your faith-vetoer's exact position. He is actively playing his stake as much as the believer is; he is backing the field against the religious hypothesis, just as the believer is backing the religious hypothesis against the field. To preach scepticism to us as a duty until "sufficient evidence" for religion be found, is tantamount therefore to telling us, when in presence of the religious hypothesis, that to yield to our fear of its being error is wiser and better than to yield to our hope that it may be true. It is not intellect against all passions, then; it is only intellect with one passion laying down its law. And by what, forsooth, is the supreme wisdom of this passion warranted? Dupery for dupery, what proof is there that dupery through hope is so much worse than dupery through fear? I, for one, can see no proof; and I simply refuse obedience to the scientist's command to imitate his kind of option, in a case where my own stake is important enough to give me the right to choose my own form of risk. If religion be true and the evidence for it be still insufficient, I do not wish, by putting your extinguisher upon my nature (which feels to me as if it had after all some business in this matter), to forfeit my sole chance in life of getting upon the winning side—that chance depending, of course, on my willingness to run the risk of acting as if my passional need of taking the world religiously might be prophetic and right.

All this is on the supposition that it really may be prophetic and right, and that, even to us who are discussing the matter, religion is a live hypothesis which may be true. Now, to most of us religion comes in a still further way that makes a veto on our active faith even more illogical. The more perfect and more eternal aspect of the universe is represented in our religions as having personal form. The universe is no longer a mere *It* to us, but a *Thou*, if we are religious; and any relation that may be possible from person to person might be possible here. For instance, although in one sense we are passive portions of the universe, in another we show a curious autonomy, as if we were small active centres on our own account. We feel, too, as if the appeal of religion to us were made to our own active good-will, as if evidence might be forever withheld from us unless we met the hypothesis half-way. To take a trivial illustration: just as a man who in a company of gentlemen made no advances, asked a warrant for every concession, and believed no one's word without proof, would cut himself off by such churlishness from all the social rewards that a more trusting spirit would earn—so here, one who should shut himself up in snarling logicality and try to make the gods extort his recognition willy-nilly, or not get it at all, might cut himself off forever from his only opportunity of making the gods' acquaintance. This feeling, forced on us we know not whence, that by obstinately believing that there are gods (although not to do so would be so easy both for our logic and our life) we are doing the universe the deepest service we can, seems part of the living essence of the religious hypothesis. If the hypothesis were true in all its parts, including this one, then pure intellectualism, with its veto on our making willing advances, would be an absurdity; and some participation of our sympathetic nature would be logically required. I, therefore, for one, cannot see my way to accepting the agnostic rules for truth-seeking, or wilfully agree to keep my willing nature out of the game. I cannot do so for this plain reason, that *a rule of thinking which would absolutely prevent me from acknowledging certain kinds of truth if those kinds of truth were really there, would be an irrational rule.* That for me is the long and short of the formal logic of the situation, no matter what the kinds of truth might materially be.

I confess I do not see how this logic can be escaped. But sad experience makes me fear that some of you may still shrink from radically saying with me, *in abstracto*, that we have the right to believe at our own risk any hypothesis that is live enough to tempt our will. I suspect, however, that if this is so, it is because you have got away from the abstract logical point of view altogether, and are thinking (perhaps without realizing it) of some particular religious hypothesis which for you is dead. The freedom to "believe what we will" you apply to the case of some patent superstition; and the faith you think of is the faith defined by the schoolboy when he said, "Faith is when you believe something that you know ain't true." I can only repeat that this is misapprehension. *In concreto*, the freedom to believe can only cover living options which the intellect of the individual cannot by itself resolve; and living options never seem absurdities to him who has them to consider. When I look at the religious question as it really puts itself to concrete men, and when I think of all the possibilities which both practically and theoretically it involves, then this command that we shall put a stopper on our heart, instincts, and courage, and *wait*—acting of course meanwhile more or less as if religion were *not* true*—till doomsday, or till such time as our intellect and senses working together may have raked in evidence enough—this command, I say, seems to me the queerest idol ever manufactured in the philosophic cave. Were we scholastic absolutists, there might be more excuse. If we had an infallible intellect with its objective certitudes, we might feel ourselves disloyal to such a perfect organ of knowledge in not trusting to it exclusively, in not waiting for its releasing word. But if we are empiricists, if we believe that no bell in us tolls to let us know for certain when truth is in our grasp, then it seems a piece of idle fantasticality to preach so solemnly our duty of waiting for the bell. Indeed we *may* wait if we will—I hope you do not think that I am denying that—but if we do so, we do so at our peril as much as if we believed. In either case we *act*, taking our life in our hands. No one of us ought to issue vetoes to the other, nor should we bandy words of abuse. We ought, on the contrary, delicately and profoundly to respect one another's mental freedom: then only shall we bring about the intellectual republic; then only shall we have that spirit of inner tolerance without which all our outer tolerance is soulless, and which is empiricism's glory; then only shall we live and let live, in speculative as well as in practical things.

. . . .

---

*Since belief is measured by action, he who forbids us to believe religion to be true, necessarily also forbids us to act as we should if we did believe it to be true. The whole defense of religious faith hinges upon action. If the action required or inspired by the religious hypothesis is in no way different from that dictated by the naturalistic hypothesis, then religious faith is a pure superfluity, better pruned away, and controversy about its legitimacy is a piece of idle trifling, unworthy of serious minds. I myself believe, of course, that the religious hypothesis gives to the world an expression which specifically determines our reactions, and makes them in a large part unlike what they might be on a purely naturalistic scheme of belief.

# The Moral Philosopher and the Moral Life*

The main purpose of this paper is to show that there is no such thing possible as an ethical philosophy dogmatically made up in advance. We all help to determine the content of ethical philosophy so far as we contribute to the race's moral life. In other words, there can be no final truth in ethics any more than in physics, until the last man has had his experience and said his say. In the one case as in the other, however, the hypotheses which we now make while waiting, and the acts to which they prompt us, are among the indispensable conditions which determine what that "say" shall be.

First of all, what is the position of him who seeks an ethical philosophy? To begin with, he must be distinguished from all those who are satisfied to be ethical sceptics. He *will* not be a sceptic; therefore so far from ethical scepticism being one possible fruit of ethical philosophizing, it can only be regarded as that residual alternative to all philosophy which from the outset menaces every would-be philosopher who may give up the quest discouraged, and renounce his original aim. That aim is to find an account of the moral relations that obtain among things, which will weave them into the unity of a stable system, and make of the world what one may call a genuine universe from the ethical point of view. So far as the world resists reduction to the form of unity, so far as ethical propositions seem unstable, so far does the philosopher fail of his ideal. The subject-matter of his study is the ideals he finds existing in the world; the purpose which guides him is this ideal of his own, of getting them into a certain form. This ideal is thus a factor in ethical philosophy whose legitimate presence must never be overlooked; it is a positive contribution which the philosopher himself necessarily makes to the problem. But it is his only positive contribution. At the outset of his inquiry he ought to have no other ideals. Were he interested peculiarly in the triumph of any one kind of good, he would *pro tanto* cease to be a judicial investigator, and become an advocate for some limited element of the case.

---

*An Address to the Yale Philosophical Club, published in the *International Journal of Ethics*, April, 1891.

There are three questions in ethics which must be kept apart. Let them be called respectively the *psychological* question, the *metaphysical* question, and the *casuistic* question. The psychological question asks after the historical *origin* of our moral ideas and judgments; the metaphysical question asks what the very *meaning* of the words "good," "ill," and "obligation" are; the casuistic question asks what is the *measure* of the various goods and ills which men recognize, so that the philosopher may settle the true order of human obligations.

. . . .

[Ed.: Although a pioneering psychologist, James here dismisses answers to the "*psychological* question" as unhelpful in theory, uncertain in fact, and irrelevant to the uses of moral ideas. He treats the "*metaphysical* question" somewhat more seriously, winding up with the nice gesture to humanism below. But the subsequent "*casuistic* question" most engages him.]

We may now consider that what we distinguished as the metaphysical question in ethical philosophy is sufficiently answered, and that we have learned what the words "good," "bad," and "obligation" severally mean. They mean no absolute natures, independent of personal support. They are objects of feeling and desire, which have no foothold or anchorage in Being, apart from the existence of actually living minds.

Wherever such minds exist, with judgments of good and ill, and demands upon one another, there is an ethical world in its essential features. Were all other things, gods and men and starry heavens, blotted out from this universe, and were there left but one rock with two loving souls upon it, that rock would have as thoroughly moral a constitution as any possible world which the eternities and immensities could harbor. It would be a tragic constitution, because the rock's inhabitants would die. But while they lived, there would be real good things and real bad things in the universe; there would be obligations, claims, and expectations; obediences, refusals, and disappointments; compunctions and longings for harmony to come again, and inward peace of conscience when it was restored; there would, in short, be a moral life, whose active energy would have no limit but the intensity of interest in each other with which the hero and heroine might be endowed.

We, on this terrestrial globe, so far as the visible facts go, are just like the inhabitants of such a rock. Whether a God exist, or whether no God exist, in yon blue heaven above us bent, we form at any rate an ethical republic here below. And the first reflection which this leads to is that ethics have as genuine and real a foothold in a universe where the highest consciousness is human, as in a universe where there is a God as well. "The religion of humanity" affords a basis for ethics as well as theism does. Whether the purely human system can gratify the philosopher's demand as well as the other is a different question, which we ourselves must answer ere we close.

# III

The last fundamental question in Ethics was, it will be remembered, the *casuistic* question. Here we are, in a world where the existence of a divine thinker has been and perhaps always will be doubted by some of the lookers-on, and where, in spite of the presence of a large number of ideals in which human beings agree, there are a mass of others about which no general consensus obtains. It is hardly necessary to present a literary picture of this, for the facts are too well known. The wars of the flesh and the spirit in each man, the concupiscences of different individuals pursuing the same unshareable material or social prizes, the ideals which contrast so according to races, circumstances, temperaments, philosophical beliefs, etc.—all form a maze of apparently inextricable confusion with no obvious Ariadne's thread to lead one out. Yet the philosopher, just because he is a philosopher, adds his own peculiar ideal to the confusion (with which if he were willing to be a sceptic he would be passably content), and insists that over all these individual opinions there is a *system of truth* which he can discover if he only takes sufficient pains.

We stand ourselves at present in the place of that philosopher, and must not fail to realize all the features that the situation comports. In the first place we will not be sceptics; we hold to it that there is a truth to be ascertained. But in the second place we have just gained the insight that that truth cannot be a self-proclaiming set of laws, or an abstract "moral reason," but can only exist in act, or in the shape of an opinion held by some thinker really to be found. There is, however, no visible thinker invested with authority. Shall we then simply proclaim our own ideals as the lawgiving ones? No; for if we are true philosophers we must throw our own spontaneous ideals, even the dearest, impartially in with that total mass of ideals which are fairly to be judged. But how then can we as philosophers ever find a test; how avoid complete moral scepticism on the one hand, and on the other escape bringing a wayward personal standard of our own along with us, on which we simply pin our faith?

The dilemma is a hard one, nor does it grow a bit more easy as we revolve it in our minds. The entire undertaking of the philosopher obliges him to seek an impartial test. That test, however, must be incarnated in the demand of some actually existent person; and how can he pick out the person save by an act in which his own sympathies and prepossessions are implied?

One method indeed presents itself, and has as a matter of history been taken by the more serious ethical schools. If the heap of things demanded proved on inspection less chaotic than at first they seemed, if they furnished their own relative test and measure, then the casuistic problem would be solved. If it were found that all goods *quâ* goods contained a common essence, then the amount of this essence involved in any one good would show its rank in the scale of goodness, and order could be quickly made; for this essence would be *the* good upon which all thinkers were agreed, the relatively objective and universal good that the philosopher seeks. Even his own private ideals would be measured by their share of it, and find their rightful place among the rest.

Various essences of good have thus been found and proposed as bases of the ethical system. Thus, to be a mean between two extremes; to be recognized by a special intuitive faculty; to make the agent happy for the moment; to make others as well as him happy in the long run; to add to his perfection or dignity; to harm no one; to follow from reason or flow from universal law; to be in accordance with the will of God; to promote the survival of the human species on this planet—are so many tests, each of which has been maintained by somebody to constitute the essence of all good things or actions so far as they are good.

No one of the measures that have been actually proposed has, however, given general satisfaction. Some are obviously not universally present in all cases—*e.g.*, the character of harming no one, or that of following a universal law; for the best course is often cruel; and many acts are reckoned good on the sole condition that they be exceptions, and serve not as examples of a universal law. Other characters, such as following the will of God, are unascertainable and vague. Others again, like survival, are quite indeterminate in their consequences, and leave us in the lurch where we most need their help: a philosopher of the Sioux Nation, for example, will be certain to use the survival-criterion in a very different way from ourselves. The best, on the whole, of these marks and measures of goodness seems to be the capacity to bring happiness. But in order not to break down fatally, this test must be taken to cover innumerable acts and impulses that never *aim* at happiness; so that, after all, in seeking for a universal principle we inevitably are carried onward to the *most* universal principle—that *the essence of good is simply to satisfy demand*. The demand may be for anything under the sun. There is really no more ground for supposing that all our demands can be accounted for by one universal underlying kind of motive than there is ground for supposing that all physical phenomena are cases of a single law. The elementary forces in ethics are probably as plural as those of physics are. The various ideals have no common character apart from the fact that they are ideals. No single abstract principle can be so used as to yield to the philosopher anything like a scientifically accurate and genuinely useful casuistic scale.

. . . .

What can he do, then, it will now be asked, except to fall back on scepticism and give up the notion of being a philosopher at all?

But do we not already see a perfectly definite path of escape which is open to him just because he is a philosopher, and not the champion of one particular ideal? Since everything which is demanded is by that fact a good, must not the guiding principle for ethical philosophy (since all demands conjointly cannot be satisfied in this poor world) be simply to satisfy at all times *as many demands as we can?* That act must be the best act, accordingly, which makes for the *best whole*, in the sense of awakening the least sum of dissatisfactions. In the casuistic scale, therefore, those ideals must be written highest which *prevail at the least cost*, or by whose realization the least possible number of other ideals are destroyed. Since victory and defeat there must be, the victory to be philosophically prayed for is that of the more inclusive side—of the side which even in the hour of triumph will to some degree do justice to the ideals in which the vanquished party's interests lay. The course of history is nothing but the story of men's struggles from generation to generation to find the more and more inclusive order. *Invent some manner* of realizing your own ideals which will also satisfy the alien demands— that and that only is the path of peace! Following this path, society has shaken itself into one sort of relative equilibrium after another by a series of social discoveries quite analogous to those of science. Polyandry and polygamy and slavery, private warfare and liberty to kill, judicial torture and arbitrary royal power have slowly succumbed to actually aroused complaints; and though some one's ideals are unquestionably the worse off for each improvement, yet a vastly greater total number of them find shelter in our civilized society than in the older savage ways. So far then, and up to date, the casuistic scale is made for the philosopher already far better than he can ever make it for himself. An experiment of the most searching kind has proved that the laws and usages of the land are what yield the maximum of satisfaction to the thinkers taken all together. The presumption in cases of conflict must always be in favor of the conventionally recognized good. The philosopher must be a conservative, and in the construction of his casuistic scale must put the things most in accordance with the customs of the community on top.

And yet if he be a true philosopher he must see that there is nothing final in any actually given equilibrium of human ideals, but that, as our present laws and customs have fought and conquered other past ones, so they will in their turn be overthrown by any newly discovered order which will hush up the complaints that they still give rise to, without producing others louder still. "Rules are made for man, not man for rules"—that one sentence is enough to immortalize Green's

*Prolegomena to Ethics.* And although a man always risks much when he breaks away from established rules and strives to realize a larger ideal whole than they permit, yet the philosopher must allow that it is at all times open to any one to make the experiment, provided he fear not to stake his life and character upon the throw. The pinch is always here. Pent in under every system of moral rules are innumerable persons whom it weighs upon, and goods which it represses; and these are always rumbling and grumbling in the background, and ready for any issue by which they may get free. See the abuses which the institution of private property covers, so that even to-day it is shamelessly asserted among us that one of the prime functions of the national government is to help the adroiter citizens to grow rich. See the unnamed and unnamable sorrows which the tyranny, on the whole so beneficent, of the marriage-institution brings to so many, both of the married and the unwed. See the wholesale loss of opportunity under our *régime* of so-called equality and industrialism, with the drummer and the counter-jumper in the saddle, for so many faculties and graces which could flourish in the feudal world. See our kindliness for the humble and the outcast, how it wars with that stern weeding out which until now has been the condition of every perfection in the breed. See everywhere the struggle and the squeeze; and everlastingly the problem how to make them less. The anarchists, nihilists, and free-lovers; the free-silverites, socialists, and single-tax men; the free-traders and civil-service reformers; the prohibitionists and anti-vivisectionists; the radical darwinians with their idea of the suppression of the weak—these and all the conservative sentiments of society arrayed against them, are simply deciding through actual experiment by what sort of conduct the maximum amount of good can be gained and kept in this world. These experiments are to be judged, not *à priori*, but by actual finding, after the fact of their making, how much more outcry or how much appeasement comes about. What closet-solutions can possibly anticipate the result of trials made on such a scale? Or what can any superficial theorist's judgment be worth, in a world where every one of hundreds of ideals has its special champion already provided in the shape of some genius expressly born to feel it, and to fight to death in its behalf? The pure philosopher can only follow the windings of the spectacle, confident that the line of least resistance will always be towards the richer and the more inclusive arrangement, and that by one tack after another some approach to the kingdom of heaven is incessantly made.

# IV

All this amounts to saying that, so far as the casuistic question goes, ethical science is just like physical science, and instead of being deducible all at once from abstract principles, must simply bide its time, and be ready to revise its conclusions from day to day. The presumption of course, in both sciences, always is that the vulgarly accepted opinions are true, and the right casuistic order that which public opinion believes in; and surely it would be folly quite as great, in most of us, to strike out independently and to aim at originality in ethics as in physics. Every now and then, however, some one is born with the right to be original, and his revolutionary thought or action may bear prosperous fruit. He may replace old "laws of nature" by better ones; he may, by breaking old moral rules in a certain place, bring in a total condition of things more ideal than would have followed had the rules been kept.

On the whole, then, we must conclude that no philosophy of ethics is possible in the old-fashioned absolute sense of the term. Everywhere the ethical philosopher must wait on facts. The thinkers who create the ideals come he knows not whence, their sensibilities are evolved he knows not how; and the question as to which of two conflicting ideals will give the best universe then and there, can be answered by him only through the aid of the experience of other men. I said some time ago, in treating of the "first" question, that the intuitional moralists deserve credit for keeping most clearly to the psychological facts. They do much to spoil this merit on the whole, however, by mixing with it that dogmatic temper which, by absolute distinctions and unconditional "thou shalt nots," changes a growing, elastic, and continuous life into a superstitious system of relics and dead bones. In point of fact, there are no absolute evils, and there are no non-moral goods; and the *highest* ethical life—however few may be called to bear its burdens—consists at all times in the breaking of rules which have grown too narrow for the actual case. There is but one unconditional commandment, which is that we should seek incessantly, with fear and trembling, so to vote and to act as to bring about the very largest total universe of good which we can see. Abstract rules indeed can help; but they help the less in proportion as our intuitions are more piercing, and our vocation is the stronger for the moral life. For every real dilemma is in literal strictness a unique situation; and the exact combination of ideals realized and ideals disappointed which each decision creates is always a universe without a precedent, and for which no adequate previous rule exists. The philosopher, then, *quâ* philosopher, is no better able to determine the best universe in the concrete emergency than other men. He sees, indeed, somewhat better than most men what the question always is— not a question of this good or that good simply taken, but of the two total universes with which these goods respectively belong. He knows that he must vote always for the richer universe, for the good which seems most organizable, most fit to enter into complex combinations, most apt to be a member of a more inclusive whole. But which particular universe this is he cannot know for certain in advance; he only knows that if he makes a bad mistake the cries of the wounded will soon inform him of the fact. In all this the philosopher is just like the rest of us non-philosophers, so far as we are just and sympathetic instinctively, and so far as we are open to the voice of complaint. His function is in fact indistinguishable from that of the best kind of statesman at the present day. His books upon ethics, therefore, so far as they truly touch the moral life, must more and more ally themselves with a literature which is confessedly tentative and suggestive rather than dogmatic—I mean with novels and dramas of the deeper sort, with sermons, with books on statecraft and philanthropy and social and economical reform. Treated in this way ethical treatises may be voluminous and luminous as well; but they never can be *final*, except in their abstractest and vaguest features; and they must more and more abandon the old-fashioned, clear-cut, and would-be "scientific" form.

# V

The chief of all the reasons why concrete ethics cannot be final is that they have to wait on metaphysical and theological beliefs. I said some time back that real ethical relations existed in a purely human world. They would exist even in what we called a moral solitude if the thinker had various ideals which took hold of him in turn. His self of one day would make demands on his self of another; and some of the demands might be urgent and tyrannical, while others were gentle and easily put aside. We call the tyrannical demands *imperatives*. If we ignore these we do not hear the last of it. The good which we have wounded returns to plague us with interminable crops of consequential damages, compunctions, and regrets. Obligation can thus exist inside a single thinker's consciousness; and perfect peace can abide with him only so far as he lives according to some sort of a casuistic scale which keeps his more imperative goods on top. It is the nature of these goods to be cruel to their rivals. Nothing shall avail when weighed in the balance against them. They call out all the mercilessness in our disposition, and do not easily forgive us if we are so soft-hearted as to shrink from sacrifice in their behalf.

The deepest difference, practically, in the moral life of man is the difference between the easy-going and the strenuous mood. When in the easy-going mood the shrinking from present ill is our ruling consideration. The strenuous mood, on the contrary, makes us quite indifferent to present ill, if only the greater ideal be attained. The capacity for the strenuous mood probably lies slumbering in every man, but it has more difficulty in some than in others in waking up. It needs the wilder passions to arouse it, the big fears, loves, and indignations; or else the deeply penetrating appeal of some one of the higher fidelities, like justice, truth, or freedom. Strong relief is a necessity of its vision; and a world where all the mountains are brought down and all the valleys are exalted is no congenial place for its habitation. This is why in a solitary thinker this mood might slumber on forever without waking. His various ideals, known to him to be mere preferences of his own, are too nearly of the same denominational value: he can play fast or loose with them at will. This too is why, in a merely human world without a God, the appeal to our moral energy falls short of its maximal stimulating power. Life, to be sure, is even in such a world a genuinely ethical symphony; but it is played in the compass of a couple of poor octaves, and the infinite scale of values fails to open up. Many of us, indeed—like Sir James Stephen in those eloquent *Essays by a Barrister*—would openly laugh at the very idea of the strenuous mood being awakened in us by those claims of remote posterity which constitute the last appeal of the religion of humanity. We do not love these men of the future keenly enough; and we love them perhaps the less the more we hear of their evolutionized perfection, their high average longevity and education, their freedom from war and crime, their relative immunity from pain and zymotic disease, and all their other negative superiorities. This is all too finite, we say; we see too well the vacuum beyond. It lacks the note of infinitude and mystery, and may all be dealt with in the don't-care mood. No need of agonizing ourselves or making others agonize for these good creatures just at present.

When, however, we believe that a God is there, and that he is one of the claimants, the infinite perspective opens out. The scale of the symphony is incalculably prolonged. The more imperative ideals now begin to speak with an altogether new objectivity and significance, and to utter the penetrating, shattering, tragically challenging note of appeal. They ring out like the call of Victor Hugo's alpine eagle, "qui parle au précipice et que le gouffre entend," and the strenuous mood awakens at the sound. It saith among the trumpets, ha, ha! it smelleth the battle afar off, the thunder of the captains and the shouting. Its blood is up; and cruelty to the lesser claims, so far from being a deterrent element, does but add to the stern joy with which it leaps to answer to the greater. All through history, in the periodical conflicts of puritanism with the don't-care temper, we see the antagonism of the strenuous and genial moods, and the contrast between the ethics of infinite and mysterious obligation from on high, and those of prudence and the satisfaction of merely finite need.

The capacity of the strenuous mood lies so deep down among our natural human possibilities that even if there were no metaphysical or traditional grounds for believing in a God, men would postulate one simply as a pretext for living hard, and getting out of the game of existence its keenest possibilities of zest. Our attitude towards concrete evils is entirely different in a world where we believe there are none but finite demanders, from what it is in one where we joyously face tragedy for an infinite demander's sake. Every sort of energy and endurance, of courage and capacity for handling life's evils, is set free in those who have religious faith. For this reason the strenuous type of character will on the battle-field of human history always outwear the easy-going type, and religion will drive irreligion to the wall.

It would seem, too—and this is my final conclusion—that the stable and systematic moral universe for which the ethical philosopher asks is fully possible only in a world where there is a divine thinker with all-enveloping demands. If such a thinker existed, his way of subordinating the demands to one another would be the finally valid casuistic scale; his claims would be the most appealing; his ideal universe would be the most inclusive realizable whole. If he now exist, then actualized in his thought already must be that ethical philosophy which we seek as the pattern which our own must evermore approach.* In the interests of our own ideal of systematically unified moral truth, therefore, we, as would-be philosophers, must postulate a divine thinker, and pray for the victory of the religious cause. Meanwhile, exactly what the thought of the infinite thinker may be is hidden from us even were we sure of his existence; so that our postulation of him after all serves only to let loose in us the strenuous mood. But this is what it does in all men, even those who have no interest in philosophy. The ethical philosopher, therefore, whenever he ventures to say which course of action is the best, is on no essentially different level from the common man. "See, I have set before thee this day life and good, and death and evil; therefore, choose life that thou and thy seed may live"—when this challenge comes to us, it is simply our total character and personal genius that are on trial; and if we invoke any so-called philosophy, our choice and use of that also are but revelations of our personal aptitude or incapacity for moral life. From this unsparing practical ordeal no professor's lectures and no array of books can save us. The solving word, for the learned and the unlearned man alike, lies in the last resort in the dumb willingnesses and unwillingnesses of their interior characters, and nowhere else. It is not in heaven, neither is it beyond the sea; but the word is very nigh unto thee, in thy mouth and in thy heart, that thou mayest do it.

---

*All this is set forth with great freshness and force in a work of my colleague, Professor Josiah Royce: *The Religious Aspect of Philosophy*, Boston, 1995.

# On a Certain Blindness in Human Beings

Our judgments concerning the worth of things, big or little, depend on the *feelings* the things arouse in us. Where we judge a thing to be precious in consequence of the *idea* we frame of it, this is only because the idea is itself associated already with a feeling. If we were radically feelingness, and if ideas were the only things our mind could entertain, we should lose all our likes and dislikes at a stroke, and be unable to point to any one situation or experience in life more valuable or significant that any other.

Now the blindness in human beings, of which this discourse will treat, is the blindness with which we all are afflicted in regard to the feelings of creatures and people different from ourselves.

We are practical beings, each of us with limited functions and duties to perform. Each is bound to feel intensely the importance of his own duties and the significance of the situations that call these forth. But this feeling is in each of us a vital secret, for sympathy with which we vainly look to others. The others are too much absorbed in their own vital secrets to take an interest in ours. Hence the stupidity and injustice of our opinions, so far as they deal with the significance of alien lives. Hence the falsity of our judgments, so far as they presume to decide in an absolute way on the value of other persons' conditions or ideals.

Take our dogs and ourselves, connected as we are by a tie more intimate than most ties in this world; and yet, outside of that tie of friendly fondness, how insensible, each of us, to all that makes life significant for the other!—we to the rapture of bones under hedges, or smells of trees and lamp-posts, they to the delights of literature and art. As you sit reading the most moving romance you ever fell upon, what sort of a judge is your fox-terrier of your behavior? With all his good will toward you, the nature of your conduct is absolutely excluded from his comprehension. To sit there like a senseless statue, when you might be taking him to walk and throwing sticks for him to catch! What queer disease is this that comes over you every day, of holding things and staring at them like that for hours together, paralyzed of motion and vacant of all conscious life? The African savages came nearer the truth; but they, too, missed it, when they gathered wonderingly round one of our American travellers who, in the interior, had just come into possession of a stray copy of the New York *Commercial Advertiser*, and was devouring it column by column. When he got through, they offered him a high price for the mysterious object; and, being asked for what they wanted it, they said: "For an eye medicine"—that being the only reason they could conceive of for the protracted bath which he had given his eyes upon its surface.

The spectator's judgment is sure to miss the root of the matter, and to possess no truth. The subject judged knows a part of the world of reality which the judging spectator fails to see, knows more while the spectator knows less; and, wherever there is conflict of opinion and difference of vision, we are bound to believe that the truer side is the side that feels the more, and not the side that feels the less.

Let me take a personal example of the kind that befalls each one of us daily:—

Some years ago, while journeying in the mountains of North Carolina, I passed by a large number of "coves," as they call them there, or heads of small valleys between the hills, which had been newly cleared and planted. The impression on my mind was one of unmitigated squalor. The settler had in every case cut down the more manageable trees, and left their charred stumps standing. The larger trees he had girdled and killed, in order that their foliage should not cast a shade. He had then built a log cabin, plastering its chinks with clay, and had set up a tall zigzag rail fence around the scene of his havoc, to keep the pigs and cattle out. Finally, he had irregularly planted the intervals between the stumps and trees with Indian corn, which grew among the chips; and there he dwelt with his wife and babes—an axe, a gun, a few utensils, and some pigs and chickens feeding in the woods, being the sum total of his possessions.

The forest had been destroyed; and what had "improved" it out of existence was hideous, a sort of ulcer, without a single element of artificial grace to make up for the loss of Nature's beauty. Ugly, indeed, seemed the life of the squatter, scudding, as the sailors say, under bare poles, beginning again away back where our first ancestors started, and by hardly a single item the better off for all the achievements of the intervening generations.

Talk about going back to nature! I said to myself, oppressed by the dreariness, as I drove by. Talk of a country life for one's old age and for one's children! Never thus, with nothing but the bare ground and one's bare hands to fight the battle! Never, without the best spoils of culture woven in! The beauties and commodities gained by the centuries are sacred. They are our heritage and birthright. No modern person ought to be willing to live a day in such a state of rudimentariness and denudation!

Then I said to the mountaineer who was driving me, "What sort of people are they who have to make these new clearings?" "All of us," he replied. "Why, we ain't happy here, unless we are getting one of these coves under cultivation." I instantly felt that I had been losing the whole inward significance of the situation. Because to me the clearings spoke of naught but denudation, I thought that to those whose sturdy arms and obedient axes had made them they could tell no other story. But, when *they* looked on the hideous stumps, what they thought of was personal victory. The chips, the girdled trees, and the vile split rails spoke of honest sweat, persistent toil and final reward. The cabin was a warrant of safety for self and wife and babes. In short, the clearing, which to me was a mere ugly picture on the retina, was to them a symbol redolent with moral memories and sang a very paean of duty, struggle, and success.

I had been as blind to the peculiar ideality of their conditions as they certainly would also have been to the ideality of mine, had they had a peep at my strange indoor academic ways of life at Cambridge.

Wherever a process of life communicates an eagerness to him who lives it, there the life becomes genuinely significant. Sometimes the eagerness is more knit up with the motor activities, sometimes with the perceptions, sometimes with the imagination, sometimes with reflective thought. But, wherever it is found, there is the zest, the tingle, the excitement of reality; and there *is* "importance" in the only real and positive sense in which importance ever anywhere can be.

[James quotes at length here from Robert Louis Stevenson's "The Latern Bearers," Tolstoy's *War and Peace,* the poetry of Wordsworth and Walt Whitman, and from other authors.—ed.]

. . . .

And now what is the result of all these considerations and quotations? It is negative in one sense, but positive in another. It absolutely forbids us to be forward in pronouncing on the meaninglessness of forms of existence other than our own; and it commands us to tolerate, respect, and indulge those whom we see harmlessly interested and happy in their own ways, however unintelligible these may be to us. Hands off: neither the whole of truth nor the whole of good is revealed to any single observer, although each observer gains a partial superiority of insight from the peculiar position in which he stands. Even prisons and sick-rooms have their special revelations. It is enough to ask of each of us that he should be faithful to his own opportunities and make the most of his own blessings, without presuming to regulate the rest of the vast field.

# THE VARIETIES OF RELIGIOUS EXPERIENCE

The material of our study of human nature is now spread before us; and in this parting hour, set free from the duty of description, we can draw our theoretical and practical conclusions. In my first lecture, defending the empirical method, I foretold that whatever conclusions we might come to could be reached by spiritual judgments only, appreciations of the significance for life of religion, taken "on the whole." Our conclusions cannot be as sharp as dogmatic conclusions would be, but I will formulate them, when the time comes, as sharply as I can.

Summing up in the broadest possible way the characteristics of the religious life, as we have found them, it includes the following beliefs:—

1. That the visible world is part of a more spiritual universe from which it draws its chief significance;

2. That union or harmonious relation with that higher universe is our true end;

3. That prayer or inner communion with the spirit thereof—be that spirit "God" or "law"—is a process wherein work is really done, and spiritual energy flows in and produces effects, psychological or material, within the phenomenal world.

Religion includes also the following psychological characteristics:—

4. A new zest which adds itself like a gift to life, and takes the form either of lyrical enchantment or of appeal to earnestness and heroism;

5. An assurance of safety and a temper of peace, and, in relation to others, a preponderance of loving affections.

In illustrating these characteristics by documents, we have been literally bathed in sentiment. In re-reading my manuscript, I am almost appalled at the amount of emotionality which I find in it. After so much of this, we can afford to be dryer and less sympathetic in the rest of the work that lies before us.

. . . .

The further limits of our being plunge, it seems to me, into an altogether other dimension of existence from the sensible and merely "understandable" world. Name it the mystical region, or the supernatural region, whichever you choose. So far as our ideal impulses originate in this region (and most of them do originate in it, for we find them possessing us in a way for which we cannot articulately account), we belong to it in a more intimate sense than that in which we belong to the visible world, for we belong in the most intimate sense wherever our ideals belong. Yet the unseen region in question is not merely ideal, for it produces effects in this world. When we commune with it, work is actually done upon our finite personality, for we are turned into new men, and consequences in the way of conduct follow in the natural world upon our regenerative change.* But that which produces effects within another reality must be termed a reality itself, so I feel as if we had no philosophic excuse for calling the unseen or mystical world unreal.

God is the natural appellation, for us Christians at least, for the supreme reality, so I will call this higher part of the universe by the name of God.** We and God have business with each other; and in opening ourselves to his influence our deepest destiny is fulfilled. The universe, at those parts of it which our personal being constitutes, takes a turn genuinely for the worse or for the better in proportion as each one of us fulfils or evades God's demands. As far as this goes I probably have you with me, for I only translate into schematic language what I may call the instinctive belief of mankind: God is real since he produces real effects.

The real effects in question, so far as I have as yet admitted them, are exerted on the personal centres of energy of the various subjects, but the spontaneous faith of most of the subjects is that they embrace a wider sphere than this. Most religious men believe (or "know," if they be mystical) that not only they themselves, but the whole universe of

---

* That the transaction of opening ourselves, otherwise called prayer, is a perfectly definite one for certain persons, appears abundantly in the preceding lectures. I append another concrete example to reinforce the impression on the reader's mind: —

"Man can learn to transcend these limitations [of finite thought] and draw power and wisdom at will. . . . The divine presence is known through experience. The turning to a higher plane is a distinct act of consciousness. It is not a vague, twilight or semi-conscious experience. It is not an ecstasy; it is not a trance. It is not super-consciousness in the Vedantic sense. It is not due to self-hypnotization. It is a perfectly calm, sane, sound, rational, common-sense shifting of consciousness from the phenomena of sense-perception to the phenomena of seership, from the thought of self to a distinctively higher realm. . . . For example, if the lower self be nervous, anxious, tense, one can in a few moments compel it to be calm. This is not done by a word amply. Again I say, it is not hypnotism. It is by the exercise of power. One feels the spirit of peace as definitely as heat is perceived on a hot summer day. The power can be as surely used as the sun's rays can be focused and made to do work, to set fire to wood." *The Higher Law*, vol. iv. pp. 4, 6, Boston, August, 1901.

** Transcendentalists are fond of the term "Over-soul," but as a rule they use it in an intellectualist sense, as meaning only a medium of communion. "God" is a causal agent as well as a medium of communion, and that is the aspect which I wish to emphasize.

beings to whom the God is present, are secure in his parental hands. There is a sense, a dimension, they are sure, in which we are *all* saved, in spite of the gates of hell and all adverse terrestrial appearances. God's existence is the guarantee of an ideal order that shall be permanently preserved. This world may indeed, as science assures us, some day burn up or freeze; but if it is part of his order, the old ideals are sure to be brought elsewhere to fruition, so that where God is, tragedy is only provisional and partial, and shipwreck and dissolution are not the absolutely final things. Only when this farther step of faith concerning God is taken, and remote objective consequences are predicted, does religion, as it seems to me, get wholly free from the first immediate subjective experience, and bring a *real hypothesis* into play. A good hypothesis in science must have other properties than those of the phenomenon it is immediately invoked to explain, otherwise it is not prolific enough. God, meaning only what enters into the religious man's experience of union, falls short of being an hypothesis of this more useful order. He needs to enter into wider cosmic relations in order to justify the subject's absolute confidence and peace.

That the God with whom, starting from the hither side of our own extra-marginal self, we come at its remoter margin into commerce should be the absolute world-ruler, is of course a very considerable over-belief. Over-belief as it is, though, it is an article of almost every one's religion. Most of us pretend in some way to prop it upon our philosophy, but the philosophy itself is really propped upon this faith. What is this but to say that Religion, in her fullest exercise of function, is not a mere illumination of facts already elsewhere given, not a mere passion, like love, which views things in a rosier light. It is indeed that, as we have seen abundantly. But it is something more, namely, a postulator of new *facts* as well. The world interpreted religiously is not the materialistic world over again, with an altered expression; it must have, over and above the altered expression, *a natural constitution* different at some point from that which a materialistic world would have. It must be such that different events can be expected in it, different conduct must be required.

This thoroughly "pragmatic" view of religion has usually been taken as a matter of course by common men. They have interpolated divine miracles into the field of nature, they have built a heaven out beyond the grave. It is only transcendentalist metaphysicians who think that, without adding any concrete details to Nature, or subtracting any, but by simply calling it the expression of absolute spirit, you make it more divine just as it stands. I believe the pragmatic way of taking religion to be the deeper way. It gives it body as well as soul, it makes it claim, as everything real must claim, some characteristic realm of fact as its very own. What the more characteristically divine facts are, apart from the actual inflow of energy in the faith-state and the prayer-state, I know not. But the over-belief on which I am ready to make my personal venture is that they exist. The whole drift of my education goes to persuade me that the world of our present consciousness is only one out of many worlds of consciousness that exist, and that those other worlds must contain experiences which have a meaning for our life also; and that although in the main their experiences and those of this world keep discrete, yet the two become continuous at certain points, and higher energies filter in. By being faithful in my poor measure to this over-belief, I seem to myself to keep more sane and true. I *can*, of course, put myself into the sectarian scientist's attitude, and imagine vividly that the world of sensations and of scientific laws and objects may be all. But whenever I do this, I hear that inward monitor of which W. K. Clifford once wrote, whispering the word "bosh!" Humbug is humbug, even though it bear the scientific name, and the total expression of human experience, as I view it objectively, invincibly urges me beyond the narrow "scientific" bounds. Assuredly, the real world is of a different temperament—more intricately built than physical science allows. So my objective and my subjective conscience both hold me to the over-belief which I express. Who knows whether the faithfulness of individuals here below to their own poor over-beliefs may not actually help God in turn to be more effectively faithful to his own greater tasks?

. . . .

In writing my concluding lecture I had to aim so much at simplification that I fear that my general philosophic position received so scant a statement as hardly to be intelligible to some of my readers. I therefore add this epilogue.... [ed.]

. . . .

Notwithstanding my own inability to accept either popular Christianity or scholastic theism, I suppose that my belief that in communion with the Ideal new force comes into the world, and new departures are made here below, subjects me to being classed among the supernaturalists of the piecemeal or crasser type....[ed.]

. . . .

I state the matter thus bluntly, because the current of thought in academic circles runs against me, and I feel like a man who must set his back against an open door quickly if he does not wish to see it closed and locked. In spite of its being so shocking to the reigning intellectual tastes, I believe that a candid consideration of piecemeal supernaturalism and a complete discussion of all its metaphysical bearings will show it to be the hypothesis by which the largest number of legitimate requirements are met. That of course would be a program for other books than this; what I now say sufficiently indicates to the philosophic reader the place where I belong.

If asked just where the differences in fact which are due to God's existence come in, I should have to say that in general I have no hypothesis to offer beyond what the phenomenon of "prayerful communion," especially when certain kinds of incursion from the subconscious region take part in it, immediately suggests. The appearance is that in this phenomenon something ideal, which in one sense is part of ourselves and in another sense is not ourselves, actually exerts an influence, raises our centre of personal energy, and produces regenerative effects unattainable in other ways. If, then, there be a wider world of being than that of our every-day consciousness, if in it there be forces whose effects on us are intermittent, if one facilitating condition of the effects be the openness of the "subliminal" door, we have the elements of a theory to which the phenomena of religious life lend plausibility. I am so impressed by the importance of these phenomena that I adopt the hypothesis which they so naturally suggest. At these places at least, I say, it would seem as though transmundane energies, God, if you will, produced immediate effects within the natural world to which the rest of our experience belongs.

The difference in natural "fact" which most of us would assign as the first difference which the existence of a God ought to make would, I imagine, be personal immortality. Religion, in fact, for the great majority of our own race *means* immortality, and nothing else. God is the producer of immortality; and whoever has doubts of immortality is written down as an atheist without farther trial. I have said nothing in my lectures about immortality or the belief therein, for to me it seems a secondary point. If only our ideals are cared for in "eternity," I do not see why we might not be willing to resign their care to other hands than ours. Yet I sympathize with the urgent impulse to be present ourselves, and in the conflict of impulses, both of them so vague yet both of them noble, I know not how to decide. It seems to me that it is eminently a case for facts to testify. Facts, I think, are yet lacking to prove "spirit-return," though I have the highest respect for the patient labors of Messrs. Myers, Hodgson, and Hyslop, and am somewhat impressed by their favorable conclusions. I consequently leave the matter open, with this brief word to save the reader from a possible perplexity as to why immortality got no mention in the body of this book.

The ideal power with which we feel ourselves in connection, the "God" of ordinary men, is, both by ordinary men and by philosophers, endowed with certain of those metaphysical attributes which in the lecture on philosophy I treated with such disrespect. He is assumed as a matter of course to be "one and only" and to be "infinite"; and the notion of many finite gods is one which hardly any one thinks it worth while to consider, and still less to uphold. Nevertheless, in the interests of intellectual clearness, I feel bound to say that religious experience, as we have studied it, cannot be cited as unequivocally supporting the infinitist belief. The only thing that it unequivocally testifies to is that we can experience union with *something* larger than ourselves and in that union find our greatest peace. Philosophy, with its passion for unity, and mysticism with its mono-ideistic bent, both "pass to the limit" and identify the something with a unique God who is the all-inclusive soul of the world. Popular opinion, respectful to their authority, follows the example which they set.

Meanwhile the practical needs and experiences of religion seem to me sufficiently met by the belief that beyond each man and in a fashion continuous with him there exists a larger power which is friendly to him and to his ideals. All that the facts require is that the power should be both other and larger than our conscious selves. Anything larger will do, if only it be large enough to trust for the next step. It need not be infinite, it need not be solitary. It might conceivably even be only a larger and more godlike self, of which the present self would then be but the mutilated expression, and the universe might conceivably be a collection of such selves, of different degrees of inclusiveness, with no absolute unity realized in it at all.* Thus would a sort of polytheism return upon us—a polytheism which I do not on this occasion defend, for my only aim at present is to keep the testimony of religious experience clearly within its proper bounds.

Upholders of the monistic view will say to such a polytheism (which, by the way, has always been the real religion of common people, and is so still to-day) that unless there be one all-inclusive God, our guarantee of security is left imperfect. In the Absolute, and in the Absolute only, *all* is saved. If there be different gods, each caring for his part, some portion of some of us might not be covered with divine protection, and our religious consolation would thus fail to be complete. It goes back to what was said on pages 131–133 [Lectures VI and VII, not included here], about the possibility of there being portions of the universe that may irretrievably be lost. Common sense is less sweeping in its demands than philosophy or mysticism have been wont to be, and can suffer the notion of this world being partly saved and partly lost. The ordinary moralistic state of mind makes the salvation of the world conditional upon the success with which each unit does its part. Partial and conditional salvation is in fact a most familiar notion when taken in the abstract, the only difficulty being to determine the details. Some men are even disinterested enough to be willing to be in the unsaved remnant as far as their persons go, if only they can be persuaded that their cause will prevail—all of us are willing, whenever our activity-excitement rises sufficiently high. I think, in fact, that a final philosophy

---

*Such a notion is suggested in my Ingersoll Lecture On Human Immortality, Boston and London, 1899.

of religion will have to consider the pluralistic hypothesis more seriously than it has hitherto been willing to consider it. For practical life at any rate, the *chance* of salvation is enough. No fact in human nature is more characteristic than its willingness to live on a chance. The existence of the chance makes the difference, as Edmund Gurney says, between a life of which the keynote is resignation and a life of which the keynote is hope.* But all these statements are unsatisfactory from their brevity, and I can only say that I hope to return to the same questions in another book.

---

*Tertium Quid, 1887, p. 99. See also pp. 148, 149.

# Part IV

# TRUTHS OF EXPERIENCE

## What Pragmatism Means

Some years ago, being with a camping party in the mountains, I returned, from a solitary ramble to find every one engaged in a ferocious metaphysical dispute. The *corpus* of the dispute was a squirrel—a live squirrel supposed to be clinging to one side of a tree-trunk; while over against the tree's opposite side a human being was imagined to stand. This human witness tries to get sight of the squirrel by moving rapidly round the tree, but no matter how fast he goes, the squirrel moves as fast in the opposite direction, and always keeps the tree between himself and the man, so that never a glimpse of him is caught. The resultant metaphysical problem now is this: *Does the man go round the squirrel or not?* He goes round the tree, sure enough, and the squirrel is on the tree; but does he go round the squirrel? In the unlimited leisure of the wilderness, discussion had been worn threadbare. Every one had taken sides, and was obstinate; and the numbers on both sides were even. Each side, when I appeared therefore appealed to me to make it a majority. Mindful of the scholastic adage that whenever you meet a contradiction you must make a distinction, I immediately sought and found one, as follows: "Which party is right," I said, "depends on what you *practically mean* by 'going round' the squirrel. If you mean passing from the north of him to the east, then to the south, then to the west, and then to the north of him again, obviously the man does go round him, for he occupies these successive positions. But if on the contrary you mean being first in front of him, then on the right of him, then behind him, then on his left, and finally in front again, it is quite as obvious that the man fails to go round him, for by the compensating movements the squirrel makes, he keeps his belly turned towards the man all the time, and his back turned away. Make the distinction, and there is no occasion for any farther dispute. You are both right and both wrong according as you conceive the verb 'to go round' in one practical fashion or the other."

Although one or two of the hotter disputants called my speech a shuffling evasion, saying they wanted no quibbling or scholastic hair-splitting, but meant just plain honest English "round," the majority seemed to think that the distinction had assuaged the dispute.

I tell this trivial anecdote because it is a peculiarly simple example of what I wish now to speak of as *the pragmatic method*. The pragmatic method is primarily a method of settling metaphysical disputes that otherwise might be interminable. Is the world one or many?—fated or free?—material or spiritual?—here are notions either of which may or may not hold good of the world; and disputes over such notions are unending. The pragmatic method in such cases is to try to interpret each notion by tracing its respective practical consequences. What difference would it practically make to any one if this notion rather than that notion were true? If no practical difference whatever can be traced, then the alternatives mean practically the same thing, and all dispute is idle. Whenever a dispute is serious, we ought to be able to show some practical difference that must follow from one side or the other's being right.

A glance at the history of the idea will show you still better what pragmatism means. The term is derived from the same Greek word πρᾶγμα, meaning action, from which our words "practice" and "practical" come. It was first introduced into philosophy by Mr. Charles Peirce in 1878. In an article entitled "How to Make Our Ideas Clear," in the *Popular Science Monthly* for January of that year,* Mr. Peirce, after pointing out that our beliefs are really rules for action, said that, to develop a thoughts meaning, we need only determine what conduct it is fitted to produce: that conduct is for us its sole significance. And the tangible fact at the root of all our thought-distinctions, however subtle, is that there is no one of them so fine as to consist in anything but a possible difference of practice. To attain perfect clearness in our thoughts of an object, then, we need only consider what conceivable effects of a practical kind the object may involve—what sensations we are to expect from it, and what reactions we must prepare. Our conception of these effects, whether immediate or remote, is then for us

---

*Translated in the *Revue Philosophique* for January, 1879 (vol. vii).

the whole of our conception of the object, so far as that conception has positive significance at all.

This is the principle of Peirce, the principle of pragmatism. It lay entirely unnoticed by any one for twenty years, until I, in an address before Professor Howison's philosophical union at the university of California, brought it forward again and made a special application of it to religion. By that date (1898) the times seemed ripe for its reception. The word "pragmatism" spread, and at present it fairly spots the pages of the philosophic journals. On all hands we find the "pragmatic movement" spoken of, sometimes with respect, sometimes with contumely, seldom with clear understanding. It is evident that the term applies itself conveniently to a number of tendencies that hitherto have lacked a collective name, and that it has "come to stay."

. . . .

It is astonishing to see how many philosophical disputes collapse into insignificance the moment you subject them to this simple test of tracing a concrete consequence. There can *be* no difference anywhere that doesn't *make* a difference elsewhere—no difference in abstract truth that doesn't express itself in a difference in concrete fact and in conduct consequent upon that fact, imposed on somebody, somehow, somewhere, and somewhen. The whole function of philosophy ought to be to find out what definite difference it will make to you and me, at definite instants of our life, if this world-formula or that world-formula be the true one.

There is absolutely nothing new in the pragmatic method. Socrates was an adept at it. Aristotle used it methodically. Locke, Berkeley, and Hume made momentous contributions to truth by its means. Shadworth Hodgson keeps insisting that realities are only what they are "known as." But these forerunners of pragmatism used it in fragments: they were a prelude only. Not until in our time has it generalized itself, become conscious of a universal mission, pretended to a conquering destiny. I believe in that destiny, and I hope I may end by inspiring you with my belief.

Pragmatism represents a perfectly familiar attitude in philosophy, the empiricist attitude, but it represents it, as it seems to me, both in a more radical and in a less objectionable form than it has ever yet assumed. A pragmatist turns his back resolutely and once for all upon a lot of inveterate habits dear to professional philosophers. He turns away from abstraction and insufficiency, from verbal solutions, from bad *a priori* reasons, from fixed principles, closed systems, and pretended absolutes and origins. He turns towards concreteness and adequacy, towards facts, towards action and towards power. That means the empiricist temper regnant and the rationalist temper sincerely given up. It means the open air and possibilities of nature, as against dogma, artificiality, and the pretence of finality in truth.

At the same time it does not stand for any special results. It is a method only. But the general triumph of that method would mean an enormous change in what I called in my last lecture the "temperament" of philosophy. Teachers of the ultra-rationalistic type would be frozen out, much as the courtier type is frozen out in republics, as the ultramontane type of priest is frozen out in protestant lands. Science and metaphysics would come much nearer together, would in fact work absolutely hand in hand.

Metaphysics has usually followed a very primitive kind of quest. You know how men have always hankered after unlawful magic, and you know what a great part in magic *words* have always played. If you have his name, or the formula of incantation that binds him, you can control the spirit, genie, afrite, or whatever the power may be. Solomon knew the names of all the spirits, and having their names, he held them subject to his will. So the universe has always appeared to the natural mind as a kind of enigma, of which the key must be sought in the shape of some illuminating or power-bringing word or name. That word names the universe's *principle*, and to possess it is after a fashion to possess the universe itself. "God," "Matter," "Reason," "the Absolute," "Energy," are so many solving names. You can rest when you have them. You are at the end of your metaphysical quest.

But if you follow the pragmatic method, you cannot look on any such word as closing your quest. You must bring out of each word its practical cash-value, set it at work within the stream of your experience. It appears less as a solution, then, than as a program for more work, and more particularly as an indication of the ways in which existing realities may be *changed*.

*Theories thus become instruments, not answers to enigmas, in which we can rest.* We don't lie back upon them, we move forward, and, on occasion, make nature over again by their aid. Pragmatism unstiffens all our theories, limbers them up and sets each one at work. Being nothing essentially new, it harmonizes with many ancient philosophic tendencies. It agrees with nominalism for instance, in always appealing to particulars; with utilitarianism in emphasizing practical aspects; with positivism in its disdain for verbal solutions, useless questions and metaphysical abstractions.

All these, you see, are *anti-intellectualist* tendencies. Against rationalism as a pretension and a method pragmatism is fully armed and militant. But, at the outset, at least, it stands for no particular results. It has no dogmas, and no doctrines save its method. As the young Italian pragmatist Papini has well said, it lies in the midst of our theories, like a corridor in a hotel. Innumerable chambers open out of it. In one you may find a man writing an atheistic volume; in the next some one on his knees praying for faith and strength; in a third a chemist investigating a body's properties. In a fourth a system of idealistic metaphysics is being excogitated; in a fifth the impossibility of metaphysics is being shown. But they all own the corridor, and all must pass through it if they want a practicable way of getting into or out of their respective rooms.

No particular results then, so far, but only an attitude of orientation, is what the pragmatic method means. *The attitude of looking away from first things, principles, "categories," supposed necessities; and of looking towards last things, fruits, consequences, facts.*

So much for the pragmatic method! You may say that I have been praising it rather than explaining it to you, but I shall presently explain it abundantly enough by showing how it works on some familiar problems. Meanwhile the word pragmatism has come to be used in a still wider sense, as meaning also a certain *theory of truth* . . . [ed.].

. . . .

I am well aware how odd it must seem to some of you to hear me say that an idea is "true" so long as to believe it is profitable to our lives. That it is *good,* for much as it profits, you will gladly admit. If what we do by its aid is good, you will allow the idea itself to be good in so far forth, for we are the better for possessing it. But is it not a strange misuse of the word "truth," you will say, to call ideas also "true" for this reason?

. . . [ed.] Let me now say only this, that truth is *one species of good,* and not, as is usually supposed, a category distinct from good, and co-ordinate with it. *The true is the name of whatever proves itself to be good in the way of belief, and good, too, for definite, assignable reasons.* Surely you must admit this, that if there were no good for life in true ideas, or if the knowledge of them were positively disadvantageous and false ideas the only useful ones, then the current notion that truth is divine and precious, and its pursuit a duty, could never have grown up or become a dogma. In a world like that, our duty would be to *shun* truth, rather. But in this world, just as certain foods are not only agreeable to our taste, but good for our teeth, our stomach, and our tissues; so certain ideas are not only agreeable to think about, or agreeable as supporting other ideas that we are fond of, but they are also helpful in life's practical struggles. If there be any life that it is really better we should lead, and if there be any idea which, if believed in, would help us to lead that life, then it would be really *better for us* to believe in that idea, *unless, indeed, belief in it incidentally clashed with other greater vital benefits.*

"What would be better for us to believe"! This sounds very like a definition of truth. It comes very near to saying "what we ought to believe": and in *that* definition none of you would find any oddity. Ought we ever not to believe what it is *better for us* to believe? And can we then keep the notion of what is better for us, and what is true for us, permanently apart?

Pragmatism says no, and I fully agree with her. . . . [ed.]

. . . .

I said just now that what is better for us to believe is true *unless the belief incidentally clashes with some other vital benefit.* Now in real life what vital benefits is any particular belief of ours most liable to clash with?

What indeed except the vital benefits yielded by *other beliefs*. In other words, the greatest enemy of any one of our truths may be the rest of our truths.

. . . .

You see by this what I meant when I called pragmatism a mediator and reconciler and said, borrowing the word from Papini, that she "unstiffens" our theories. She has in fact no prejudices whatever, no obstructive dogmas, no rigid canons of what shall count as proof. She is completely genial. She will entertain any hypothesis, she will consider any evidence. It follows that in the religious field she is at a great advantage both over positivistic empiricism, with its anti-theological bias, and over religious rationalism, with its exclusive interest in the remote, the noble, the simple, and the abstract in the way of conception.

In short, she widens the field of search for God. Rationalism sticks to logic and the empyrean. Empiricism sticks to the external senses. Pragmatism is willing to take anything, to follow either logic or the senses and to count the humblest and most personal experiences. She will count mystical experiences if they have practical consequences. She will take a God who lives in the very dirt of private fact—if that should seem a likely place to find him.

Her only test of probable truth is what works best in the way of leading us, what fits every part of life best and combines with the collectivity of experience's demands, nothing being omitted. If theological ideas should do this, if the notion of God, in particular, should prove to do it, how could pragmatism possibly deny God's existence? She could see no meaning in treating as "not true" a notion that was pragmatically so successful. What other kind of truth could there be, for her, than all this agreement with concrete reality?

. . . .

# PRAGMATISM'S CONCEPTION OF TRUTH

. . . .

I fully expect to see the pragmatist view of truth run through the classic stages of a theory's career. First, you know, a new theory is attacked as absurd; then it is admitted to be true, but obvious and insignificant; finally it is seen to be so important that its adversaries claim that they themselves discovered it. Our doctrine of truth is at present in the first of these three stages, with symptoms of the second stage having begun in certain quarters. I wish that this lecture might help it beyond the first stage in the eyes of many of you.

Truth, as any dictionary will tell you, is a property of certain of our ideas. It means their "agreement," as falsity means their disagreement, with "reality." Pragmatists and intellectualists both accept this definition as a matter of course. They begin to quarrel only after the question is raised as to what may precisely be meant by the term "agreement," and what by the term "reality," when reality is taken as something for our ideas to agree with.

In answering these questions the pragmatists are more analytic and painstaking, the intellectualists more offhand and irreflective. The popular notion is that a true idea must copy its reality. Like other popular views, this one follows the analogy of the most usual experience. Our true ideas of sensible things do indeed copy them. Shut your eyes and think of yonder clock on the wall, and you get just such a true picture or copy of its dial. But your idea of its "works" (unless you are a clock-maker) is much less of a copy, yet it passes muster, for it in no way clashes with the reality. Even though it should shrink to the mere word "works," that word still serves you truly; and when you speak of the "time-keeping function" of the clock, or of its spring's "elasticity," it is hard to see exactly what your ideas can copy.

You perceive that there is a problem here. Where our ideas cannot copy definitely their object, what does agreement with that object mean? Some idealists seem to say that they are true whenever they are what God means that we ought to think about that object. Others hold the copy-view all through, and speak as if our ideas possessed truth just in proportion as they approach to being copies of the Absolute's eternal way of thinking.

These views, you see, invite pragmatistic discussion. But the great assumption of the intellectualists is that truth means essentially an inert static relation. When you've got your true idea of anything, there's an end of the matter. You're in possession; you *know*, you have fulfilled your thinking destiny. You are where you ought to be mentally; you have obeyed your categorical imperative; and nothing more need follow on that climax of your rational destiny. Epistemologically you are in stable equilibrium.

Pragmatism, on the other hand, asks its usual question. "Grant an idea or belief to be true," it says, "what concrete difference will its being true make in any one's actual life? How will the truth be realized? What experiences will be different from those which would obtain if the belief were false? What, in short, is the truth's cash-value in experiential terms?"

The moment pragmatism asks this question, it sees the answer: *True ideas are those that we can assimilate, validate, corroborate and verify. False ideas are those that we can not.* That is the practical difference it makes to us to have true ideas; that, therefore, is the meaning of truth, for it is all that truth is known-as.

This thesis is what I have to defend. The truth of an idea is not a stagnant property inherent in it. Truth *happens* to an idea. It *becomes* true, is *made* true by events. Its verity is in fact an event, a process: the process namely of its verifying itself, its veri-*fication*. Its validity is the process of its valid-*ation*.

But what do the words verification and validation themselves pragmatically mean? They again signify certain practical consequences of the verified and validated idea. It is hard to find any one phrase that characterizes these consequences better than the ordinary agreement-formula—just such consequences being what we have in mind whenever we say that our ideas "agree" with reality. They lead us, namely, through the acts and other ideas which they instigate, into or up to, or towards, other parts of experience with which we feel all the while—such feeling being among our potentialities—that the original ideas remain in agreement. The connexions and transitions come to us from point to point as being progressive, harmonious, satisfactory. This function of agreeable leading is what we mean by an idea's verification. Such an account is vague and it sounds at first quite trivial, but it has results which it will take the rest of my hour to explain.

Let me begin by reminding you of the fact that the possession of true thoughts means everywhere the possession of invaluable instruments of action; and that our duty to gain truth, so far from being a blank command from out of the blue, or a "stunt" self-imposed by our intellect, can account for itself by excellent practical reasons.

The importance to human life of having true beliefs about matters of fact is a thing too notorious. We live in a world of realities that can be infinitely useful or infinitely harmful. Ideas that tell us which of them to expect count as the true ideas in all this primary sphere of verification, and the pursuit of such ideas is a primary human duty. The possession of truth, so far from being here an end in itself, is only a preliminary means towards other vital satisfactions. If I am lost in the woods and starved, and find what looks like a cow-path, it is of the utmost importance that I should think of a human habitation at the end of it, for if I do so and follow it, I save myself. The true thought is useful here because the house which is its object is useful. The practical value of true ideas is thus primarily derived from the practical importance of their objects to us. Their objects are, indeed, not important at all times. I may on another occasion have no use for the house; and then my idea of it, however verifiable, will be practically irrelevant, and had better remain latent. Yet since almost any object may some day become temporarily important, the advantage of having a general stock of *extra* truths, of ideas that shall be true of merely possible situations, is obvious. We store such extra truths away in our memories, and with the overflow we fill our books of reference. Whenever such an extra truth becomes practically relevant to one of our emergencies, it passes from cold-storage to do work in the world and our belief in it grows active. You can say of it then either that "it is useful because it is true" or that "it is true because it is useful." Both these phrases mean exactly the same thing, namely that here is an idea that gets fulfilled and can be verified. True is the name for whatever idea starts the verification-process, useful is the name for its completed function in experience. True ideas would never have been singled out as such, would never have acquired a class-name, least of all a name suggesting value, unless they had been useful from the outset in this way.

From this simple cue pragmatism gets her general notion of truth as something essentially bound up with the way in which one moment in our experience may lead us towards other moments which it will be worth while to have been led to. Primarily, and on the common-sense level, the truth of a state of mind means this function of a *leading that is worth while*. When a moment in our experience, of any kind whatever, inspires us with a thought that is true, that means that sooner or later we dip by that thought's guidance into the particulars of experience again and make advantageous connexion with them. This is a vague enough statement, but I beg you to retain it, for it is essential.

. . . .

Truth lives, in fact, for the most part on a credit system. Our thoughts and beliefs "pass" so long as nothing challenges them, just as bank-notes pass so long as nobody refuses them. But this all points to direct face-to-face verifications somewhere, without which the fabric of truth collapses like a financial system with no cash-basis whatever. You accept my verification of one thing, I yours of another. We trade on each other's truth. But beliefs verified concretely by *somebody* are the posts of the whole superstructure.

. . . .

. . . [ed] Any idea that helps us to *deal*, whether practically or intellectually, with either the reality or its belongings, that doesn't entangle our progress in frustrations, that fits, in fact, and adapts our life to the reality's whole setting, will agree sufficiently to meet the requirement. It will hold true of that reality.

. . . .

. . . [ed.] Truth in science is what gives us the maximum possible sum of satisfactions, taste included, but consistency both with previous truth and with novel fact is always the most imperious claimant.

I have led you through a very sandy desert. But now, if I may be allowed so vulgar an expression, we begin to taste the milk in the cocoanut. Our rationalist critics here discharge their batteries upon us, and to reply to them will take us out from all this dryness into full sight of a momentous philosophical alternative.

Our account of truth is an account of truths in the plural, of processes of leading, realized *in rebus*, and having only this quality in common, that they *pay*. They pay by guiding us into or towards some part of a system that dips at numerous points into sense-percepts, which we may copy mentally or not, but with which at any rate we are now in the kind of commerce vaguely designated as verification. Truth for us is simply a collective name for verification-processes, just as health, wealth, strength, etc., are names for other processes connected with life, and also pursued because it pays to pursue them. Truth is *made*, just as health, wealth and strength are made, in the course of experience.

Here rationalism is instantaneously up in arms against us. I can imagine a rationalist to talk as follows:

"Truth is not made," he will say; "it absolutely obtains, being a unique relation that does not wait upon any process, but shoots straight over the head of experience, and hits its reality every time. Our belief that yon thing on the wall is a clock is true already, altho no one in the whole history of the world should verify it. The bare quality of standing in that transcendent relation is what makes any thought true that possesses it, whether or not there be verification. You pragmatists put the cart before the horse in making truth's being reside in verification-processes. These are merely signs of its being, merely our lame ways of ascertaining after the fact, which of our ideas already has possessed the wondrous quality. The quality itself is timeless, like all essences and natures. Thoughts partake of it directly, as they partake of falsity or of irrelevancy. It can't be analyzed away into pragmatic consequences."

The whole plausibility of this rationalist tirade is due to the fact to which we have already paid so much attention. In our world, namely, abounding as it does in things of similar kinds and similarly associated, one verification serves for others of its kind, and one great use of knowing things is to be led not so much to them as to their associates, especially to human talk about them. The quality of truth, obtaining *ante rem*, pragmatically means, then, the fact that in such a world innumerable ideas work better by their indirect or possible than by their direct and actual verification. Truth *ante rem* means only verifiability, then; or else it is a case of the stock rationalist trick of treating the *name* of a concrete phenomenal reality as an independent prior entity, and placing it behind the reality as its explanation. . . . [ed.]

In the case of "wealth" we all see the fallacy. We know that wealth is but a name for concrete processes that certain men's lives play a part in, and not a natural excellence found in Messrs. Rockefeller and Carnegie, but not in the rest of us.

Like wealth, health also lives *in rebus*. It is a name for processes, as digestion, circulation, sleep, etc., that go on happily, tho in this instance we are more inclined to think of it as a principle and to say the man digests and sleeps so well because he is so healthy.

With "strength" we are, I think, more rationalistic still, and decidedly inclined to treat it as an excellence pre-existing in the man and explanatory of the herculean performances of his muscles.

With "truth" most people go over the border entirely, and treat the rationalistic account as self-evident. But really all these words in *th* are exactly similar. Truth exists *ante rem* just as much and as little as the other things do.

The scholastics, following Aristotle, made much of the distinction between habit and act. Health *in tutu* means, among other things, good sleeping and digesting. But a healthy man need not always be sleeping, or always digesting, any more than a wealthy man need be always handling money, or a strong man always lifting weights. All such qualities sink to the status of "habits" between their times of exercise; and similarly truth becomes a habit of certain of our ideas and beliefs in their intervals of rest from their verifying activities. But those activities are the root of the whole matter, and the condition of there being any habit to exist in the intervals.

*"The true" to put it very briefly, is only the expedient in the way of our*

*thinking, just as "the right" is only the expedient in the way of our behaving.*
Expedient in almost any fashion; and expedient in the long run and on
the whole of course; for what meets expediently all the experience in
sight won't necessarily meet all farther experiences equally satisfactorily.
Experience, as we know, has ways of *boiling over*, and making us correct
our present formulas.

The "absolutely" true, meaning what no farther experience will ever
alter, is that ideal vanishing-point towards which we imagine that all
our temporary truths will some day converge. It runs on all fours with
the perfectly wise man, and with the absolutely complete experience;
and, if these ideals are ever realized, they will all be realized together.
Meanwhile we have to live to-day by what truth we can get to-day, and
be ready to-morrow to call it falsehood. Ptolemaic astronomy, euclidean
space, aristotelian logic, scholastic metaphysics, were expedient for
centuries, but human experience has boiled over those limits, and we
now call these things only relatively true, or true within those borders
of experience. "Absolutely" they are false; for we know that those limits
were casual, and might have been transcended by past theorists just as
they are by present thinkers.

When new experiences lead to retrospective judgments, using the
past tense, what these judgments utter *was* true, even tho no past thinker
had been led there. We live forwards, a Danish thinker has said, but
we understand backwards. The present sheds a backward light on the
world's previous processes. They may have been truth-processes for the
actors in them. They are not so for one who knows the later revelations
of the story.

This regulative notion of a potential better truth to be established
later, possibly to be established some day absolutely, and having powers
of retroactive legislation, turns its face, like all pragmatist notions,
towards concreteness of fact, and towards the future. Like the half-
truths, the absolute truth will have to be *made*, made as a relation
incidental to the growth of a mass of verification-experience, to which
the half-true ideas are all along contributing their quota.

I have already insisted on the fact that truth is made largely out of
previous truths. Men's beliefs at any time are so much experience *funded.*
But the beliefs are themselves parts of the sum total of the world's

experience, and become matter, therefore, for the next day's funding operations. So far as reality means experienceable reality, both it and the truths men gain about it are everlastingly in process of mutation— mutation towards a definite goal, it may be—but still mutation.

Mathematicians can solve problems with two variables. On the Newtonian theory, for instance, acceleration varies with distance, but distance also varies with acceleration. In the realm of truth-processes facts come independently and determine our beliefs provisionally. But these beliefs make us act, and as fast as they do so, they bring into sight or into existence new facts which re-determine the beliefs accordingly. So the whole coil and ball of truth, as it rolls up, is the product of a double influence. Truths emerge from facts; but they dip forward into facts again and add to them; which facts again create or reveal new truth (the word is indifferent) and so on indefinitely. The "facts" themselves meanwhile are not *true*. They simply *are*. Truth is the function of the beliefs that start and terminate among them.

The case is like a snowball's growth, due as it is to the distribution of the snow on the one hand, and to the successive pushes of the boys on the other, with these factors co-determining each other incessantly.

The most fateful point of difference between being a rationalist and being a pragmatist is now fully in sight. Experience is in mutation, and our psychological ascertainments of truth are in mutation—so much rationalism will allow; but never that either reality itself or truth itself is mutable. Reality stands complete and ready-made from all eternity, rationalism insists, and the agreement of our ideas with it is that unique unanalyzable virtue in them of which she has already told us. As that intrinsic excellence, their truth has nothing to do with our experiences. It adds nothing to the content of experience. It makes no difference to reality itself; it is supervenient, inert, static, a reflexion merely. It doesn't *exist*, it *holds* or *obtains*, it belongs to another dimension from that of either facts or fact-relations, belongs, in short, to the epistemological dimension—and with that big word rationalism closes the discussion.

Thus, just as pragmatism faces forward to the future, so does rationalism here again face backward to a past eternity. True to her inveterate habit, rationalism reverts to "principles," and thinks that when an abstraction once is named, we own an oracular solution.

. . . .

I have honestly tried to stretch my own imagination and to read the best possible meaning into the rationalist conception, but I have to confess that it still completely baffles me. The notion of a reality calling on us to "agree" with it, and that for no reasons, but simply because its claim is "unconditional" or "transcendent," is one that I can make neither head nor tail of. . . . [ed.]

Surely in this field of truth it is the pragmatists and not the rationalists who are the more genuine defenders of the universe's rationality.

# A Pluralistic Universe

. . . .

Pragmatically interpreted, pluralism or the doctrine that it is many means only that the sundry parts of reality *may be externally related.* Everything you can think of, however vast or inclusive, has on the pluralistic view a genuinely "external" environment of some sort or amount. Things are "with" one another in many ways, but nothing includes everything, or dominates over everything. The word "and" trails along after every sentence. Something always escapes. "Ever not quite" has to be said of the best attempts made anywhere in the universe at attaining all-inclusiveness. The pluralistic world is thus more like a federal republic than like an empire or a kingdom. However much may be collected, however much may report itself as present at any effective centre of consciousness or action, something else is self-governed and absent and unreduced to unity.

Monism, on the other hand, insists that when you come down to reality as such, to the reality of realities, *everything* is present to everything else in one vast instantaneous co-implicated completeness— nothing can in *any* sense, functional or substantial, be really absent from anything else, all things interpenetrate and telescope together in the great total conflux.

For pluralism, all that we are required to admit as the constitution of reality is what we ourselves find empirically realized in every minimum of finite life. Briefly it is this, that nothing real is absolutely simple, that every smallest bit of experience is a *multum in parvo* plurally related, that each relation is one aspect, character, or function, way of its being taken, or way of its taking something else; and that a bit of reality when actively engaged in one of these relations is not *by that very fact* engaged in all the other relations simultaneously. The relations are not *all* what the French call *solidaires* with one another. Without losing its identity a thing can either take up or drop another thing, like the log I spoke of, which by taking up new carriers and dropping old ones can travel anywhere with a light escort.

For monism, on the contrary, everything, whether we realize it or not, drags the whole universe along with itself and drops nothing. The log starts and arrives with all its carriers supporting it. If a thing were once disconnected, it could never be connected again, according to monism. The pragmatic difference between the two systems is thus a definite one. It is just thus, that if *a* is once out of sight of *b* or out of touch with it, or, more briefly, "out" of it at all, then, according to monism, it must always remain so, they can never get together; whereas pluralism admits that on another occasion they may work together, or in some way be connected again. Monism allows for no such things as "other occasions" in reality—in *real* or absolute reality, that is.

The difference I try to describe amounts, you see, to nothing more than the difference between what I formerly called the each-form and the all-form of reality. Pluralism lets things really exist in the each-form or distributively. Monism thinks that the all-form or collective-unit form is the only form that is rational. The all-form allows of no taking up and dropping of connexions, for in the all the parts are essentially and eternally co-implicated. In the each-form, on the contrary, a thing may be connected by intermediary things, with a thing with which it has no immediate or essential connexion. It is thus at all times in many possible connexions which are not necessarily actualized at the moment. They depend on which actual path of intermediation it may functionally strike into: the word "or" names a genuine reality. Thus, as I speak here, I may look ahead *or* to the right *or* to the left, and in either case the intervening space and air and ether enable me to see the faces of a different portion of this audience. My being here is independent of any one set of these faces.

If the each-form be the eternal form of reality no less than it is the form of temporal appearance, we still have a coherent world, and not an incarnate incoherence, as is charged by so many absolutists. Our "multiverse" still makes a "universe"; for every part, tho it may not be in actual or immediate connexion, is nevertheless in some possible or mediated connexion, with every other part however remote, through the fact that each part hangs together with its very next neighbors in inextricable interfusion. The type of union, it is true, is different here from the monistic type of *all-einheit*. It is not a universal co-implication, or integration of all things *durcheinander*. It is what I call the strung-along type, the type of continuity, contiguity, or concatenation. If you prefer greek words, you may call it the synechistic type. At all events, you see that it forms a definitely conceivable alternative to the through-and-through unity of all things at once, which is the type opposed to it by monism. You see also that it stands or falls with the notion I have taken such pains to defend, of the through-and-through union of adjacent minima of experience, of the confluence of every passing moment of concretely felt experience with its immediately next neighbors. The recognition of this fact of coalescence of next with next in concrete experience, so that all the insulating cuts we make there are artificial products of the conceptualizing faculty, is what distinguishes the empiricism which I call "radical," from the bugaboo empiricism of the traditional rationalist critics, which (rightly or wrongly) is accused of chopping up experience into atomistic sensations, incapable of union with one another until a purely intellectual principle has swooped down upon them from on high and folded them in its own conjunctive categories. Here, then, you have the plain alternative, and the full mystery of the difference between pluralism and monism, as clearly as I can set it forth on this occasion. It packs up into a nutshell:—Is the manyness in oneness that indubitably characterizes the world we inhabit, a property only of the absolute whole of things, so that you must postulate that one-enormous-whole indivisibly as the *prius* of there being any many at all—in other words, start with the rationalistic block-universe, entire, unmitigated, and complete?—or can the finite elements have their own aboriginal forms of manyness in oneness, and where they have no immediate oneness still be continued into one another by intermediary terms—each one of these terms being one with its next neighbors, and yet the total "oneness" never getting absolutely complete?

The alternative is definite. It seems to me, moreover, that the two horns of it make pragmatically different ethical appeals—at least they *may* do so, to certain individuals. But if you consider the pluralistic horn to be intrinsically irrational, self-contradictory, and absurd, I can now say no more in its defence. Having done what I could in my earlier lectures to break the edge of the intellectualistic *reductiones ad absurdum*, I must leave the issue in your hands. Whatever I may say, each of you will be sure to take pluralism or leave it, just as your own sense of rationality moves and inclines. The only thing I emphatically insist upon is that it is a fully co-ordinate, hypothesis with monism. This world *may*, in the last resort, be a block-universe; but on the other hand it *may* be a universe only strung-along, not rounded in and closed. Reality *may* exist distributively just as it sensibly seems to, after all. On that possibility I do insist.

One's general vision of the probable usually decides such alternatives. They illustrate what I once wrote of as the "will to believe." In some of my lectures at Harvard I have spoken of what I call the "faith-ladder," as something quite different from the *sorites* of the logic-books, yet seeming to have an analogous form. I think you will quickly recognize in yourselves, as I describe it, the mental process to which I give this name.

A conception of the world arises in you somehow, no matter how. Is it true or not? you ask.

It *might* be true somewhere, you say, for it is not self-contradictory.

It *may* be true, you continue, even here and now.

It is *fit* to be true, it would be *well if it were true*, it *ought* to be true, you presently feel.

It *must* be true, something persuasive in you whispers next; and then—as a final result—

It shall be *held for true*, you decide; it *shall be* as if true, for *you*.

And your acting thus may in certain special cases be a means of making it securely true in the end.

Not one step in this process is logical, yet it is the way in which monists and pluralists alike espouse and hold fast to their visions. It is life exceeding logic, it is the practical reason for which the theoretic reason finds arguments after the conclusion is once there. In just this way do some of us hold to the unfinished pluralistic universe; in just this way do others hold to the timeless universe eternally complete.

Meanwhile the incompleteness of the pluralistic universe, thus assumed and held to as the most probable hypothesis, is also represented by the pluralistic philosophy, as being self-reparative through us, as getting its disconnections remedied in part by our behavior. "We use what we are and have, to know; and what we know, to be and have still more."* Thus do philosophy and reality, theory and action, work in the same circle indefinitely.

*Blondel: *Annales de Philosophie Chrétienne*, June, 1906, p. 241.

# The Meaning of Truth

The pivotal part of my book named *Pragmatism* is its account of the relation called "truth" which may obtain between an idea (opinion, belief, statement, or what not) and its object.

. . . .

This account of truth, following upon the similar ones given by Messrs. Dewey and Schiller, has occasioned the liveliest discussion. Few critics have defended it, most of them have scouted it. It seems evident that the subject is a hard one to understand, under its apparent simplicity; and evident also, I think, that the definitive settlement of it will mark a turning-point in the history of epistemology, and consequently in that of general philosophy. . . . [ed.]

One of the accusations which I oftenest have had to meet is that of making the truth of our religious beliefs consist in their "feeling good" to us, and in nothing else. I regret to have given some excuse for this charge, by the unguarded language in which, in the book *Pragmatism*, I spoke of the truth of the belief of certain philosophers in the absolute. Explaining why I do not believe in the absolute myself . . . [ed.], yet finding that it may secure "moral holidays" to those who need them, and is true in so far forth (if to gain moral holidays be a good), I offered this as a conciliatory olive-branch to my enemies. But they, as is only too common with such offerings, trampled the gift under foot and turned and rent the giver. I had counted too much on their good will— oh for the rarity of christian charity under the sun! Oh for the rarity of ordinary secular intelligence also! I had supposed it to be matter of common observation that, of two competing views of the universe which in all other respects are equal, but of which the first denies some vital human need while the second satisfies it, the second will be favored by sane men for the simple reason that it makes the world seem more rational. To choose the first view under such circumstances would be an ascetic act, an act of philosophic self-denial of which no normal human being would be guilty. Using the pragmatic test of the meaning of concepts, I had shown the concept of the absolute to *mean* nothing but the holiday giver, the banisher of cosmic fear. One's objective deliverance, when one says "the absolute exists," amounted, on my showing, just to this, that "some justification of a feeling of security in presence of the universe," exists, and that systematically to refuse to cultivate a feeling of security would be to do violence to a tendency in one's emotional life which might well be respected as prophetic.

Apparently my absolutist critics fail to see the workings of their own minds in any such picture, so all that I can do is to apologize, and take my offering back. The absolute is true in no way then, and least of all, by the verdict of the critics, in the way which I assigned!

My treatment of "God," "freedom," and "design" was similar. Reducing, by the pragmatic test, the meaning of each of these concepts to its positive experienceable operation, I showed them all to mean the same thing, viz., the presence of "promise" in the world. "God or no God?" means "promise or no promise?" It seems to me that the alternative is objective enough, being a question as to whether the cosmos has one character or another, even though our own provisional answer be made on subjective grounds. Nevertheless christian and non-christian critics alike accuse me of summoning people to say "God exists," *even when he doesn't exist*, because forsooth in my philosophy the "truth" of the saying doesn't really mean that he exists in any shape whatever, but only that to say so feels good.

Most of the pragmatist and anti-pragmatist warfare is over what the word "truth" shall be held to signify, and not over any of the facts embodied in truth-situations; for both pragmatists and anti-pragmatists believe in existent objects, just as they believe in our ideas of them. The difference is that when the pragmatists speak of truth, they mean exclusively something about the ideas, namely their workableness; whereas when anti-pragmatists speak of truth they seem most often to mean something about the objects. Since the pragmatist, if he agrees that an idea is "really" true, also agrees to whatever it says about its object; and since most anti-pragmatists have already come round to agreeing that, if the object exists, the idea that it does so is workable; there would seem so little left to fight about that I might well be asked why instead of reprinting my share in so much verbal wrangling, I do not show my sense of "values" by burning it all up.

I understand the question and I will give my answer. I am interested in another doctrine in philosophy to which I give the name of radical empiricism, and it seems to me that the establishment of the pragmatist theory of truth is a step of first-rate importance in making radical empiricism prevail. Radical empiricism consists first of a postulate, next of a statement of fact, and finally of a generalized conclusion.

The postulate is that the only things that shall be debatable among philosophers shall be things definable in terms drawn from experience. [Things of an unexperienceable nature may exist *ad libitum*, but they form no part of the material for philosophic debate.]

The statement of fact is that the relations between things, conjunctive as well as disjunctive, are just as much matters of direct particular experience, neither more so nor less so, than the things themselves.

The generalized conclusion is that therefore the parts of experience hold together from next to next by relations that are themselves parts of experience. The directly apprehended universe needs, in short, no extraneous trans-empirical connective support, but possesses in its own right a concatenated or continuous structure.

The great obstacle to radical empiricism in the contemporary mind is the rooted rationalist belief that experience as immediately given is all disjunction and no conjunction, and that to make one world out of this separateness, a higher unifying agency must be there. In the prevalent idealism this agency is represented as the absolute all-witness which "relates" things together by throwing "categories" over them like a net. The most peculiar and unique, perhaps, of all these categories is supposed to be the truth-relation, which connects parts of reality in pairs, making of one of them a knower, and of the other a thing known, yet which is itself contentless experientially, neither describable, explicable, nor reduceable to lower terms, and denotable only by uttering the name "truth."

The pragmatist view, on the contrary, of the truth-relation is that it has a definite content, and that everything in it is experienceable. Its whole nature can be told in positive terms. The "workableness" which ideas must have, in order to be true, means particular workings, physical or intellectual, actual or possible, which they may set up from next to next inside of concrete experience. Were this pragmatic contention admitted, one great point in the victory of radical empiricism would also be scored, for the relation between an object and the idea that truly knows it, is held by rationalists to be nothing of this describable sort, but to stand outside of all possible temporal experience; and on the relation, so interpreted, rationalism is wonted to make its last most obdurate rally.

Now the anti-pragmatist contentions which I try to meet in this volume can be so easily used by rationalists as weapons of resistance, not only to pragmatism but to radical empiricism also (for if the truth-relation were transcendent, others might be so too), that I feel strongly the strategical importance of having them definitely met and got out of the way. What our critics most persistently keep saying is that though workings go with truth, yet they do not constitute it. It is numerically additional to them, prior to them, explanatory *of* them, and in no wise to be explained *by* them, we are incessantly told. The first point for our enemies to establish, therefore, is that *something* numerically additional and prior to the workings is involved in the truth of an idea. Since the *object* is additional, and usually prior, most rationalists plead *it*, and boldly accuse us of denying it. This leaves on the bystanders the impression—since we cannot reasonably deny the existence of the object—that our account of truth breaks down, and that our critics have driven us from the field. Altho in various places in this volume I try to refute the slanderous charge that we deny real existence, I will say here again, for the sake of emphasis, that the existence of the object, whenever the idea asserts it "truly," is the only reason, in innumerable cases, why the idea does work successfully, if it work at all; and that it seems an abuse of language, to say the least, to transfer the word " truth" from the idea to the object's existence, when the falsehood of ideas that won't work is explained by that existence as well as the truth of those that will.

I find this abuse prevailing among my most accomplished adver-saries. But once establish the proper verbal custom, let the word "truth" represent a property of the idea, cease to make it something mysteriously connected with the object known, and the path opens fair and wide, as I believe, to the discussion of radical empiricism on its merits. The truth of an idea will then mean only its workings, or that in it which by ordinary psychological laws sets up those workings; it will mean neither the idea's object, nor anything "salutatory" inside the idea, that terms drawn from experience cannot describe.

. . . .

PART V

# THE STRENUOUS LIFE AND ITS REWARDS

## ON SOME MENTAL EFFECTS OF THE EARTHQUAKE*

When I departed from Harvard for Stanford University last December, almost the last good-by I got was that of my old Californian friend B: "I hope they'll give you a touch of earthquake while you're there, so that you may also become acquainted with *that* Californian institution."

Accordingly, when, lying awake at about half past five on the morning of April 18 in my little "flat" on the campus of Stanford, I felt the bed begin to waggle, my first consciousness was one of gleeful recognition of the nature of the movement. "By Jove," I said to myself, "here's B's old earthquake, after all!" And then, as it went *crescendo*, "And a jolly good one it is, too!" I said.

Sitting up involuntarily, and taking a kneeling position, I was thrown down on my face as it went *fortior* shaking the room exactly as a terrier shakes a rat. Then everything that was on anything else slid off to the floor, over went bureau and chiffonier with a crash, as the *fortissimo* was reached; plaster cracked, an awful roaring noise seemed to fill the outer air, and in an instant all was still again, save the soft babble of human voices from far and near that soon began to make itself heard, as the inhabitants in costumes *negligés* in various degrees sought the greater safety of the street and yielded to the passionate desire for sympathetic communication.

The thing was over, as I understand the Lick Observatory to have declared, in forty-eight seconds. To me it felt as if about that length of time, although I have heard others say that it seemed to them longer. In my case, sensation and emotion were so strong that little thought, and no reflection or volition, were possible in the short time consumed by the phenomenon.

---

*At the time of the San Francisco earthquake the author was at Leland Stanford University nearby. He succeeded in getting into San Francisco on the morning of the earthquake, and spent the remainder of the day in the city. These observations appeared in the *Youth's Companion* for June 7, 1906.

The emotion consisted wholly of glee and admiration; glee at the vividness which such an abstract idea or verbal term as "earthquake" could put on when translated into sensible reality and verified concretely; and admiration at the way in which the frail little wooden house could hold itself together in spite of such a shaking. I felt no trace whatever of fear; it was pure delight and welcome.

"*Go* it," I almost cried aloud, "and go it *stronger!*"

I ran into my wife's room, and found that she, although awakened from sound sleep, had felt no fear, either. Of all the persons whom I later interrogated, very few had felt any fear while the shaking lasted, although many had had a "turn," as they realized their narrow escapes from bookcases or bricks from chimney-breasts falling on their beds and pillows an instant after they had left them.

As soon as I could think, I discerned retrospectively certain peculiar ways in which my consciousness had taken in the phenomenon. These ways were quite spontaneous, and, so to speak, inevitable and irresistible.

First, I personified the earthquake as a permanent individual entity. It was *the* earthquake of my friend B's augury, which had been lying low and holding itself back during all the intervening months, in order, on that lustrous April morning, to invade my room, and energize the more intensely and triumphantly. It came, moreover, directly to *me*. It stole in behind my back, and once inside the room, had me all to itself, and could manifest itself convincingly. Animus and intent were never more present in any human action, nor did any human activity ever more definitely point back to a living agent as its source and origin.

All whom I consulted on the point agreed as to this feature in their experience. "It expressed intention," "It was vicious," "It was bent on destruction," "It wanted to show its power," or what not. To me, it wanted simply to manifest the full meaning of its *name*. But what was this "It"? To some, apparently, a vague demonic power; to me an individualized being, B's earthquake, namely.

One informant interpreted it as the end of the world and the beginning of the final judgment. This was a lady in a San Francisco hotel, who did not think of its being an earthquake till after she had got into the street and some one had explained it to her. She told me that the theological interpretation had kept fear from her mind, and made her take the shaking calmly. For "science," when the tensions in the earth's crust reach the breaking-point, and strata fall into an altered equilibrium, earthquake is simply the collective *name* of all the cracks and shakings and disturbances that happen. They *are* the earthquake. But for me *the* earthquake was the *cause* of the disturbances, and the perception of it as a living agent was irresistible. It had an overpowering dramatic convincingness.

I realize now better than ever how inevitable were men's earlier mythologic versions of such catastrophes, and how artificial and against the grain of our spontaneous perceiving are the later habits into which science educates us. It was simply impossible for untutored men to take earthquakes into their minds as anything but supernatural warnings or retributions.

A good instance of the way in which the tremendousness of a catastrophe may banish fear was given me by a Stanford student. He was in the fourth story of Encina Hall, an immense stone dormitory building. Awakened from sleep, he recognized what the disturbance was, and sprang from the bed, but was thrown off his feet in a moment, while his books and furniture fell round him. Then, with an awful, sinister, grinding roar, everything gave way, and with chimneys, floor-beams, walls and all, he descended through the three lower stories of the building into the basement. "This is my end, this is my death," he felt; but all the while no trace of fear. The experience was too overwhelming for anything but passive surrender to it. (Certain heavy chimneys had fallen in, carrying the whole centre of the building with them.)

Arrived at the bottom, he found himself with rafters and débris round him, but not pinned in or crushed. He saw daylight, and crept toward it through the obstacles. Then, realizing that he was in his nightgown, and feeling no pain anywhere, his first thought was to get back to his room and find some more presentable clothing. The stairways at Encina Hall are at the ends of the building. He made his way to one of them, and went up the four flights, only to find his room no longer extant. Then he noticed pain in his feet, which had been injured, and came down the stairs with difficulty. When he talked with me ten days later he had been in hospital a week, was very thin and pale, and went on crutches, and was dressed in borrowed clothing.

So much for Stanford, where all our experiences seem to have been very similar. Nearly all our chimneys went down, some of them disintegrating from top to bottom; parlor floors were covered with bricks; plaster strewed the floors; furniture was everywhere upset and dislocated; but the wooden dwellings sprang back to their original position, and in house after house not a window stuck or a door scraped at top or bottom. Wood architecture was triumphant! Everybody was excited, but the excitement at first, at any rate, seemed to be almost joyous. Here at last was a *real* earthquake after so many years of harmless waggle! Above all, there was an irresistible desire to talk about it, and exchange experiences.

Most people slept outdoors for several subsequent nights, partly to be safer in case of a recurrence, but also to work off their emotion, and get the full unusualness out of the experience. The vocal babble of early-waking girls and boys from the gardens of the campus, mingling with the birds' songs and the exquisite weather, was for three or four days a delightful sunrise phenomenon.

Now turn to San Francisco, thirty-five miles distant, from which an automobile ere long brought us the dire news of a city in ruins, with fires beginning at various points, and the water-supply interrupted. I was fortunate enough to board the only train of cars—a very small one—that got up to the city; fortunate enough also to escape in the evening by the only train that left it. This gave me and my valiant feminine escort some four hours of observation. My business is with "subjective" phenomena exclusively; so I will say nothing of the material ruin that greeted us on every hand—the daily papers and the weekly journals have done full justice to that topic. By midday, when we reached the city, the pall of smoke was vast and the dynamite detonations had begun, but the troops, the police and the firemen seemed to have established order, dangerous neighborhoods were roped off everywhere and picketed, saloons closed, vehicles impressed, and every one at work who *could* work.

It was indeed a strange sight to see an entire population in the streets, busy as ants in an uncovered ant-hill scurrying to save their eggs and larvae. Every horse, and everything on wheels in the city, from hucksters' wagons to automobiles, was being loaded with what effects could be scraped together from houses which the advancing flames were threatening. The sidewalks were covered with well-dressed men and women, carrying baskets, bundles, valises, or dragging trunks to spots of greater temporary safety, soon to be dragged farther, as the fire kept spreading!

In the safer quarters, every doorstep was covered with the dwelling's tenants, sitting surrounded, with their more indispensable chattels, and ready to flee at a minute's notice. I think every one must have fasted on that day, for I saw no one eating. There was no appearance of general dismay, and little of chatter or of incoördinated excitement.

Every one seemed doggedly bent on achieving the job which he had set himself to perform; and the faces, although somewhat tense and set and grave, were inexpressive of emotion. I noticed only three persons overcome, two Italian women, very poor, embracing an aged fellow countrywoman, and all weeping. Physical fatigue and *seriousness* were the only inner states that one could read on countenances.

With lights forbidden in the houses, and the streets lighted only by the conflagration, it was apprehended that the criminals of San Francisco would hold high carnival on the ensuing night. But whether they feared the disciplinary methods of the United States troops, who were visible everywhere, or whether they were themselves solemnized by the immensity of the disaster, they lay low and did not "manifest," either then or subsequently.

The only very discreditable thing to human nature that occurred was later, when hundreds of lazy "bummers" found that they could keep camping in the parks, and make alimentary storage-batteries of their stomachs, even in some cases getting enough of the free rations in their huts or tents to last them well into the summer. This charm of pauperized vagabondage seems all along to have been Satan's most serious bait to human nature. There was theft from the outset, but confined, I believe, to petty pilfering.

Cash in hand was the only money, and millionaires and their families were no better off in this respect than any one. Whoever got a vehicle could have the use of it; but the richest often went without, and spent the first two nights on rugs on the bare ground, with nothing but what their own arms had rescued. Fortunately, those nights were dry and comparatively warm, and Californians are accustomed to camping conditions in the summer, so suffering from exposure was less great than it would have been elsewhere. By the fourth night, which was rainy, tents and huts had brought most campers under cover.

I went through the city again eight days later. The fire was out, and about a quarter of the area stood unconsumed. Intact skyscrapers dominated the smoking level majestically and superbly—they and a few walls that had survived the overthrow. Thus has the courage of our architects and builders received triumphant vindication!

The inert elements of the population had mostly got away, and those that remained seemed what Mr. H. G. Wells calls "efficients." Sheds were already going up as temporary starting-points of business. Every one looked cheerful, in spite of the awful discontinuity of past and future, with every familiar association with material things dissevered; and the discipline and order were practically perfect.

As these notes of mine must be short, I had better turn to my more generalized reflections.

Two things in retrospect strike me especially, and are the most emphatic of all my impressions. Both are reassuring as to human nature. The first of these was the rapidity of the improvisation of order out of chaos. It is clear that just as in every thousand human beings there will be statistically so many artists, so many athletes, so many thinkers, and so many potentially good soldiers, so there will be so many potential organizers in times of emergency. In point of fact, not only in the great city, but in the outlying towns, these natural ordermakers, whether amateurs or officials, came to the front immediately. There seemed to be no possibility which there was not some one there to think of, or which within twenty-four hours was not in some way provided for.

A good illustration is this: Mr. Keith is the great landscape-painter of the Pacific slope, and his pictures, which are many, are artistically and pecuniarily precious. Two citizens, lovers of his work, early in the day diverted their attention from all other interests, their own private ones included, and made it their duty to visit every place which they knew to contain a Keith painting. They cut them from their frames, rolled them up, and in this way got all the more important ones into a place of safety.

When they then sought Mr. Keith, to convey the joyous news to him, they found him still in his studio, which was remote from the fire, beginning a new painting. Having given up his previous work for lost, he had resolved to lose no time in making what amends he could for the disaster.

The completeness of organization at Palo Alto, a town of ten thousand inhabitants close to Stanford University, was almost comical. People feared exodus on a large scale of the rowdy elements of San Francisco. In point of fact, very few refugees came to Palo Alto. But within twenty-four hours, rations, clothing, hospital, quarantine, disinfection, washing, police, military, quarters in camp and in houses, printed information, employment, all were provided for under the care of so many volunteer committees.

Much of this readiness was American, much of it Californian; but I believe that every country in a similar crisis would have displayed it in a way to astonish the spectators. Like soldiering, it lies always latent in human nature.

The second thing that struck me was the universal equanimity. We soon got letters from the East, ringing with anxiety and pathos; but I now know fully what I have always believed, that the pathetic way of feeling great disasters belongs rather to the point of view of people at a distance than to the immediate victims. I heard not a single really pathetic or sentimental word in California expressed by any one.

The terms "awful," "dreadful" fell often enough from people's lips, but always with a sort of abstract meaning, and with a face that seemed to admire the vastness of the catastrophe as much as it bewailed its cuttingness. When talk was not directly practical, I might almost say that it expressed (at any rate in the nine days I was there) a tendency more toward nervous excitement than toward grief. The hearts concealed private bitterness enough, no doubt, but the tongues disdained to dwell on the misfortunes of self, when almost everybody one spoke to had suffered equally.

Surely the cutting edge of all our usual misfortunes comes from their character of loneliness. We lose our health, our wife or children die, our house burns down, or our money is made way with, and the world goes on rejoicing, leaving us on one side and counting us out from all its business. In California every one, to some degree, was suffering, and one's private miseries were merged in the vast general sum of privation and in the all-absorbing practical problem of general recuperation. The cheerfulness, or, at any rate, the steadfastness of tone, was universal. Not a single whine or plaintive word did I hear from the hundred losers whom I spoke to. Instead of that there was a temper of helpfulness beyond the counting.

It is easy to glorify this as something characteristically American, or especially Californian. Californian education has, of course, made the thought of all possible recuperations easy. In an exhausted country, with no marginal resources, the outlook on the future would be much darker. But I like to think that what I write of is a normal and universal trait of human nature. In our drawing-rooms and offices we wonder how people ever *do* go through battles, sieges and shipwrecks. We quiver and sicken in imagination, and think those heroes superhuman. Physical pain, whether suffered alone or in company, is always more or less unnerving and intolerable. But mental pathos and anguish, I fancy, are usually effects of distance. At the place of action, where all are concerned together, healthy animal insensibility and heartiness take their place. At San Francisco the need will continue to be awful, and there will doubtless be a crop of nervous wrecks before the weeks and months are over, but meanwhile the commonest men, simply because they are men, will go on, singly and collectively, showing this admirable fortitude of temper.

# The Energies of Men[*]

. . . .

I wish to spend this hour on one conception of functional psychology, a conception never once mentioned or heard of in laboratory circles, but used perhaps more than any other by common, practical men—I mean the conception of the *amount of energy available* for running one's mental and moral operations by. Practically every one knows in his own person the difference between the days when the tide of this energy is high in him and those when it is low, though no one knows exactly what reality the term energy covers when used here, or what its tides, tensions, and levels are in themselves. This vagueness is probably the reason why our scientific psychologists ignore the conception altogether. It undoubtedly connects itself with the energies of the nervous system, but it presents fluctuations that cannot easily be translated into neural terms. It offers itself as the notion of a quantity, but its ebbs and floods produce extraordinary qualitative results. To have its level raised is the most important thing that can happen to a man, yet in all my reading I know of no single page or paragraph of a scientific psychology book in which it receives mention—the psychologists have left it to be treated by the moralists and mind-curers and doctors exclusively.

Every one is familiar with the phenomenon of feeling more or less alive on different days. Every one knows on any given day that there are energies slumbering in him which the incitements of that day do not call forth, but which he might display if these were greater. Most of us feel as if we lived habitually with a sort of cloud weighing on us, below our highest notch of clearness in discernment, sureness in reasoning, or firmness in deciding. Compared with what we ought to be, we are only half-awake. Our fires are damped, our drafts are checked. We are making use of only a small part of our possible mental and physical resources. In some persons this sense of being cut off from their rightful resources is

---

[*]Delivered as the Presidential Address before the American Philosophical Association at Columbia University, December 28, 1906.

extreme, and we then get the formidable neurasthenic and psychasthenic conditions, with life grown into one tissue of impossibilities, that the medical books describe.

Part of the imperfect vitality under which we labor can be explained by scientific psychology. It is the result of the inhibition exerted by one part of our ideas on other parts. Conscience makes cowards of us all. Social conventions prevent us from telling the truth after the fashion of the heroes and heroines of Bernard Shaw. Our scientific respectability keeps us from exercising the mystical portions of our nature freely. If we are doctors, our mind-cure sympathies, if we are mind-curists, our medical sympathies are tied up. We all know persons who are models of excellence, but who belong to the extreme philistine type of mind. So deadly is their intellectual respectability that we can't converse about certain subjects at all, can't let our minds play over them, can't even mention them in their presence. I have numbered among my dearest friends persons thus inhibited intellectually, with whom I would gladly have been able to talk freely about certain interests of mine, certain authors, say, as Bernard Shaw, Chesterton, Edward Carpenter, H. G. Wells, but it wouldn't do, it made them too uncomfortable, they wouldn't play, I had to be silent. An intellect thus tied down by literality and decorum makes on one the same sort of impression that an able-bodied man would who should habituate himself to do his work with only one of his fingers, locking up the rest of his organism and leaving it unused. . . . [ed.]

The existence of reservoirs of energy that habitually are not tapped is most familiar to us in the phenomenon of "second wind." Ordinarily we stop when we meet the first effective layer, so to call it, of fatigue. We have then walked, played, or worked "enough" and desist. That amount of fatigue is an efficacious obstruction, on this side of which our usual life is cast. But if an unusual necessity forces us to press onward, a surprising thing occurs. The fatigue gets worse up to a certain critical point, when gradually or suddenly it passes away, and we are fresher than before. We have evidently tapped a level of new energy, masked until then by the fatigue-obstacle usually obeyed. There may be layer after layer of this experience. A third and a fourth "wind" may supervene. Mental activity shows the phenomenon as well as physical, and in exceptional cases we may find, beyond the very extremity of fatigue distress, amounts of ease and power that we never dreamed ourselves to own, sources of strength habitually not taxed at all, because habitually we never push through the obstruction, never pass those early critical points.

When we do pass, what makes us do so ?

Either some unusual stimulus fills us with emotional excitement, or some unusual idea of necessity induces us to make an extra effort of will. *Excitements, ideas, and efforts,* in a word, are what carry us over the dam.

In those hyperesthetic conditions which chronic invalidism so often brings in its train, the dam has changed its normal place. The pain-threshold is abnormally near. The slightest functional exercise gives a distress which the patient yields to and stops. In such cases of "habit-neurosis" a new range of power often comes in consequence of the bullying-treatment, of efforts which the doctor obliges the patient, against his will, to make. First comes the very extremity of distress, then follows unexpected relief. There seems no doubt that we are each and all of us to some extent victims of habit-neurosis. We have to admit the wider potential range and the habitually narrow actual use. We live subject to inhibition by degrees of fatigue which we have come only from habit to obey. Most of us may learn to push the barrier farther off, and to live in perfect comfort on much higher levels of power. . . . [ed.]

The excitements that carry us over the usually effective dam are most often the classic emotional ones, love, anger, crowd-contagion, or despair. Life's vicissitudes bring them in abundance. . . . [ed.]

. . . [ed.] People must have been appalled lately in San Francisco to find the stores of bottled up energy and endurance they possessed.

Wars, of course, and shipwrecks, are the great revealers of what men and women are able to do and bear.

. . . .

Such experiences show how profound is the alternation in the manner in which, under excitement, our organism will sometimes perform its physiological work. The metabolisms become different when the reserves have to be used, and for weeks and months the deeper use may go on. . . . [ed.]

. . . [ed.] We are all to some degree oppressed, unfree. We don't come to our own. It is there, but we don't get at it. The threshold must be made to shift. Then many of us find that an excentric activity—a "spree," say—relieves. There is no doubt that to some men sprees and excesses or almost any kind are medicinal, temporarily at any rate, in spite of what the moralists and doctors say.

But when the normal tasks and stimulations of life don't put a man's deeper levels of energy on tap, and he requires distinctly deleterious excitements, his constitution verges on the abnormal. The normal opener of deeper and deeper levels of energy is the will. The difficulty is to use it; to make the effort which the word volition implies. But if we *do* make it (or if a god, though he were only the god Chance, makes it through us), it will act dynamogenically on us for a month. It is notorious that a single successful effort of moral volition, such as saying "no" to some habitual temptation, or performing some courageous act, will launch a man on a higher level of energy for days and weeks, will give him a new range of power.

The emotions and excitements due to usual situations are the usual inciters of the will. But these act discontinuously; and in the intervals the shallower levels of life tend to close in and shut us off. Accordingly the best practical knowers of the human soul have invented the thing known as methodical ascetic discipline to keep the deeper levels constantly in reach. Beginning with easy tasks, passing to harder ones, and exercising day by day, it is, I believe, admitted that disciples of asceticism can reach very high levels of freedom and power of will.

Ignatius Loyola's spiritual exercises must have produced this result in innumerable devotees. But the most venerable ascetic system, and the one whose results have the most voluminous experimental corroboration, is undoubtedly the Yoga system in Hindostan. From time immemorial, by Hatha Yoga, Raja Yoga, Karma Yoga, or whatever code of practice it might be, Hindu aspirants to perfection have trained themselves, month in and out, for years. The result claimed, and certainly in many cases accorded by impartial judges, is strength of character, personal power, unshakability of soul. But it is not easy to disentangle fact from

tradition in Hindu affairs. So I am glad to have a European friend who has submitted to Hatha Yoga training, and whose account of the results I am privileged to quote. I think you will appreciate the light it throws on the question of our unused reservoirs of power.
[Here follows the friend's account.—ed.]

. . . .

I wrote to him that I couldn't possibly attribute any sacramental value to the particular Hatha Yoga processes, the postures, breathings, fastings, and the like, and that they seemed to me but so many manners, available in his case and his chela's, but not for everybody, of breaking through the barriers which life's routine had concreted round the deeper strata of the will, and gradually bringing its unused energies into action.

He replied as follows: "You are quite right that the Yoga exercises are nothing else than a methodical way of increasing our will. Because we are unable to will at once the most difficult things, we must imagine steps leading to them. Breathing being the easiest of the bodily activities, it is very natural that it offers a good scope for exercise of will. The control of thought could be gained without breathing-discipline, but it is simply easier to control thought simultaneously with the control of breath. Anyone who can think clearly and persistently of one thing needs not breathing exercises. You are quite right that we are not using all our power and that we often learn how much we *can* only when we *must*. . . . The power that we do not use up completely can be brought [more and more] into use by what we call *faith*. Faith is like the manometer of the will, registering its pressure. . . . [ed.]

Allowance made for every enthusiasm and exaggeration, there can be no doubt of my friend's regeneration—relatively, at any rate. . . . [ed.] There is, in fact, no doubt that profound modification has occurred in the running of his mental machinery. The gearing has changed, and his will is available otherwise than it was. Available without any new ideas, beliefs, or emotions, so far as I can make out, having been implanted in him. He is simply more balanced where he was more unbalanced.

You will remember that he speaks of faith, calling it a "manometer" of the will. It sounds more natural to call our will the manometer of our faiths. Ideas set free beliefs, and the beliefs set free our wills (I use these terms with no pretension to be "psychological"), so the will-acts register the faith-pressure within. Therefore, having considered the liberation of our stored-up energy by emotional excitements and by efforts, whether methodical or unmethodical, I must now say a word about *ideas* as our third great dynamogenic agent. Ideas contradict other ideas and keep us from believing them. An idea that thus negates a first idea may itself in turn be negated by a third idea, and the first idea may thus regain its natural influence over our belief and determine our behavior. Our philosophic and religious development proceeds thus by credulities, negations, and the negating of negations.

But whether for arousing or for stopping belief, ideas may fail to be efficacious, just as a wire at one time alive with electricity, may at another time be dead. Here our insight into causes fails us, and we can only note results in general terms. In general, whether a given idea shall be a live idea, depends more on the person into whose mind it is injected than on the idea itself. The whole history of "suggestion" opens out here. Which are the suggestive ideas for this person, and which for that? Beside the susceptibilities determined by one's education and by one's original peculiarities of character, there are lines along which men simply as men tend to be inflammable by ideas. As certain objects naturally awaken love, anger, or cupidity, so certain ideas naturally awaken the energies of loyalty, courage, endurance, or devotion. When these ideas are effective in an individual's life, their effect is often very great indeed. They may transfigure it, unlocking innumerable powers which, but for the idea, would never have come into play. "Fatherland," "The Union," "Holy Church," the "Monroe Doctrine," "Truth," "Science," "Liberty," Garibaldi's phrase "Rome or Death," etc., are so many examples of energy-releasing abstract ideas. The *social* nature of all such phrases is an essential factor of their dynamic power. They are forces of detent in situations in which no other force produces equivalent effects, and each is a force of detent only in a specific group of men.

The memory that an oath or vow has been made will nerve one to abstinences and efforts otherwise impossible: witness the "pledge" in the history of the temperance movement. A mere promise to his sweetheart will clean up a youth's life all over—at any rate for a time. For such effects an educated susceptibility is required. The idea of one's "honour," for example, unlocks energy only in those who have had the education of a gentleman, so called.

That delightful being, Prince Pueckler-Muskau, writes to his wife from England that he has invented "a sort of artificial resolution respecting things that are difficult of performance." " My device," he says, "is this: I give my word of honour most solemnly to myself to do or to leave undone this or that. I am of course extremely cautious in the use of this expedient, but when once the word is given, even though I afterwards think I have been precipitate or mistaken, I hold it to be perfectly irrevocable, whatever inconveniences I foresee likely to result. If I were capable of breaking my word after such mature consideration, I should lose all respect for myself—and what man of sense would not prefer death to such an alternative? . . . When the mysterious formula is pronounced, no alteration in my own views, nothing short of physical impossibility, must, for the welfare of my soul, alter my will. . . . I find something very satisfactory in the thought that man has the power of framing such props and weapons out of the most trivial materials, indeed out of nothing, merely by the force of his will, which thereby truly deserves the name of omnipotent."*

*Conversions*, whether they be political, scientific, philosophic, or religious, form another way in which bound energies are let loose. They unify, and put a stop to ancient mental interferences. The result is freedom, and often a great enlargement of power. A belief that thus settles upon an individual always acts as a challenge to his will. But, for the particular challenge to operate, he must be the right challeng*ee*. In religious conversions we have so fine an adjustment that the idea may be in the mind of the challengee for years before it exerts effects; and why it should do so then is often so far from obvious that the event is taken for a miracle of grace, and not a natural occurrence. Whatever it is, it may be a highwater mark of energy, in which "noes," once impossible, are easy, and in which a new range of "yeses" gain the right of way.

---

*Tour in England, Ireland, and France*, Philadelphia, 1833, p. 435.

. . . .

I have thus brought a pretty wide induction to bear upon my thesis, and it appears to hold good. The human individual lives usually far within his limits; he possesses powers of various sorts which he habitually fails to use. He energizes below his maximum, and he behaves below his optimum. In elementary faculty, in coordination, in power of inhibition and control, in every conceivable way, his life is contracted like the field of vision of an hysteric subject—but with less excuse, for the poor hysteric is diseased, while in the rest of us it is only an inveterate *habit*—the habit of inferiority to our full self—that is bad.

Expressed in this vague manner, everyone must admit my thesis to be true. The terms have to remain vague; for though every man of woman born knows what is meant by such phrases as having a good vital tone, a high tide of spirits, an elastic temper, as living energetically, working easily, deciding firmly, and the like, we should all be put to our trumps if asked to explain in terms of scientific psychology just what such expressions mean. We can draw some child-like psychophysical diagrams, and that is all. In physics the conception of "energy" is perfectly defined. It is correlated with the conception of "work." But mental work and moral work, although we cannot live without talking about them, are terms as yet hardly analyzed, and doubtless mean several heterogeneous elementary things. Our muscular work is a voluminous physical quantity, but our ideas and volitions are minute forces of release, and by "work" here we mean the substitution of higher *kinds* for lower *kinds* of detent. Higher and lower here are qualitative terms, not translatable immediately into quantities, unless indeed they should prove to mean newer or older forms of cerebral organization, and unless newer should then prove to mean cortically more superficial, older, cortically more deep. Some anatomists, as you know, have pretended this; but it is obvious that the intuitive or popular idea of mental work, fundamental and absolutely indispensable as it is in our lives, possesses no degree whatever of scientific clearness to-day.

Here, then, is the first problem that emerges from our study. Can any one of us refine upon the conceptions of mental work and mental energy, so as later to be able to throw some definitely analytic light on what we mean by "having a more elastic moral tone," or by "using higher levels of power and will"? I imagine that we may have to wait long before progress in this direction is made. The problem is too homely; one doesn't see just how to get in the electric keys and revolving drums that alone make psychology scientific to-day.

My fellow-pragmatist in Florence, G. Papini, has adopted a new conception of philosophy. He calls it the *doctrine of action* in the widest sense, the study of all human powers and means (among which latter, *truths* of every kind whatsoever figure, of course, in the first rank). From this point of view philosophy is a *Pragmatic*, comprehending, as tributary departments of itself, the old disciplines of logic, metaphysic, physic, and ethic.

And here, after our first problem, two other problems burst upon our view. My belief that these two problems form a program of work well worthy of the attention of a body as learned and earnest as this audience, is, in fact, what has determined me to choose this subject, and to drag you through so many familiar facts during the hour that has sped.

The first of the two problems is *that of our powers*, the second *that of our means*. We ought somehow to get a topographic survey made of the limits of human power in every conceivable direction, something like an ophthalmologist's chart of the limits of the human field of vision; and we ought then to construct a methodical inventory of the paths of access, or keys, differing with the diverse types of individual, to the different kinds of power. This would be an absolutely concrete study, to be carried on by using historical and biographical material mainly. The limits of power must be limits that have been realized in actual persons, and the various ways of unlocking the reserves of power must have been exemplified in individual lives. Laboratory experimentation can play but a small part. Your psychologist's *Versuchsthier*, outside of hypnosis, can never be called on to tax his energies in ways as extreme as those which the emergencies of life will force on him.

So here is a program of concrete individual psychology, at which anyone in some measure may work. It is replete with interesting facts, and points to practical issues superior in importance to anything we know. I urge it therefore upon your consideration. In some shape we have all worked at it in a more or less blind and fragmentary way; yet before Papini mentioned it I had never thought of it, or heard it broached by anyone, in the generalized form of a program such as I now suggest, a program that might with proper care be made to cover the whole field of psychology, and might show us parts of it in a very fresh light.

It is just the generalizing of the problem that seems to me to make so strong an appeal. I hope that in some of you the conception may unlock unused reservoirs of investigating power.

# THE MORAL EQUIVALENT OF WAR*

The war against war is going to be no holiday excursion or camping party. The military feelings are too deeply grounded to abdicate their place among our ideals until better substitutes are offered than the glory and shame that come to nations as well as to individuals from the ups and downs of politics, and the vicissitudes of trade. There is something highly paradoxical in the modern man's relation to war. Ask all our millions, north and south, whether they would vote now (were such a thing possible) to have our war for the Union expunged from history, and the record of a peaceful transition to the present time substituted for that of its marches and battles, and probably hardly a handful of eccentrics would say yes. Those ancestors, those efforts, those memories and legends, are the most ideal part of what we now own together, a sacred spiritual possession worth more than all the blood poured out. Yet ask those same people whether they would be willing in cold blood to start another civil war now to gain another similar possession, and not one man or woman would vote for the proposition. In modern eyes, precious though wars may be, they must not be waged solely for the sake of the ideal harvest. Only when forced upon one, only when an enemy's injustice leaves us no alternative, is a war now thought permissible.

It was not thus in ancient times. The earlier men were hunting men, and to hunt a neighboring tribe, kill the males, loot the village and possess the females, was the most profitable, as well as the most exciting, way of living. Thus were the more martial tribes selected, and in chiefs and peoples a pure pugnacity and love of glory came to mingle with the more fundamental appetite for plunder.

Modern war is so expensive that we feel trade to be a better avenue to plunder; but modern man inherits all the innate pugnacity and all the love of glory of his ancestors. Showing war's irrationality and horror is of no effect upon him. The horrors make the fascination. War is the

---

*Written for and first published by the Association for International Conciliation (Leaflet No. 27) [February, 1910] and also published in *Maclure's Magazine*, August, 1910, and *The Popular Science Monthly*, October, 1910.

*strong* life; it is life *in extremis*; war-taxes are the only ones men never hesitate to pay, as the budgets of all nations show us.

History is a bath of blood. The *Iliad* is one long recital of how Diomedes and Ajax, Sarpedon and Hector *killed*. No detail of the wounds they made is spared us, and the Greek mind fed upon the story. Greek history is a panorama of jingoism and imperialism—war for war's sake, all the citizens being warriors. It is horrible reading, because of the irrationality of it all—save for the purpose of making "history"—and the history is that of the utter ruin of a civilization in intellectual respects perhaps the highest the earth has ever seen.

Those wars were purely piratical. Pride, gold, women, slaves, excitement, were their only motives. In the Peloponnesian war, for example, the Athenians ask the inhabitants of Melos (the island where the "Venus of Milo" was found), hitherto neutral, to own their lordship. The envoys meet, and hold a debate which Thucydides gives in full, and which, for sweet reasonableness of form, would have satisfied Matthew Arnold. "The powerful exact what they can," said the Athenians, "and the weak grant what they must." When the Meleans say that sooner than be slaves they will appeal to the gods, the Athenians reply: "Of the gods we believe and of men we know that, by a law of their nature, wherever they can rule they will. This law was not made by us, and we are not the first to have acted upon it; we did but inherit it, and we know that you and all mankind, if you were as strong as we are, would do as we do. So much for the gods; we have told you why we expect to stand as high in their good opinion as you." Well, the Meleans still refused, and their town was taken. "The Athenians," Thucydides quietly says, "thereupon put to death all who were of military age and made slaves of the women and children. They then colonized the island, sending thither five hundred settlers of their own."

Alexander's career was piracy pure and simple, nothing but an orgy of power and plunder, made romantic by the character of the hero. There was no rational principle in it, and the moment he died his generals and governors attacked one another. The cruelty of those times is incredible. When Rome finally conquered Greece, Paulus Aemilius was told by the Roman Senate to reward his soldiers for their toil by "giving" them the old kingdom of Epirus. They sacked seventy cities and carried off a hundred and fifty thousand inhabitants as slaves. How many they killed I know not; but in Etolia they killed all the senators, five hundred and fifty in number. Brutus was "the noblest Roman of them all," but to reanimate his soldiers on the eve of Philippi he similarly promises to give them the cities of Sparta and Thessalonica to ravage, if they win the fight.

Such was the gory nurse that trained societies to cohesiveness. We inherit the warlike type; and for most of the capacities of heroism that the human race is full of we have to thank this cruel history. Dead men tell no tales, and if there were any tribes of other type than this they have left no survivors. Our ancestors have bred pugnacity into our bone and marrow, and thousands of years of peace won't breed it out of us. The popular imagination fairly fattens on the thought of wars. Let public opinion once reach a certain fighting pitch, and no ruler can withstand it. In the Boer war both governments began with bluff but couldn't stay there, the military tension was too much for them. In 1898 our people had read the word "WAR" in letters three inches high for three months in every newspaper. The pliant politician McKinley was swept away by their eagerness, and our squalid war with Spain became a necessity.

At the present day, civilized opinion is a curious mental mixture. The military instincts and ideals are as strong as ever, but are confronted by reflective criticisms which sorely curb their ancient freedom. Innumerable writers are showing up the bestial side of military service. Pure loot and mastery seem no longer morally avowable motives, and pretexts must be found for attributing them solely to the enemy. England and we, our army and navy authorities repeat without ceasing, arm solely for "peace," Germany and Japan it is who are bent on loot and glory. "Peace" in military mouths to-day is a synonym for "war expected." The word has become a pure provocative, and no government wishing peace sincerely should allow it ever to be printed in a newspaper. Every up-to-date dictionary should say that "peace" and "war" mean the same thing, now *in posse*, now *in actu*. It may even reasonably be said that the intensely sharp competitive *preparation* for war by the nations *is the real war*, permanent, unceasing; and that the battles are only a sort of public verification of the mastery gained during the "peace"-interval.

It is plain that on this subject civilized man has developed a sort of double personality. If we take European nations, no legitimate interest of any one of them would seem to justify the tremendous destructions which a war to compass it would necessarily entail. It would seem as though common sense and reason ought to find a way to reach agreement in every conflict of honest interests. I myself think it our bounden duty to believe in such international rationality as possible. But, as things stand, I see how desperately hard it is to bring the peace-party and the war-party together, and I believe that the difficulty is due to certain deficiencies in the program of pacificism which set the militarist imagination strongly, and to a certain extent justifiably, against it. In the whole discussion both sides are on imaginative and sentimental ground. It is but one utopia against another, and everything one says must be abstract and hypothetical. Subject to this criticism and caution, I will try to characterize in abstract strokes the opposite imaginative forces, and point out what to my own very fallible mind seems the best utopian hypothesis, the most promising line of conciliation.

In my remarks, pacificist though I am, I will refuse to speak of the bestial side of the war-régime (already done justice to by many writers) and consider only the higher aspects of militaristic sentiment. Patriotism no one thinks discreditable; nor does any one deny that war is the romance of history. But inordinate ambitions are the soul of every patriotism, and the possibility of violent death the soul of all romance. The militarily patriotic and romantic-minded everywhere, and especially the professional military class, refuse to admit for a moment that war may be a transitory phenomenon in social evolution. The notion of a sheep's paradise like that revolts, they say, our higher imagination. Where then would be the steeps of life? If war had ever stopped, we should have to reinvent it, on this view, to redeem life from flat degeneration.

Reflective apologists for war at the present day all take it religiously. It is a sort of sacrament. Its profits are to the vanquished as well as to the victor; and quite apart from any question of profit, it is an absolute good, we are told, for it is human nature at its highest dynamic. Its "horrors" are a cheap price to pay for rescue from the only alternative supposed, of a world of clerks and teachers, of co-education and zoophily, of "consumer's leagues" and "associated charities," of industrialism unlimited, and feminism unabashed. No scorn, no hardness, no valor any more! Fie upon such a cattleyard of a planet!

So far as the central essence of this feeling goes, no healthy minded person, it seems to me, can help to some degree partaking of it. Militarism is the great preserver of our ideals of hardihood, and human life with no use for hardihood would be contemptible. Without risks or prizes for the darer, history would be insipid indeed; and there is a type of military character which every one feels that the race should never cease to breed, for every one is sensitive to its superiority. The duty is incumbent on mankind of keeping military characters in stock—of keeping them, if not for use, then as ends in themselves and as pure pieces of perfection—so that Roosevelt's weaklings and mollycoddles may not end by making everything else disappear from the face of nature.

This natural sort of feeling forms, I think, the innermost soul of army-writings. Without any exception known to me, militarist authors take a highly mystical view of their subject, and regard war as a biological or sociological necessity, uncontrolled by ordinary psychological checks and motives. When the time of development is ripe the war must come, reason or no reason, for the justifications pleaded are invariably fictitious. War is, in short, a permanent human *obligation*. General Homer Lea, in his recent book *The Valor of Ignorance*, plants himself squarely on this ground. Readiness for war is for him the essence of nationality, and ability in it the supreme measure of the health of nations.

Nations, General Lea says, are never stationary—they must necessarily expand or shrink, according to their vitality or decrepitude. Japan now is culminating; and by the fatal law in question it is impossible that her statesmen should not long since have entered, with extraordinary foresight, upon a vast policy of conquest—the game in which the first moves were her wars with China and Russia and her treaty with England, and of which the final objective is the capture of the Philippines, the Hawaiian Islands, Alaska, and the whole of our Coast west of the Sierra Passes. This will give Japan what her ineluctable vocation as a state absolutely forces her to claim, the possession of the entire Pacific Ocean; and to oppose these deep designs we Americans have, according to our author, nothing but our conceit, our ignorance, our commercialism, our corruption, and our feminism. General Lea makes a minute technical comparison of the military strength which we at present could oppose to the strength of Japan, and concludes that the islands, Alaska, Oregon, and Southern California, would fall almost without resistance, that San Francisco must surrender in a fortnight to a Japanese investment, that in three or four months the war would be over, and our republic, unable to regain what it had heedlessly neglected to protect sufficiently, would then "disintegrate," until perhaps some Caesar should arise to weld us again into a nation.

A dismal forecast indeed! Yet not unplausible, if the mentality of Japan's statesmen be of the Caesarian type of which history shows so many examples, and which is all that General Lea seems able to imagine. But there is no reason to think that women can no longer be the mothers of Napoleonic or Alexandrian characters; and if these come in Japan and find their opportunity, just such surprises as *The Valor of Ignorance* paints may lurk in ambush for us. Ignorant as we still are of the innermost recesses of Japanese mentality, we may be foolhardy to disregard such possibilities.

Other militarists are more complex and more moral in their considerations. The *Philosophie des Krieges*, by S. R. Steinmetz is a good example. War, according to this author, is an ordeal instituted by God, who weighs the nations in its balance. It is the essential form of the State, and the only function in which peoples can employ all their powers at once and convergently. No victory is possible save as the resultant of a totality of virtues, no defeat for which some vice or weakness is not responsible. Fidelity, cohesiveness, tenacity, heroism, conscience, education, inventiveness, economy, wealth; physical health and vigor— there isn't a moral or intellectual point of superiority that doesn't tell, when God holds his assizes and hurls the peoples upon one another. *Die Weltgeschichte ist das Weltgericht*; and Dr. Steinmetz does not believe that in the long run chance and luck play any part in apportioning the issues.

The virtues that prevail, it must be noted, are virtues anyhow, su-periorities that count in peaceful as well as in military competition; but the strain on them, being infinitely intenser in the latter case, makes war infinitely more searching as a trial. No ordeal is comparable to its winnowings. Its dread hammer is the welder of men into cohesive states, and nowhere but in such states can human nature adequately develop its capacity. The only alternative is "degeneration."

Dr. Steinmetz is a conscientious thinker, and his book, short as it is, takes much into account. Its upshot can, it seems to me, be summed up in Simon Patten's word, that mankind was nursed in pain and fear, and that the transition to a "pleasure-economy" may be fatal to a being wielding no powers of defense against its disintegrative influences. If we speak of the *fear of emancipation from the fear-régime,* we put the whole situation into a single phrase; fear regarding ourselves now taking the place of the ancient fear of the enemy.

Turn the fear over as I will in my mind, it all seems to lead back to two unwillingnesses of the imagination, one aesthetic, and the other moral; unwillingness, first to envisage a future in which army-life, with its many elements of charm, shall be forever impossible, and in which the destinies of peoples shall nevermore be decided quickly, thrillingly, and tragically, by force, but only gradually and insipidly by "evolution"; and, secondly, unwillingness to see the supreme theatre of human strenuousness closed, and the splendid military aptitudes of men doomed to keep always in a state of latency and never show themselves in action. These insistent unwillingnesses, no less than other aesthetic and ethical insistencies have, it seems to me, to be listened to and respected. One cannot meet them effectively by mere counter-insistency on war's expensiveness and horror. The horror makes the thrill; and when the question is of getting the extremest and supremest out of human nature, talk of expense sounds ignominious. The weakness of so much merely negative criticism is evident—pacificism makes no converts from the military party. The military party denies neither the bestiality nor the horror, nor the expense; it only says that these things tell but half the story. It only says that war is *worth* them; that, taking human nature as a whole, its wars are its best protection against its weaker and more cowardly self, and that mankind cannot *afford* to adopt a peace-economy.

Pacificists ought to enter more deeply into the aesthetical and ethical point of view of their opponents. Do that first in any controversy, says J. J. Chapman, *then move the point,* and your opponent will follow.

So long as anti-militarists propose no substitute for war's disciplinary function, no *moral equivalent* of war, analogous, as one might say, to the mechanical equivalent of heat, so long they fail to realize the full inwardness of the situation. And as a rule they do fail. The duties, penalties, and sanctions pictured in the utopias they paint are all too weak and tame to touch the military-minded. Tolstoi's pacificism is the only exception to this rule, for it is profoundly pessimistic as regards all this world's values, and makes the fear of the Lord furnish the moral spur provided elsewhere by the fear of the enemy. But our socialistic peace-advocates all believe absolutely in this world's values; and instead of the fear of the Lord and the fear of the enemy, the only fear they reckon with is the fear of poverty if one be lazy. This weakness pervades all the socialistic literature with which I am acquainted. Even in Lowes Dickinson's exquisite dialogue,* high wages and short hours are the only forces invoked for overcoming man's distaste for repulsive kinds of labor. Meanwhile men at large still live as they always have lived, under a pain-and-fear economy—for those of us who live in an ease-economy are but an island in the stormy ocean—and the whole atmosphere of present-day utopian literature tastes mawkish and dishwatery to people who still keep a sense for life's more bitter flavors. It suggests, in truth, ubiquitous inferiority.

Inferiority is always with us, and merciless scorn of it is the keynote of the military temper. "Dogs, would you live forever?" shouted Frederick the Great. "Yes," say our utopians, "let us live forever, and raise our level gradually." The best thing about our "inferiors" to-day is that they are as tough as nails, and physically and morally almost as insensitive. Utopianism would see them soft and squeamish, while militarism would keep their callousness, but transfigure it into a meritorious characteristic, needed by "the service," and redeemed by that from the suspicion of inferiority. All the qualities of a man acquire dignity when he knows that the service of the collectivity that owns him needs them. If proud of the collectivity, his own pride rises in proportion. No collectivity is like an army for nourishing such pride; but it has to be confessed that the

---

* Justice and Liberty, N. Y. 1909.

only sentiment which the image of pacific cosmopolitan industrialism is capable of arousing in countless worthy breasts is shame at the idea of belonging to *such* a collectivity. It is obvious that the United States of America as they exist to-day impress a mind like General Lea's as so much human blubber. Where is the sharpness and precipitousness, the contempt for life, whether one's own, or another's? Where is the savage "yes" and "no," the unconditional duty? Where is the conscription? Where is the blood-tax? Where is anything that one feels honored by belonging to?

Having said thus much in preparation, I will now confess my own utopia. I devoutly believe in the reign of peace and in the gradual advent of some sort of a socialistic equilibrium. The fatalistic view of the war-function is to me nonsense, for I know that war-making is due to definite motives and subject to prudential checks and reasonable criticisms, just like any other form of enterprise. And when whole nations are the armies, and the science of destruction vies in intellectual refinement with the sciences of production, I see that war becomes absurd and impossible from its own monstrosity. Extravagant ambitions will have to be replaced by reasonable claims, and nations must make common cause against them. I see no reason why all this should not apply to yellow as well as to white countries, and I look forward to a future when acts of war shall be formally outlawed as between civilized peoples.

All these beliefs of mine put me squarely into the anti-militarist party. But I do not believe that peace either ought to be or will be permanent on this globe, unless the states pacifically organized preserve some of the old elements of army-discipline. A permanently successful peace-economy cannot be a simple pleasure-economy. In the more or less socialistic future towards which mankind seems drifting we must still subject ourselves collectively to those severities which answer to our real position upon this only partly hospitable globe. We must make new energies and hardihoods continue the manliness to which the military mind so faithfully clings. Martial virtues must be the enduring cement; intrepidity, contempt of softness, surrender of private interest, obedience to command, must still remain the rock upon which states are built— unless, indeed, we wish for dangerous reactions against commonwealths fit only for contempt, and liable to invite attack whenever a centre of crystallization for military-minded enterprise gets formed anywhere in their neighborhood.

The war-party is assuredly right in affirming and reaffirming that the martial virtues, although originally gained by the race through war, are absolute and permanent human goods. Patriotic pride and ambition in their military form are, after all, only specifications of a more general competitive passion. They are its first form, but that is no reason for supposing them to be its last form. Men now are proud of belonging to a conquering nation, and without a murmur they lay down their persons and their wealth, if by so doing they may fend off subjection. But who can be sure that *other aspects of one's country* may not, with time and education and suggestion enough, come to be regarded with similarly effective feelings of pride and shame? Why should men not some day feel that it is worth a blood-tax to belong to a collectivity superior in *any* ideal respect? Why should they not blush with indignant shame if the community that owns them is vile in any way whatsoever? Individuals, daily more numerous, now feel this civic passion. It is only a question of blowing on the spark till the whole population gets incandescent, and on the ruins of the old morals of military honor, a stable system of morals of civic honor builds itself up. What the whole community comes to believe in grasps the individual as in a vise. The war-function has grasped us so far; but constructive interests may some day seem no less imperative, and impose on the individual a hardly lighter burden.

Let me illustrate my idea more concretely. There is nothing to make one indignant in the mere fact that life is hard, that men should toil and suffer pain. The planetary conditions once for all are such, and we can stand it. But that so many men, by mere accidents of birth and opportunity, should have a life of *nothing else* but toil and pain and hardness and inferiority imposed upon them, should have *no* vacation, while others natively no more deserving never get any taste of this campaigning life at all—*this* is capable of arousing indignation in reflective minds. It may end by seeming shameful to all of us that some of us have nothing but campaigning, and others nothing but unmanly ease. If now—and this is my idea—there were, instead of military conscription a conscription of the whole youthful population to form for a certain number of years a part of the army enlisted against *Nature*, the injustice would tend to be evened out, and numerous other goods to the commonwealth would follow. The military ideals of hardihood and discipline would be wrought into the growing fibre of the people; no one would remain blind as the luxurious classes now are blind, to man's real relations to the globe he lives on, and to the permanently sour and hard foundations of his higher life. To coal and iron mines, to freight trains, to fishing fleets in December, to dishwashing, clothes-washing, and window-washing, to road-building and tunnel-making, to foundries and stoke-holes, and to the frames of skyscrapers, would our gilded youths be drafted off, according to their choice, to get the childishness knocked out of them, and to come back into society with healthier sympathies and soberer ideas. They would have paid their blood-tax, done their own part in the immemorial human warfare against nature; they would tread the earth more proudly, the women would value them more highly, they would be better fathers and teachers of the following generation.

Such a conscription, with the state of public opinion that would have required it, and the many moral fruits it would bear, would preserve in the midst of a pacific civilization the manly virtues which the military party is so afraid of seeing disappear in peace. We should get toughness without callousness, authority with as little criminal cruelty as possible, and painful work done cheerily because the duty is temporary, and threatens not, as now, to degrade the whole remainder of one's life. I spoke of the "moral equivalent" of war. So far, war has been the only force that can discipline a whole community, and until an equivalent discipline is organized, I believe that war must have its way. But I have no serious doubt that the ordinary prides and shames of social man, once developed to a certain intensity, are capable of organizing such a moral equivalent as I have sketched, or some other just as effective for preserving manliness of type. It is but a question of time, of skillful propagandism, and of opinion-making men seizing historic opportunities.

The martial type of character can be bred without war. Strenuous honor and disinterestedness abound elsewhere. Priests and medical men are in a fashion educated to it, and we should all feel some degree of it imperative if we were conscious of our work as an obligatory service to the stare. We should be *owned*, as soldiers are by the army, and our pride would rise accordingly. We could be poor, then, without humiliation, as army officers now are. The only thing needed henceforward is to inflame the civic temper as past history has inflamed the military temper.

[A long quotation from H. G. Wells on military discipline follows.—ed.]

. . . .

It would be simply preposterous if the only force that could work ideals of honor and standards of efficiency into English or American natures should be the fear of being killed by the Germans or the Japanese. Great indeed is Fear; but it is not, as our military enthusiasts believe and try to make us believe, the only stimulus known for awakening the higher ranges of men's spiritual energy. The amount of alteration in public opinion which my utopia postulates is vastly less than the difference between the mentality of those black warriors who pursued Stanley's party on the Congo with their cannibal war-cry of "Meat! Meat" and that of the "general-staff" of any civilized nation. History has seen the latter interval bridged over: the former one can be bridged over much more easily.

# WHAT MAKES A LIFE SIGNIFICANT?

In my previous talk, "On a Certain Blindness," I tried to make you feel how soaked and shot-through life is with values and meanings which we fail to realize because of our external and insensible point of view. The meanings are there for the others, but they are not there for us. There lies more than a mere interest of curious speculation in understanding this. It has the most tremendous practical importance. I wish that I could convince you of it as I feel it myself. It is the basis of all our tolerance, social, religious, and political. The forgetting of it lies at the root of every stupid and sanguinary mistake that rulers over subject-peoples make. The first thing to learn in intercourse with others is noninterference with their own peculiar ways of being happy, provided those ways do not assume to interfere by violence with ours. No one has insight into all the ideals. No one should presume to judge them off-hand. The pretension to dogmatize about them in each other is the root of most human injustices and cruelties, and the trait in human character most likely to make the angels weep.

Every Jack sees in his own particular Jill charms and perfections to the enchantment of which we stolid onlookers are stone-cold. And which has the superior view of the absolute truth, he or we? Which has the more vital insight into the nature of Jill's existence, as a fact? Is he in excess, being in this matter a maniac? or are we in defect, being victims of a pathological anaesthesia as regards Jill's magical importance? Surely the latter; surely to Jack are the profounder truths revealed; surely poor Jill's palpitating little life-throbs *are* among the wonders of creation, *are* worthy of this sympathetic interest; and it is to our shame that the rest of us cannot feel like Jack. For Jack realizes Jill concretely, and we do not. He struggles toward a union with her inner life, divining her feelings, anticipating her desires, understanding her limits as manfully as he can, and yet inadequately, too; for he is also afflicted with some blindness, even here. Whilst we, dead clods that we are, do not even seek after these things, but are contented that that portion of eternal fact named Jill should be for us as if it were not. Jill, who knows her inner life, knows that Jack's way of taking it—so importantly—is the true and serious way; and she responds to the truth in him by taking him truly and seriously, too. May the ancient blindness never wrap its clouds about either of them again! Where would any of *us* be, were there no one willing to know us as we really are or ready to repay us for *our* insight by making recognizant return? We ought, all of us, to realize each other in this intense, pathetic, and important way.

If you say that this is absurd, and that we cannot be in love with everyone at once, I merely point out to you that, as a matter of fact, certain persons do exist with an enormous capacity for friendship and for taking delight in other people's lives; and that such persons know more of truth than if their hearts were not so big. The vice of ordinary Jack and Jill affection is not its intensity, but its exclusions and its jealousies. Leave those out, and you see that the ideal I am holding up before you, however impracticable to-day, yet contains nothing intrinsically absurd.

We have unquestionably a great cloud-bank of ancestral blindness weighing down upon us, only transiently riven here and there by fitful revelations of the truth. It is vain to hope for this state of things to alter much. Our inner secrets must remain for the most part impenetrable by others, for beings as essentially practical as we are are necessarily short of sight. But, if we cannot gain much positive insight into one another, cannot we at least use our sense of our own blindness to make us more cautious in going over the dark places? Cannot we escape some of those hideous ancestral intolerances and cruelties, and positive reversals of the truth?

For the remainder of this hour I invite you to seek with me some principle to make our tolerance less chaotic. And, as I began my previous lecture by a personal reminiscence, I am going to ask your indulgence for a similar bit of egotism now.

A few summers ago I spent a happy week at the famous Assembly Grounds on the borders of Chautauqua Lake. The moment one treads that sacred enclosure, one feels one's self in an atmosphere of success. Sobriety and industry, intelligence and goodness, orderliness and ideality, prosperity and cheerfulness, pervade the air. It is a serious and studious picnic on a gigantic scale. Here you have a town of many thousands of inhabitants, beautifully laid out in the forest and drained, and equipped with means for satisfying all the necessary lower and most of the superfluous higher wants of man. You have a first-class college in full blast. You have magnificent music—a chorus of seven hundred voices, with possibly the most perfect open-air auditorium in the world. You have every sort of athletic exercise from sailing, rowing, swimming, bicycling, to the ball-field and the more artificial doings which the gymnasium affords. You have kindergartens and model secondary schools. You have general religious services and special club-houses for the several sects. You have perpetually running soda-water fountains, and daily popular lectures by distinguished men. You have the best of company, and yet no effort. You have no zymotic diseases, no poverty, no drunkenness, no crime, no police. You have culture, you have kindness, you have cheapness, you have equality, you have the best fruits of what mankind has fought and bled and striven for under the name of civilization for centuries. You have, in short, a foretaste of what human society might be, were it all in the light, with no suffering and no dark corners.

I went in curiosity for a day. I stayed for a week, held spell-bound by the charm and ease of everything, by the middle-class paradise, without a sin, without a victim, without a blot, without a tear.

And yet what was my own astonishment, on emerging into the dark and wicked world again, to catch myself quite unexpectedly and involuntarily saying: "Ouf! what a relief! Now for something primordial and savage, even though it were as bad as an Armenian massacre, to set the balance straight again. This order is too tame, this culture too second-rate, this goodness too uninspiring. This human drama without a villain or a pang; this community so refined that ice-cream soda-water is the utmost offering it can make to the brute animal in man; this city simmering in the tepid lakeside sun; this atrocious harmlessness of all things—I cannot abide with them. Let me take my chances again in the big outside worldly wilderness with all its sins and sufferings. There are the heights and depths, the precipices and the steep ideals, the gleams of the awful and the infinite; and there is more hope and help a thousand times than in this dead level and quintessence of every mediocrity."

Such was the sudden right-about-face performed for me by my lawless fancy! There had been spread before me the realization—on a small, sample scale of course—of all the ideals for which our civilization has been striving: security, intelligence, humanity, and order; and here was the instinctive hostile reaction, not of the natural man, but of a so-called cultivated man upon such a Utopia. There seemed thus to be a self-contradiction and paradox somewhere, which I, as a professor drawing a full salary, was in duty bound to unravel and explain, if I could.

So I meditated. And, first of all, I asked myself what the thing was that was so lacking in this Sabbatical city, and the lack of which kept one forever falling short of the higher sort of contentment. And I soon recognized that it was the element that gives to the wicked outer world all its moral style, expressiveness and picturesqueness—the element of precipitousness, so to call it, of strength and strenuousness, intensity and danger. What excites and interests the looker-on at life, what the romances and the statues celebrate and the grim civic monuments remind us of, is the everlasting battle of the powers of light with those of darkness; with heroism, reduced to its bare chance, yet ever and anon snatching victory from the jaws of death. But in this unspeakable Chautauqua there was no potentiality of death in sight anywhere, and no point of the compass visible from which danger might possibly appear. The ideal was so completely victorious already that no sign of any previous battle remained, the place just resting on its oars. But what our human emotions seem to require is the sight of the struggle going on. The moment the fruits are being merely eaten, things become ignoble. Sweat and effort, human nature strained to its uttermost and on the rack, yet getting through alive, and then turning its back on its success to pursue another more rare and arduous still—this is the sort of thing the presence of which inspires us, and the reality of which it seems to be the function of all the higher forms of literature and fine art to bring home to us and suggest. At Chautauqua there were no racks, even in the place's historical museum; and no sweat, except possibly the gentle moisture on the brow of some lecturer, or on the sides of some player in the ball-field.

Such absence of human nature *in extremis* anywhere seemed, then, a sufficient explanation for Chautauqua's flatness and lack of zest.

But was not this a paradox well calculated to fill one with dismay? It looks indeed, thought I, as if the romantic idealists with their pessimism about our civilization were, after all, quite right. An irremediable flatness is coming over the world. Bourgeoisie and mediocrity, church sociables and teachers' conventions, are taking the place of the old heights and depths and romantic chiaroscuro. And, to get human life in its wild intensity, we must in future turn more and more away from the actual, and forget it, if we can, in the romancer's or the poet's pages. The whole world, delightful and sinful as it may still appear for a moment to one just escaped from the Chautauquan enclosure, is nevertheless obeying more and more just those ideals that are sure to make of it in the end a mere Chautauqua Assembly on an enormous scale. *Was im Gesang soll leben muss im Leben untergehn.* Even now, in our own country, correctness, fairness, and compromise for every small advantage are crowding out all other qualities. The higher heroisms and the old rare flavors are passing out of life.*

With these thoughts in my mind, I was speeding with the train toward Buffalo, when, near that city, the sight of a workman doing something on the dizzy edge of a sky-scaling iron construction brought me to my senses very suddenly. And now I perceived, by a flash of insight, that I had been steeping myself in pure ancestral blindness, and looking at life with the eyes of a remote spectator. Wishing for heroism and the spectacle of human nature on the rack, I had never noticed the great fields of heroism lying round about me, I had failed to see it present and alive. I could only think of it as dead and embalmed, labelled and costumed, as it is in the pages of romance. And yet there it was before me in the daily lives of the laboring classes. Not in clanging fights and desperate marches only is heroism to be looked for, but on every railway bridge and fire-proof building that is going up to-day. On freight-trains, on the decks of vessels, in cattle-yards and mines, on lumber-rafts, among the firemen and the policemen, the demand for courage is incessant; and the supply never fails. There, every day of the year somewhere, is human nature *in extremis* for you. And wherever a scythe, an axe, a pick, or a shovel is wielded, you have it sweating and aching and with its powers of patient endurance racked to the utmost under the length of hours of the strain.

---

*This address was composed before the Cuban and Philippine wars. Such outbursts of the passion of mastery are, however, only episodes in a social process which in the long run seems everywhere tending toward the Chatauquan ideals.

As I awoke to all this unidealized heroic life around me, the scales seemed to fall from my eyes; and a wave of sympathy greater than anything I had ever before felt with the common life of common men began to fill my soul. It began to seem as if virtue with horny hands and dirty skin were the only virtue genuine and vital enough to take account of. Every other virtue poses; none is absolutely unconscious and simple, and unexpectant of decoration or recognition, like this. These are our soldiers, thought I, these our sustainers, these the very parents of our life.

Many years ago, when in Vienna, I had had a similar feeling of awe and reverence in looking at the peasant-women, in from the country on their business at the market for the day. Old hags many of them were, dried and brown and wrinkled, kerchiefed and short-petticoated, with thick wool stockings on their bony shanks, stumping through the glittering thoroughfares, looking neither to the right nor the left, bent on duty, envying nothing, humble-hearted, remote—and yet at bottom, when you came to think of it, bearing the whole fabric of the splendors and corruptions of that city on their laborious backs. For where would any of it have been without their unremitting, unrewarded labor in the fields? And so with us: not to our generals and poets, I thought, but to the Italian and Hungarian laborers in the Subway, rather, ought the monuments of gratitude and reverence of a city like Boston to be reared.

. . . .

If any of you have been readers of Tolstoi, you will see that I passed into a vein of feeling similar to his, with its abhorrence of all that conventionally passes for distinguished, and its exclusive deification of the bravery, patience, kindliness, and dumbness of the unconscious natural man.

Where now is *our* Tolstoi, I said, to bring the truth of all this home to our American bosoms, fill us with a better insight, and wean us away from that spurious literary romanticism on which our wretched culture—as it calls itself—is fed? Divinity lies all about us, and culture is too hidebound to even suspect the fact. Could a Howells or a Kipling be enlisted in this mission? or are they still too deep in the ancestral blindness, and not humane enough for the inner joy and meaning of the laborer's existence to be really revealed? Must we wait for some one born and bred and living as a laborer himself, but who, by grace of Heaven, shall also find a literary voice?

And there I rested on that day, with a sense of widening of vision, and with what it is surely fair to call an increase of religious insight into life. In God's eyes the differences of social position, of intellect, of culture, of cleanliness, of dress, which different men exhibit, and all the other rarities and exceptions on which they so fantastically pin their pride, must be so small as practically quite to vanish; and all that should remain is the common fact that here we are, a countless multitude of vessels of life, each of us pent in to peculiar difficulties, with which we must severally struggle by using whatever of fortitude and goodness we can summon up. The exercise of the courage, patience, and kindness, must be the significant portion of the whole business; and the distinctions of position can only be a manner of diversifying the phenomenal surface upon which these underground virtues may manifest their effects. At this rate, the deepest human life is everywhere, is eternal. And, if any human attributes exist only in particular individuals, they must belong to the mere trapping and decoration of the surface-show.

Thus are men's lives levelled up as well as levelled down—levelled up in their common inner meaning, levelled down in their outer gloriousness and show. Yet always, we must confess, this levelling insight tends to be obscured again; and always the ancestral blindness returns and wraps us up, so that we end once more by thinking that creation can be for no other purpose than to develop remarkable situations and conventional distinctions and merits. And then always some new leveller in the shape of a religious prophet has to arise—the Buddha, the Christ, or some Saint Francis, some Rousseau or Tolstoi—to redispel our blindness. Yet, little by little, there comes some stable gain; for the world does get more humane, and the religion of democracy tends toward permanent increase.

This, as I said, became, for a time my conviction, and gave me great content. I have put the matter into the form of a personal reminiscence, so that I might lead you into it more directly and completely, and so save time. But now I am going to discuss the rest of it with you in a more impersonal way.

Tolstoi's levelling philosophy began long before he had the crisis of melancholy commemorated in that wonderful document of his entitled *My Confession*, which led the way to his more specifically religious works. In his masterpiece *War and Peace*—assuredly the greatest of human novels—the role of the spiritual hero is given to a poor little soldier named Karataieff, so helpful, so cheerful, and so devout that, in spite of his ignorance and filthiness, the sight of him opens the heavens, which have been closed, to the mind of the principal character of the book; and his example evidently is meant by Tolstoi to let God into the world again for the reader. Poor little Karataieff is taken prisoner by the French; and, when too exhausted by hardship and fever to march, is shot as other prisoners were in the famous retreat from Moscow. The last view one gets of him is his little figure leaning against a white birch-tree, and uncomplainingly awaiting the end.

"The more," writes Tolstoi in the work *My Confession*, "the more I examined the life of these laboring folks, the more persuaded I became that they veritably have faith, and get from it alone the sense and the possibility of life. . . . Contrariwise to those of our own class, who protest against destiny and grow indignant at its rigor, these people receive maladies and misfortunes without revolt, without opposition, and with a firm and tranquil confidence that all had to be like that, could not be otherwise, and that it is all right so. . . . The more we live by our intellect, the less we understand the meaning of life. We see only a cruel jest in suffering and death, whereas these people live, suffer, and draw near to death with tranquillity, and oftener than not with joy. . . . There are enormous multitudes of them happy with the most perfect happiness, although deprived of what for us is the sole good of life. Those who understand life's meaning, and know how to live and die thus, are to be counted not by twos, threes, tens, but by hundreds, thousands, millions. They labor quietly, endure privations and pains, live and die, and throughout everything see the good without seeing the vanity. I had to love these people. The more I entered into their life, the more I loved them; and the more it became possible for me to live, too. It came about not only that the life of our society, of the learned and of the rich, disgusted me—more than that, it lost all semblance of meaning in my eyes. All our actions, our deliberations, our sciences, our arts, all appeared to me with a new significance. I understood that these things might be charming pastimes, but that one need seek in them no depth, whereas the life of the hard-working populace, of that multitude of human beings who really contribute to existence, appeared to me in its true light. I understood that there veritably is life, that the meaning which life there receives is the truth; and I accepted it."*

In a similar way does [Robert Louis] Stevenson appeal to our piety toward the elemental virtue of mankind.

"What a wonderful thing," he writes,** "is this Man! How surprising are his attributes! Poor soul, here for so little, cast among so many hardships, savagely surrounded, savagely descended, irremediably condemned to prey upon his fellow-lives—who should have blamed him, had he been of a piece with his destiny and a being merely barbarous? . . . [Yet] it matters not where we look, under what climate we observe him, in what stage of society, in what depth of ignorance, burdened with what erroneous morality; in ships at sea, a man inured to hardship and vile pleasures, his brightest hope a fiddle in a tavern, and a bedizened trull who sells herself to rob him, and he, for all that, simple, innocent, cheerful, kindly like a child, constant to toil, brave to drown, for others; . . . in the slums of cities, moving among indifferent millions to mechanical employments, without hope of change in the future, with scarce a pleasure in the present, and yet true to his virtues, honest up to his lights, kind to his neighbors, tempted perhaps in vain by the bright gin-palace, . . . often repaying the world's scorn with service, often standing firm upon a scruple; . . . everywhere some virtue cherished or affected, everywhere some decency of thought and courage, everywhere the ensign of man's ineffectual goodness—ah! if I could show you this! If I could show you these men and women all the world over, in every stage of history, under every abuse of error, under every circumstance of failure, without hope, without help, without thanks, still obscurely

---

*My Confession. X. (condensed).
**Across the Plains: "Pulvis et Umbra" (abridged).

fighting the lost fight of virtue, still clinging to some rag of honor, the poor jewel of their souls."

All this is as true as it is splendid, and terribly do we need our Tolstois and Stevensons to keep our sense for it alive. Yet you remember the Irishman who, when asked, "Is not one man as good as another?" replied, "Yes; and a great deal better, too!" Similarly (it seems to me) does Tolstoi overcorrect our social prejudices, when he makes his love of the peasant so exclusive, and hardens his heart toward the educated man as absolutely as he does. Grant that at Chautauqua there was little moral effort, little sweat or muscular strain in view. Still, deep down in the souls of the participants we may be sure that something of the sort was hid, some inner stress, some vital virtue not found wanting when required. And, after all, the question recurs, and forces itself upon us, Is it so certain that the surroundings and circumstances of the virtue do make so little difference in the importance of the result? Is the functional utility, the worth to the universe of a certain definite amount of courage, kindliness, and patience, no greater if the possessor of these virtues is in an educated situation, working out far-reaching tasks, than if he be an illiterate nobody, hewing wood and drawing water, just to keep himself alive? Tolstoi's philosophy, deeply enlightening though it certainly is, remains a false abstraction. It savors too much of that Oriental pessimism and nihilism of his, which declares the whole phenomenal world and its facts and their distinctions to be a cunning fraud.

A mere bare fraud is just what our Western common sense will never believe the phenomenal world to be. It admits fully that the inner joys and virtues are the *essential* part of life's business, but it is sure that *some* positive part is also played by the adjuncts of the show. If it is idiotic in romanticism to recognize the heroic only when it sees it labelled and dressed-up in books, it is really just as idiotic to see it only in the dirty boots and sweaty shirt of some one in the fields. It is with us really under every disguise: at Chautauqua; here in your college; in the stock-yards and on the freight-trains; and in the czar of Russia's court. But, instinctively, we make a combination of two things in judging the total significance of a human being. We feel it to be some sort of a product (if such a product only could be calculated) of his inner virtue *and* his outer place,—neither singly taken, but both conjoined. If the outer differences had no meaning for life, why indeed should all this immense variety of them exist? They *must* be significant elements of the world as well.

Just test Tolstoi's deification of the mere manual laborer by the facts. This is what Mr. Walter Wyckoff, after working as an unskilled laborer in the demolition of some buildings at West Point, writes of the spiritual condition of the class of men to which he temporarily chose to belong:

"The salient features of our condition are plain enough. We are grown men, and are without a trade. In the labor market we stand ready to sell to the highest bidder our mere muscular strength for so many hours each day. We are thus in the lowest grade of labor. And, selling our muscular strength in the open market for what it will bring, we sell it under peculiar conditions. It is all the capital that we have. We have no reserve means of subsistence, and cannot, therefore, stand off for a "reserve price." We sell under the necessity of satisfying imminent hunger. Broadly speaking, we must sell our labor or starve; and, as hunger is a matter of a few hours, and we have no other way of meeting this need, we must sell at once for what the market offers for our labor.

"Our employer is buying labor in a dear market, and he will certainly get from us as much work as he can at the price. The gang-boss is secured for this purpose, and thoroughly does he know his business. He has sole command of us. He never saw us before, and he will discharge us all when the debris is cleared away. In the mean time he must get from us, if he can, the utmost of physical labor which we, individually and collectively, are capable of. If he should drive some of us to exhaustion, and we should not be able to continue at work, he would not be the loser; for the market would soon supply him with others to take our places.

"We are ignorant men, but so much we clearly see—that we have sold our labor where we could sell it dearest, and our employer has bought it where he could buy it cheapest. He has paid high, and he must get all the labor that he can; and, by a strong instinct which possesses us, we shall part with as little as we can. From work like ours there seems to us to have been eliminated every element which constitutes the nobility of labor. We feel no personal pride in its progress, and no community of interest with our employer. There is none of the joy of responsibility, none of the sense of achievement, only the dull monotony of grinding toil, with the longing for the signal to quit work, and for our wages at the end.

"And being what we are, the dregs of the labor-market, and having no certainty of permanent employment, and no organization among ourselves, we must expect to work under the watchful eye of a gang-boss, and be driven, like the wage-slaves that we are, through our tasks.

"All this is to tell us, in effect, that our lives are hard, barren, hopeless lives."

And such hard, barren, hopeless lives, surely, are not lives in which one ought to be willing permanently to remain. And why is this so? Is it because they are so dirty? Well, Nansen grew a great deal dirtier on his polar expedition; and we think none the worse of his life for that. Is it the insensibility? Our soldiers have to grow vastly more insensible, and we extol them to the skies. Is it the poverty? Poverty has been reckoned the crowning beauty of many a heroic career. Is it the slavery to a task, the loss of finer pleasures? Such slavery and loss are of the very essence of the higher fortitude, and are always counted to its credit—read the records of missionary devotion all over the world. It is not any one of these things, then, taken by itself—no, nor all of them together—that make such a life undesirable. A man might in truth live like an unskilled laborer, and do the work of one, and yet count as one of the noblest of God's creatures. Quite possibly there were some such persons in the gang that our author describes; but the current of their souls ran underground; and he was too steeped in the ancestral blindness to discern it.

If there *were* any such morally exceptional individuals, however, what made them different from the rest? It can only have been this—that their souls worked and endured in obedience to some inner *ideal*, while their comrades were not actuated by anything worthy of that name. These ideals of other lives are among those secrets that we can almost never penetrate, although something about the man may often tell us when they are there. In Mr. Wyckoff's own case we know exactly what the self-imposed ideal was. Partly he had stumped himself, as the boys say, to carry through a strenuous achievement; but mainly he wished to enlarge his sympathetic insight into fellow-lives. For this his sweat and toil acquire a certain heroic significance, and make us accord to him exceptional esteem. But it is easy to imagine his fellows with various other ideals. To say nothing of wives and babies, one may have been a convert of the Salvation Army, and had a nightingale singing of expiation and forgiveness in his heart all the while he labored. Or there might have been an apostle like Tolstoi himself, or his compatriot Bondareff, in the gang, voluntarily embracing labor as their religious mission. Class-loyalty was undoubtedly an ideal with many. And who knows how much of that higher manliness of poverty, of which Phillips Brooks has spoken so penetratingly, was or was not present in that gang?

"A rugged, barren land," says Phillips Brooks, "is poverty to live in—a land where I am thankful very often if I can get a berry or a root to eat. But living in it really, letting it bear witness to me of itself, not dishonoring it all the time by judging it after the standard of the other lands, gradually there come out its qualities. Behold! no land like this barren and naked land of poverty could show the moral geology of the world. See how the hard ribs . . . stand out strong and solid. No life like poverty could so get one to the heart of things and make men know their meaning, could so let us feel life and the world with all the soft cushions stripped off and thrown away. . . . Poverty makes men come very near each other, and recognize each other's human hearts; and poverty, highest and best of all, demands and cries out for faith in God. . . . I know how superficial and unfeeling, how like mere mockery, words in praise of poverty may seem. . . . But I am sure that the poor man's dignity and freedom, his self-respect and energy, depend upon his cordial knowledge that his poverty is a true region and kind of life, with its own chances of character, its own springs of happiness and revelations of God. Let him resist the characterlessness which often goes with being poor. Let him insist on respecting the condition where he lives. Let him learn to love it, so that by and by, [if] he grows rich, he shall go out of the low door of the old familiar poverty with a true pang of regret, and with a true honor for the narrow home in which he has lived so long."*

*Sermons, 5th Series, New York, 1893 [1891], pp. 166, 167

The barrenness and ignobleness of the more usual laborer's life consist in the fact that it is moved by no such ideal inner springs. The backache, the long hours, the danger, are patiently endured—for what? To gain a quid of tobacco, a glass of beer, a cup of coffee, a meal, and a bed, and to begin again the next day and shirk as much as one can. This really is why we raise no monument to the laborers in the Subway, even though they be our conscripts, and even though after a fashion our city is indeed based upon their patient hearts and enduring backs and shoulders. And this is why we do raise monuments to our soldiers, whose outward conditions were even brutaller still. The soldiers are supposed to have followed an ideal, and the laborers are supposed to have followed none.

You see, my friends, how the plot now thickens; and how strangely the complexities of this wonderful human nature of ours begin to develop under our hands. We have seen the blindness and deadness to each other which are our natural inheritance; and, in spite of them, we have been led to acknowledge an inner meaning which passeth show, and which may be present in the lives of others where we least descry it. And now we are led to say that such inner meaning can be *complete* and *valid for us also*, only when the inner joy, courage, and endurance are joined with an ideal.

But what, exactly, do we mean by an ideal? Can we give no definite account of such a word?

To a certain extent we can. An ideal, for instance, must be something intellectually conceived, something of which we are not unconscious, if we have it; and it must carry with it that sort of outlook, uplift, and brightness that go with all intellectual facts. Secondly, there must be *novelty* in an ideal—novelty at least for him whom the ideal grasps. Sodden routine is incompatible with ideality, although what is sodden routine for one person may be ideal novelty for another. This shows that there is nothing absolutely ideal: ideals are relative to the lives that entertain them. To keep out of the gutter is for us here no part of consciousness at all, yet for many of our brethren it is the most legitimately engrossing of ideals.

Now, taken nakedly, abstractly, and immediately, you see that mere ideals are the cheapest things in life. Everybody has them in some shape or other, personal or general, sound or mistaken, low or high; and the most worthless sentimentalists and dreamers, drunkards, shirks and verse-makers, who never show a grain of effort, courage, or endurance, possibly have them on the most copious scale. Education, enlarging as it does our horizon and perspective, is a means of multiplying our ideals, of bringing new ones into view. And your college professor, with a starched shirt and spectacles, would, if a stock of ideals were all alone by itself enough to render a life significant, be the most absolutely and deeply significant of men. Tolstoi would be completely blind in despising him for a prig, a pedant and a parody; and all our new insight into the divinity of muscular labor would be altogether off the track of truth.

But such consequences as this, you instinctively feel, are erroneous. The more ideals a man has, the more contemptible, on the whole, do you continue to deem him, if the matter ends there for him, and if none of the laboring man's virtues are called into action on his part—no courage shown, no privations undergone, no dirt or scars contracted in the attempt to get them realized. It is quite obvious that something more than the mere possession of ideals is required to make a life significant in any sense that claims the spectator's admiration. Inner joy, to be sure, it may *have*, with its ideals; but that is its own private sentimental matter. To extort from us, outsiders as we are, with our own ideals to look after, the tribute of our grudging recognition, it must back its ideal visions with what the laborers have, the sterner stuff of manly virtue; it must multiply their sentimental surface by the dimension of the active will, if we are to have *depth*, if we are to have anything cubical and solid in the way of character.

The significance of a human life for communicable and publicly recognizable purposes is thus the offspring of a marriage of two different parents, either of whom alone is barren. The ideals taken by themselves give no reality, the virtues by themselves no novelty. And let the orientalists and pessimists say what they will, the thing of deepest—or, at any rate, of comparatively deepest—significance in life does seem to be its character of *progress*, or that strange union of reality with ideal novelty which it continues from one moment to another to present. To recognize ideal novelty is the task of what we call intelligence. Not every one's intelligence can tell which novelties are ideal. For many the ideal thing will always seem to cling still to the older more familiar good. In this case character, though not significant totally, may be still significant pathetically. So, if we are to choose which is the more essential factor of human character, the fighting virtue or the intellectual breadth, we must side with Tolstoi, and choose that simple faithfulness to his light or darkness which any common unintellectual man can show.

But, with all this beating and tacking on my part, I fear you take me to be reaching a confused result. I seem to be just taking things up and dropping them again. First I took up Chautauqua, and dropped that; then Tolstoi and the heroism of common toil, and dropped them; finally, I took up ideals, and seem now almost dropping those. But please observe in what sense it is that I drop them. It is when they pretend *singly* to redeem life from insignificance. Culture and refinement all alone are not enough to do so. Ideal aspirations are not enough, when uncombined with pluck and will. But neither are pluck and will, dogged endurance and insensibility to danger enough, when taken all alone. There must be some sort of fusion, some chemical combination among these principles, for a life objectively and thoroughly significant to result.

Of course, this is a somewhat vague conclusion. But in a question of significance, of worth, like this, conclusions can never be precise. The answer of appreciation, of sentiment, is always a more or a less, a balance struck by sympathy, insight, and good will. But it is an answer, all the same, a real conclusion. And, in the course of getting it, it seems to me that our eyes have been opened to many important things. Some of you are, perhaps, more livingly aware than you were an hour ago of the depths of worth that lie around you, hid in alien lives. And, when you ask how much sympathy you ought to bestow, although the amount is, truly enough, a matter of ideal on your own part, yet in this notion of the combination of ideals with active virtues you have a rough standard for shaping your decision. In any case, your imagination is extended. You divine in the world about you matter for a little more humility on your own part, and tolerance, reverence, and love for others; and you gain a certain inner joyfulness at the increased importance of our common life. Such joyfulness is a religious inspiration and an element of spiritual health, and worth more than large amounts of that sort of technical and accurate information which we professors are supposed to be able to impart.

To show the sort of thing I mean by these words, I will just make one brief practical illustration and then close.

We are suffering to-day in America from what is called the labor-question; and, when you go out into the world, you will each and all of you be caught up in its perplexities. I use the brief term labor-question to cover all sorts of anarchistic discontents and socialistic projects, and the conservative resistances which they provoke. So far as this conflict is unhealthy and regrettable—and I think it is so only to a limited extent—the unhealthiness consists solely in the fact that one-half of our fellow-countrymen remain entirely blind to the internal significance of the lives of the other half. They miss the joys and sorrows, they fail to feel the moral virtue, and they do not guess the presence of the intellectual ideals. They are at cross-purposes all along the line, regarding each other as they might regard a set of dangerously gesticulating automata, or, if they seek to get at the inner motivation, making the most horrible mistakes. Often all that the poor man can think of in the rich man is a cowardly greediness for safety, luxury, and effeminacy, and a boundless affectation. What he is, is not a human being, but a pocket-book, a bank-account. And a similar greediness, turned by disappointment into envy, is all that many rich men can see in the state of mind of the dissatisfied poor. And, if the rich man begins to do the sentimental act over the poor man, what senseless blunders does he make, pitying him for just those very duties and those very immunities which, rightly taken, are the condition of his most abiding and characteristic joys! Each, in short, ignores the fact that happiness and unhappiness and significance are a vital mystery; each pins them absolutely on some ridiculous feature of the external situation; and everybody remains outside of everybody else's sight.

Society has, with all this, undoubtedly got to pass toward some newer and better equilibrium, and the distribution of wealth has doubtless slowly got to change: such changes have always happened, and will happen to the end of time. But if, after all that I have said, any of you expect that they will make any genuine vital difference on a large scale, to the lives of our descendants, you will have missed the significance of my entire lecture. The solid meaning of life is always the same eternal thing—the marriage, namely, of some unhabitual ideal, however special, with some fidelity, courage, and endurance; with some man's or woman's pains.—And, whatever or wherever life may be, there will always be the chance for that marriage to take place.

Fitzjames Stephen wrote many years ago words to this effect more eloquent than any I can speak: "The 'Great Eastern,' or some of her successors," he said, "will perhaps defy the roll of the Atlantic, and cross the seas without allowing their passengers to feel that they have left the firm land. The voyage from the cradle to the grave may come to be performed with similar facility. Progress and science may perhaps enable untold millions to live and die without a care, without a pang, without an anxiety. They will have a pleasant passage and plenty of brilliant conversation. They will wonder that men ever believed at all in clanging fights and blazing towns and sinking ships and praying hands; and, when they come to the end of their course, they will go their way, and the place thereof will know them no more. But it seems unlikely that they will have such a knowledge of the great ocean on which they sail, with its storms and wrecks, its currents and icebergs, its huge waves and mighty winds, as those who battled with it for years together in the little craft, which, if they had few other merits, brought those who navigated them full into the presence of time and eternity, their maker and themselves, and forced them to have some definite view of their relations to them and to each other."*

In this solid and tridimensional sense, so to call it, those philosophers are right who contend that the world is a standing thing, with no progress, no real history. The changing conditions of history touch only the surface of the show. The altered equilibriums and redistributions only diversify our opportunities and open chances to us for new ideals. But, with each new ideal that comes into life, the chance for a life based

---

*Essays by a Barrister*, London, 1862, p. 318.

on some old ideal will vanish; and he would needs be a presumptuous calculator who should with confidence say that the total sum of significances is positively and absolutely greater at any one epoch than at any other of the world.

I am speaking broadly, I know, and omitting to consider certain qualifications in which I myself believe. But one can only make one point in one lecture, and I shall be well content if I have brought my point home to you this evening in even a slight degree. *There are compensations*; and no outward changes of condition in life can keep the nightingale of its eternal meaning from singing in all sorts of different men's hearts. That is the main fact to remember. If we could not only admit it with our lips, but really and truly believe it, how our convulsive insistencies, how our antipathies and dreads of each other, would soften down! If the poor and the rich could look at each other in this way, *sub specie aeternitatis*, how gentle would grow their disputes! what tolerance and good humor, what willingness to live and let live, would come into the world!

# IS LIFE WORTH LIVING?[*]

When Mr. Mallock's book with this title appeared some fifteen years ago, the jocose answer that "it depends on the *liver*" had great currency in the newspapers. The answer which I propose to give to-night cannot be jocose. In the words of one of Shakespeare's prologues—

> I come no more to make you laugh; things now,
> That bear a weighty and a serious brow,
> Sad, high, and working, full of state and woe,

must be my theme. In the deepest heart of all of us there is a corner in which the ultimate mystery of things works sadly; and I know not what such an association as yours intends, nor what you ask of those whom you invite to address you, unless it be to lead you from the surface-glamour of existence, and for an hour at least to make you heedless to the buzzing and jigging and vibration of small interests and excitements that form the tissue of our ordinary consciousness. Without further explanation or apology, then, I ask you to join me in turning an attention, commonly too unwilling, to the profounder bass-note of life. Let us search the lonely depths for an hour together, and see what answers in the last folds and recesses of things our question may find.

. . . .

To come immediately to the heart of my theme, then, what I propose is to imagine ourselves reasoning with a fellow-mortal who is on such terms with life that the only comfort left him is to brood on the assurance, "You may end it when you will." What reasons can we plead that may render such a brother (or sister) willing to take up the burden again? . . . [ed.]

. . . .

---

[*]An Address to the Harvard Young Men's Christian Association. Published in the *International Journal of Ethics* for October, 1895, and as a pocket volume by S. B. Weston, Philadelphia, 1896

And now the application comes directly home to you and me. Probably to almost every one of us here the most adverse life would seem well worth living, if we only could be *certain* that our bravery and patience with it were terminating and eventuating and bearing fruit somewhere in an unseen spiritual world. But granting we are not certain, does it then follow that a bare trust in such a world is a fool's paradise and lubberland, or rather that it is a living attitude in which we are free to indulge? Well, we are free to trust at our own risks anything that is not impossible, and that can bring analogies to bear in its behalf. That the world of physics is probably not absolute, all the converging multitude of arguments that make in favor of idealism tend to prove; and that our whole physical life may lie soaking in a spiritual atmosphere, a dimension of being that we at present have no organ for apprehending, is vividly suggested to us by the analogy of the life of our domestic animals. Our dogs, for example, are in our human life but not of it. They witness hourly the outward body of events whose inner meaning cannot, by any possible operation, be revealed to their intelligence—events in which they themselves often play the cardinal part. My terrier bites a teasing boy, for example, and the father demands damages. The dog may be present at every step of the negotiations, and see the money paid, without an inkling of what it all means, without a suspicion that it has anything to do with *him*; and he never *can* know in his natural dog's life. Or take another case which used greatly to impress me in my medical-student days. Consider a poor dog whom they are vivisecting in a laboratory. He lies strapped on a board and shrieking at his executioners, and to his own dark consciousness is literally in a sort of hell. He cannot see a single redeeming ray in the whole business; and yet all these diabolical-seeming events are often controlled by human intentions with which, if his poor benighted mind could only be made to catch a glimpse of them, all that is heroic in him would religiously acquiesce. Healing truth, relief to future sufferings of beast and man, are to be bought by them. It may be genuinely a process of redemption. Lying on his back on the board there he may be performing a function incalculably higher than any that prosperous canine life admits of; and yet, of the whole performance, this function is the one portion that must remain absolutely beyond his ken.

Now turn from this to the life of man. In the dog's life we see the world invisible to him because we live in both worlds. In human life, although we only see our world, and his within it, yet encompassing both these worlds a still wider world may be there, as unseen by us as our world is by him; and to believe in that world *may* be the most essential function that our lives in this world have to perform. But *"may* be! *may* be!" one now hears the positivist contemptuously exclaim; "what use can a scientific life have for maybes?" Well, I reply, the "scientific" life itself has much to do with maybes, and human life at large has everything to do with them. So far as man stands for anything, and is productive or originative at all, his entire vital function may be said to have to deal with maybes. Not a victory is gained, not a deed of faithfulness or courage is done, except upon a maybe; not a service, not a sally of generosity, not a scientific exploration or experiment or text-book, that may not be a mistake. It is only by risking our persons from one hour to another that we live at all. And often enough our faith beforehand in an uncertified result *is the only thing that makes the result come true.* Suppose, for instance, that you are climbing a mountain, and have worked yourself into a position from which the only escape is by a terrible leap. Have faith that you can successfully make it, and your feet are nerved to its accomplishment. But mistrust yourself, and think of all the sweet things you have heard the scientists say of *maybes*, and you will hesitate so long that, at last, all unstrung and trembling, and launching yourself in a moment of despair, you roll in the abyss. In such a case (and it belongs to an enormous class), the part of wisdom as well as of courage is to *believe what is in the line of your needs*, for only by such belief is the need fulfilled. Refuse to believe, and you shall indeed be right, for you shall irretrievably perish. But believe, and again you shall be right, for you shall save yourself. You make one or the other of two possible universes true by your trust or mistrust—both universes having been only *maybes*, in this particular, before you contributed your act.

Now, it appears to me that the question whether life is worth living is subject to conditions logically much like these. It does, indeed, depend on you *the liver*. If you surrender to the nightmare view and crown the evil edifice by your own suicide, you have indeed made a picture totally black. Pessimism, completed by your act, is true beyond a doubt, so far as your world goes. Your mistrust of life has removed whatever worth your own enduring existence might have given to it; and now, throughout the whole sphere of possible influence of that existence, the mistrust has proved itself to have had divining power. But suppose, on the other hand, that instead of giving way to the nightmare view you cling to it that this world is not the *ultimatum*. Suppose you find yourself a very well-spring, as Wordsworth says, of—

> Zeal, and the virtue to exist by faith
> As soldiers live by courage; as, by strength
> Of heart, the sailor fights with roaring seas.

Suppose, however thickly evils crowd upon you, that your unconquerable subjectivity proves to be their match, and that you find a more wonderful joy than any passive pleasure can bring in trusting ever in the larger whole. Have you not now made life worth living on these terms? What sort of a thing would life really be, with your qualities ready for a tussle with it, if it only brought fair weather and gave these higher faculties of yours no scope? Please remember that optimism and pessimism are definitions of the world, and that our own reactions on the world, small as they are in bulk, are integral parts of the whole thing, and necessarily help to determine the definition. They may even be the decisive elements in determining the definition. A large mass can have its unstable equilibrium overturned by the addition of a feather's weight; a long phrase may have its sense reversed by the addition of the three letters *n-o-t*. This life is worth living, we can say, *since it is what we make it, from the moral point of view*; and we are determined to make it from that point of view, so far as we have anything to do with it, a success.

Now, in this description of faiths that verify themselves I have assumed that our faith in an invisible order is what inspires those efforts and that patience which make this visible order good for moral men. Our faith in the seen world's goodness (goodness now meaning fitness for successful moral and religious life) has verified itself by leaning on our faith in the unseen world. But will our faith in the unseen world similarly verify itself? Who knows?

Once more it is a case of *maybe*; and once more *maybes* are the essence of the situation. I confess that I do not see why the very existence of an invisible world may not in part depend on the personal response which any one of us may make to the religious appeal. God himself, in short, may draw vital strength and increase of very being from our fidelity. For my own part, I do not know what the sweat and blood and tragedy of this life mean, if they mean anything short of this. If this life be not a real fight, in which something is eternally gained for the universe by success, it is no better than a game of private theatricals from which one may withdraw at will. But it *feels* like a real fight—as if there were something really wild in the universe which we, with all our idealities and faithfulnesses, are needed to redeem; and first of all to redeem our own hearts from atheisms and fears. For such a half-wild, half-saved universe our nature is adapted. The deepest thing in our nature is this *Binnenleben* (as a German doctor lately has called it), this dumb region of the heart in which we dwell alone with our willingnesses and unwillingnesses, our faiths and fears. As through the cracks and crannies of caverns those waters exude from the earth's bosom which then form the fountain-heads of springs, so in these crepuscular depths of personality the sources of all our outer deeds and decisions take their rise. Here is our deepest organ of communication with the nature of things; and compared with these concrete movements of our soul all abstract statements and scientific arguments—the veto, for example, which the strict positivist pronounces upon our faith—sound to us like mere chatterings of the teeth. For here possibilities, not finished facts, are the realities with which we have actively to deal; and to quote my friend William Salter, of the Philadelphia Ethical Society, "as the essence of courage is to stake one's life on a possibility, so the essence of faith is to believe that the possibility exists."

These, then, are my last words to you: Be not afraid of life. Believe that life *is* worth living, and your belief will help create the fact. The "scientific proof" that you are right may not be clear before the day of judgment (or some stage of being which that expression may serve to symbolize) is reached. But the faithful fighters of this hour, or the beings that then and there will represent them, may then turn to the faint-hearted, who here decline to go on, with words like those with which Henry IV greeted the tardy Crillon after a great victory had been gained: "Hang yourself, brave Crillon! we fought at Arques, and you were not there."

# NOTE ON THE TEXTS

Here are the sources, with page numbers, from which the selections in this anthology come. I list them in the order of their appearance.

I have made some incidental changes in the texts, bringing to contemporary standards a few outmoded practices—such as italicizing book titles where James does not and modernizing one or two quirks of punctuation. And I have corrected a handful of typographical and spelling errors, usually indicated in brackets. I have also consulted the scholarly edition of William James's works published by Harvard University Press, and in a couple of instances have incorporated in brackets corrections made in this edition to errors in the originals. But I have not expunged every eccentricity and have left James's quotations of other authors intact even when tinkered with in that scholarly edition. When those quotations run long, I have indented them for clarity, as James sometimes did not.

Habit, *Psychology.* American Science Series—Briefer Course. New
    York: Henry Holt and Co., 1908 [1892], Ch. X complete,
    pp. 134–50
Habit, *The Principles of Psychology.* American Science Series—
    Advanced Course. New York: Henry Holt & Co., 1890.
    Two volumes, vol. I, ch. IV, pp. 104, 106–07, 117
The Laws of Habit, *Talks to Teachers on Psychology: And to Students
    on Some of Life's Ideals.* New York: Henry Holt and Co., 1920
    [1899, 1900], ch. VIII complete, pp. 64–78
Genius and Old-Fogeyism, *Psychology* [Briefer Course]. See above,
    Ch. XX, pp. 327–28
The Stream of Consciousness, Ibid., Ch. XI, pp. 152–54, 159, 160,
    165–66, 170–75
Attention and Free Will, Ibid., Ch. XIII, pp. 237–38
Will, Ibid., Ch. XXVI, pp. 415–16, 434–35, 442–44, 448–60
The Sentiment of Rationality, *The Will to Believe and Other Essays in
    Popular Philosophy.* New York: Longmans, Green, & Co. 1899
    [1897], 63–70, 74–79, 85–100, 102, 103, 107
The Will to Believe, Ibid., pp. 1–11, 19–30

The Moral Philosopher and the Moral Life, Ibid., pp. 184–85,
197–201, 204–15

On a Certain Blindness in Human Beings, *Talks to Teachers*, see
above, 229–34, 263–64

Conclusions and Postscript, *The Varieties of Religious Experience.
A Study in Human Nature*. Being the Gifford Lectures on Natural
Religion Delivered at Edinburgh in 1901–1902. London:
Longmans, Green, and Co. 1904 [1902], pp. 485–86, 515–19,
520, 521, 523–27

What Pragmatism Means, *Pragmatism. A New Name for Some
Old Ways of Thinking. Popular Lectures on Philosophy*. New York:
Longmans, Green, and Co., 1907, pp. 43–47, 49–55, 75–76,
77–78, 79–80

Pragmatism's Conception of Truth, Ibid., pp. 198–205, 207–08,
213, 217–27

Conclusions, *A Pluralistic Universe*. Hibbert Lectures at Manchester
College on the Present Situation in Philosophy. New York:
Longmans, Green, and Co., 1916 [1909], pp. 321–25, 326–30

Preface, *The Meaning of Truth. A Sequel to Pragmatism*. New York:
Longmans, Green, and Co. 1909, Preface, pp. v, vii, xvi

On Some Mental Effects of the Earthquake, *Memories and Studies*,
New York: Longmans, Green & Co. 1911. Complete,
pp. 209–26

The Energies of Men, *The Philosophical Review*, Vol. XVI, No. 1,
January 1907, pp. 2–4, 4–5, 6, 8–9, 13, 14–16, 17–20. Portions
of this original text appear below. But the version of this essay
most commonly reprinted, beginning in *American Magazine*,
October 1907, under the title "The Powers of Men," and later
under its original title in *Memories and Studies*, was extensively
revised.

The Moral Equivalent of War, *Memories and Studies*. See above.
Complete, pp. 267–96

What Makes a Life Significant? *Talks to Teachers*. See above.
Complete, pp. 265–301

   **Note:** The original edition of *Talks to Teachers on Psychology:
And to Students on Some of Life's Ideals* lists this essay in the

Contents with a question mark at the end, but the title page of the essay itself carries no question mark. Later editions differ in their use of the mark—the Harvard scholarly edition, adopted in volume one of the Library of America edition, does not have it, but the editor gives no explanation for the choice. Because the title reads like a question (akin to the essay "Is Life Worth Living?"), and the essay largely treats it as one, it is likely that James thought of it that way, as do most readers. Hence I use the mark.

Is Life Worth Living? *The Will to Believe*, see above, pp. 57–62, 32, 38

# INDEX

Wellington, [Arthur Wellesley]
Duke of: on habit, *21*, 87,
94
Wells, H. G.: WJ on 233, 234
Wesley, John: and will, 133
Whitman, Walt: WJ on 142,
146, 192–93
Wigan, Dr.: and will, WJ on,
121–22
Wilde, Oscar: WJ and, *3*
Will: and free will, *2, 8, 10,
14, 18*, 111, 122–24, 138,
168; and habit, *10, 24, 37,
42*, 92; and attention and
effort, *26–27, 52, 54*, 107,
111, 114–22, 123, 135–36;
exercise of, and ideas, *11,
26–27, 53–54*, 117, 120–22,
128–31, 135–36; and
morality, *29–30*, 172; and
truth, *30*, 165; and belief/
faith, *30–31*, 163, 165, 168,
240–42; and energy, *42–43*,
239–40; and rationality, *65n*;
and character, 91, 97, 131;
and consciousness, 83, 107;
conceptions of, 127–30;
types of, 131–33, 138–39;
education of, 133–37; our
willing nature and, 168–69;
force of, 242
Wilson, Bill: and WJ and Alcoholics Anonymous, *40*
Wordsworth, [William]: WJ and,
*11*; WJ on, 146, 192–93, 280
Wycoff, Walter: WJ on, 268–69